# CELTIC & ME

# CELTIC&ME

## CONFESSIONS FROM THE JUNGLE

# DOMINIK DIAMOND

BLACK & WHITE PUBLISHING

First published 2010
by Black & White Publishing Ltd
29 Ocean Drive, Edinburgh EH6 6JL

1 3 5 7 9 10 8 6 4 2    10 11 12 13

ISBN: 978 1 84502 293 8

Typeset by Ellipsis Books Limited, Glasgow
Printed and bound by MPG Books Ltd, Bodmin, Cornwall

# CONTENTS

# ACKNOWLEDGEMENTS

Many thanks to the following friends and colleagues who helped, gaving up their time when I emailed them explaining how drunk I'd been and could they tell me my whereabouts on the night in question, sometimes with photographic evidence: Jo Treharne, Jonny Ffinch, Ian Brown, Phil Sibson, Rikki Brown, Michael Wilson, Sad Andy, Romano Petrucci, Mark Fishman, Jack Templeton and Sally Mais.

Archie Lacey was no help at all, as he couldn't remember a thing either.

Thank you to the people who run www.kerrydalestreet.com – an incredible database of memory-jogging stats for the forgetful Fenian.

For some reason I kept bumping into Stan Mackay from Milton on away trips in Europe. He kept taking photos. He kindly let me use some of these in the book.

Thanks, finally, to Richard Wilkinson who at Beat 106 was the strictest, most anal boss I ever had and therefore the perfect choice for proofreading this book.

# DEDICATION

Dedicated to any Celtic fan who ever came up and shook me by the hand. It meant the world to me. More than the board, the manager or even the team it is YOU who are Celtic Football Club.

# FOREWORD

## By Frankie Boyle

I don't care what anybody says, I think Dominik is alright. That's probably only because I don't know him very well and haven't had to put up with his tantrums, his sectarianism, his drunkenly sending me texts meant for his mistress, or whatever the fuck he does. He's probably okay.

I used to write jokes for Dom when he presented a comedy quiz show in Scotland. It was this fucking terrible thing where he asked Scottish nonlebrities questions about archive Scottish TV footage. The viewing public enjoyed it like a kick in the balls. On my first day they showed us a clip of an old Scott's Porridge Oats ad where a family eat their porridge then all do a mad Highland jig. We had to think of a question. 'Name five dancing families,' I suggested sarcastically. Bang! That went in the show. That was the start of the first episode. We might as well have got Gunther von Hagens to do an on-air abortion.

Dom would always be teeth-grindingly high on Red Bull. He'd often give me a lift to the train station, slaloming erratically from lane to lane and occasionally screaming abuse at other drivers. He would always drop me a few streets from the actual station, because he couldn't be fucked to actually go all the way there.

One time I went round to his house to watch the Cup Final. I remember us both pissing ourselves laughing at John Hartson performing an astonishing WWF style takedown where he slammed Lorenzo Amoruso's head off the ground. I thought, this is pretty cool, watching the Scottish Cup Final with the guy from *Gamesmaster*! Except Celtic got beat and the other guy there, Rikki Brown, had only just about managed not to turn up in his sash and apron. It was shite actually.

Dom has now moved to the middle of nowhere in Canada or something. Good for him. It's not every celebrity that can pick up on how the public feel about them. I honestly wouldn't be that surprised if he wrote a great novel, or did some pioneering radio show out there.

Although I'd be a lot less surprised if I heard that he'd killed someone.

# 1

## I WAS A TEENAGE RANGERS FAN

The boy picked up the ball on the left, knocked it past the first opponent and ran round him, narrowly avoiding the dog turd steaming happily in the summer heat. He used his right foot to knock it inside past a discarded brick and headed towards the goal. His pace took him past the defender, although the defender was picking his nose at the time, just Duffy to beat now. Duffy was a year older and the best goalie on the Kirkton council estate in Arbroath. The boy dropped his right shoulder and shaped to shoot to Duffy's left, then just as the goalie committed himself and shifted his not inconsiderable weight to that side the boy flicked the ball the other way off the outside of his left foot. The ball slipped inside the blue cagoule that was being used as a goalpost as the boy wheeled off in the opposite direction, right hand in the air.

'Davie Cooper!' he screamed in ecstasy. Davie Cooper was the boy's football hero. The boy was a Rangers fan. The boy was me.

Yes. The boy who would become the man who was one of the very few Scottish people in the media to publicly nail their colours to the mast belonging to one half of the Old Firm actually grew up supporting the other lot. But it wasn't my fault, honest – a big boy did it and ran away.

The big boy in question was on the school bus that was taking the seven-year-old version of me from Kirkton down to Ladyloan School in Arbroath. He was carrying out an Arbroath school bus version of a High Street survey. It's like when those people with clipboards stop you in the road when you're rushing to get a Gregg's sausage roll at lunchtime and ask you if you think it's fair that 90% of the world's population are illiterate then ask you for a donation to Amnesty International to buy them a book. (Why? I always wonder. How are they going to read it? Surely we should be buying them a DVD or a videogame instead?)

Anyway this guy on the bus didn't have a clipboard, he had a fist. And he wasn't asking moral questions about illiteracy. He was asking 'What fucking team do you support?'

The correct answer was Rangers. The wrong answer was anything else. The correct answer got you a ruffle of your hair and an enthusiastic cry of 'Good man!' A wrong answer got the booby prize of a good old-fashioned punch in the pus. I've always been good at quizzes, even aged seven, so I gave the correct answer.

And that was it. That was all it took to make me a Rangers fan. If you think this is pathetic, then I'll tell you something that makes it even worse. I had in my pocket at the time a key ring of a footballer in a Celtic kit. My Auntie Wanda had given it to me and I carried it everywhere – ate with it, slept with it, bathed with it. It was a mass produced affair popular at the time featuring a short, chubby player, as wide as he was tall, with a ball stuck to his right foot. The Celtic-stripped version looked for all the world like Johannes Edvaldsson, the first foot-baller whose name I ever knew. Why him? Because not only was I a clever child, I was a dreadful show-off. Not for me a Miller or a Smith, oh no. I went Scandinavian just so I could have more consonants than the other kids.

I still have a page in a School Memories folder my mum put together where I have drawn this very hooped key ring and underneath it written that I supported Celtic. OK? They *were* my first team, OK?

So Dominik Diamond the Ubermediatim was actually a weak, spineless, scared seven-year-old who betrayed his auntie and his team and became a Rangers fan just to escape a punch in the pus. Why did he not simply go back to supporting Celtic when he got off the bus?

How the hell do I know? I was only seven for God's sake. At that age I still thought the tooth fairy was real, the moon was inhabited by clangers and that any day a bite from a radioactive spider would enable me to shoot webs from my wrists.

What did I know of Rangers? Nothing. Could I name one of their players? No. All I knew was that if I supported them there would be less chance of getting a smack in the face on the school bus. Then Stephen MacLeod moved to our estate.

Stephen came from the isle of Lewis and despite not understanding a word he said for the first year, we became best friends. I had no idea where Lewis was but the fact that Stephen's mum was beautiful and his dad was Kenny MacLeod, a DJ on Radio Tay, made me assume it must be some exotic Scottish Narnia where unicorns ran along the beach jostling with troll archers and country music DJs. By dint of this Stephen was the most interesting kid in the whole estate.

He was also the first kid I knew that owned *Subutteo*, the greatest football game in the world until *Sensible Soccer* came out on the Amiga (and it's absolutely no coincidence that the players in *Sensible Soccer* looked like their flick-to-kick brothers-in-arms).

Stephen and his big brother Kenny played their own version of the *Subutteo* rules: you could pick up and move all your players at the kick-off to wherever you wanted and then with each turn you got three chances to move your player to the ball before shooting or passing. It was a much easier way of playing the game because it didn't require half the finger jointed laser-accuracy of the proper rules. In fact most of the time we didn't even flick to kick, but nudged the players along instead. This did mean that no matter how good we got there was no way we could ever compete in *Subutteo* at the officially-sanctioned international level. I can't help but wonder if it was exactly this kind of mindset that made our generation of kids produce such a woeful Scottish football team when we reached adulthood.

Most of our *Subutteo* games ended in riots, thanks to the fact that Stephen's brother Kenny supported Celtic. He and Stephen used to fight like two angry raptors in a sack over this. All it would take was a casual comment from one sibling to the other on the failings of Celtic or Rangers as witnessed by their performance in the current *Subutteo* game and before you know it you had a bar-room brawl, with me comically diving around their flailing limbs trying to protect those ridiculously fragile football figures. I remember at the end of one 'season' John Greig and Peter McCloy were the only members of the Rangers squad not held together by sellotape.

The MacLeod brotherly battles only cemented my new support for Rangers in my head because of the Rule No 1 of Being Eight Years Old: *your best pal's big brother is an arsehole*, especially if they were fat like Kenny.

Celtic was the team Stephen's big fat brother supported. They could not therefore be cool. That was therefore that as far as I was concerned. That said, Kenny was responsible for the funniest joke I heard as a child.

'Who's got a big nose and eleven tits?' he asked me one day. I shrugged.

'Jock Wallace!' he cried. I laughed my head off at that.

When Kenny asked me 'Do you get it?' I was still laughing

as I eventually replied no, and still laughing when he explained it to me.

'How can you laugh at that if you're a Rangers fan?' he asked.

I now know there are two possible explanations. One is that my subconscious knew deep down I was a Tim who was merely on loan to the dark side and this laughter was, in classic Freudian terms, my id triumphing over my ego. The other is that it was because he used the word 'tits'.

Through Stephen MacLeod I was taught the names of the Rangers players of the day: John Greig; Peter McCloy; Derek Johnstone; Sandy Jardine etc.

I hated Sandy Jardine. Seriously. Even at eight years old I despised the man. Not because of anything to do with his playing ability, but rather what I perceived to be his personality from a questionnaire I read with him in *Shoot* magazine at the time. It went like this:

Name: Sandy Jardine
DOB: 31/12/48 (for the sectarian amongst you can I point out that the acronym stands for Date of Birth)
Club: Rangers
Nickname: Sandy

Eh? I thought. That's strange, his name and his nickname are exactly the same. I imagined it was for one of two reasons. Either he was so insufferably dull he had never done anything interesting enough to warrant a nickname, or he was some kind of bullying killjoy who'd made it clear on day one at the club that NOBODY was to give him a nickname or they'd be in trouble.

'Alright lads?' I imagined him saying as he strode into the Ibrox changing room. 'The name's Sandy. Sandy Jardine.'

'What's your nickname?' John Greig would ask.

'Just Sandy.'

'But you've got a girly perm and really big teeth; surely we can get an angle there?'

At that point Sandy would put someone through a wall and he would be simply Sandy forevermore. It was only in later years I discovered his name was actually William and Sandy was a nickname he'd been given when he was young because he had sandy-coloured hair.

The fact that by the time he played for Rangers he had black hair must have made this a right pain in the backside for William Jardine. I can't imagine the amount of times he must have had to sit and explain that his real name was William but he was called Sandy because he had light-brown hair and no, he knew that he didn't have it now but he did back on the day when nicknames were given out. The poor man must have dreaded that *Shoot* questionnaire. He probably kept putting it off until the Ibrox marketing men said, 'Come on Sandy, or William, or whatever you're calling yourself this week, you're the only player who's not done that *Shoot* questionnaire yet. Even Doug Robertson's done one and he's so obscure that years from now that Dominik Diamond chap will have to Google him just to make a lousy gag work.'

One Rangers player who certainly wasn't boring was Davie Cooper. In fact it's probably more accurate to say that from the ages of eight to sixteen I wasn't so much a Rangers fan as a Davie Cooper fan. Actually that's not true, I'm just trying to make it sound better than it was. You can't blame me for trying.

Anyway every time I saw Rangers on *Scotsport* or *Sportscene* Davie dazzled even more than Arthur Montford's jackets. He dribbled and dodged through legions of opposition players in that effortless way that marks the truly great artists in any field, the ball seemingly attached by an invisible thread. Whenever he was on screen it was like the rest of the picture went all fuzzy and indistinct, leaving the bit he was dancing around sharply in focus. Mind you, we lived on a council estate and had a cheap telly, so there might have been a far less magical reason for this.

Whenever I played football at what we called The Dip, a field at the bottom of our estate fenced into a natural pitch-shape by two roads, a hill and a load of wasp-infested broken masonry, it was only natural that I was always Davie Cooper. If I scored a goal, I screamed 'Davie Cooper!' If I made a pass I screamed 'Davie Cooper!' If I brought the milk in from the doorstep in the morning I plumped it on the table with a cry of 'Davie Cooper! Gets the milk!'

In my defence I never at any point consummated my support by going to Ibrox and supporting them from the stands so, in many ways my 'affair' with Rangers was like a married man who really fancies a woman he works with and hangs around, chatting away about stuff that makes her laugh and maybe even goes out for the odd drink after work with her. He might even think about her as he soaps himself in the shower, but he never actually has sex with her. Does that mean he's being unfaithful to his wife? Is that wrong? And why does Sandy Jardine's curly hair and big teeth keep popping into my head during that analogy?

Anyway, so now you know. I was a teenage Rangers fan, but it wasn't my fault. It was Stephen MacLeod and the big pus-punching boy on the bus. Luckily a few years down the line another big boy would save my soul.

## SEEING THE LIGHT IN STRANRAER

'So you're the dirty Orange bastard trying to shag my sister's pal?'

As greetings went, I'd had warmer in my sixteen years on the planet. What made this one even more menacing was that the man offering the greeting had a big knife in one hand and a pan of hot fat in the other. This was looking for all the world like a scene from *Scarface*, albeit a version set in a chip shop in Stranraer. I looked at the guy's sister. And her best pal. And raised my eyebrows as if to say, 'Gonnae help me out here? Please. Before this mad wee Italian bastard chibs me?'

'Romano, for fuck's sake, don't give him a hard time,' said his sister, Maria.

The guy smiled and put down the offensive weapons.

'I'm only joking with you Dominik. How do you do?' My sphincter relaxed, I took his offered hand and shook it. He gripped it just a bit too tightly and his smile faded again. 'Ya fucking Hun bastard. And don't use that language in here Maria; this is where your mother works.'

This set the tone for the first month of our relationship. Romano would smile and make a joke with me, then those dark Italian eyes would cloud over and he'd utter another threat. I never knew where I stood with the guy. I know now he was

8

just trying to mess with my head. I knew then he was a roaring success at it.

'Sit down guys and I'll bring you some fish and chips,' he said and dropped a pan of cut potatoes into the fryer. I went to take my seat at one of the tables in Petrucci's Café.

'Where the fuck do you think you're going?' he barked.

'You said to sit down and you'd get me fish and . . .'

'I said to the Tims in the room I'd get them fish and chips. Not the wee Orange bastards who are trying to shag my sister's best pal, which you can forget all about doing by the way.'

This was a total nightmare. I was so desperate for this guy to like me. Like everything in my life when I was seventeen, this was all to do with a girl.

I had started going out with Rachel Smith at the beginning of 1987 when we were both at Strathallan School where I was the token 'poor council estate scholarship boy' in my year. Rachel had blue eyes, one of those sexy west coast accents with a hint of cigarette-raspiness and hair so blonde it was almost white. I'd got to know her when she played violin in the orchestra for the school play that year, where I was a ridiculously melodramatic Mozart in *Amadeus*.

Most importantly, Rachel was a Celtic fan, and a pretty hard-core one at that. In fact sometimes a little too hardcore (it was incredibly off-putting as a hormone-addled seventeen-year-old to be snogging someone and, when you both surface for air, all they did was talk about how much they fancied Derek Whyte).

I liked Rachel a lot. I liked her best friend Maria even more. Maria went to Kilgraston Convent, just down the road from Strathallan. The proper Catholics went to Mass there every Sunday while the rest of us restricted ourselves to the annual St Andrews night dance with them.

Maria was the girl I'd waited my whole life to meet, jaw-droppingly beautiful in that classic Italian style: long dark hair, bottomless eyes and what gentlemen the world over refer to in glowing terms as 'huge fucking diddies'. She was funny, opinionated, loud and swore a lot. I had never met a girl like her in my life but it never amounted to anything other than friendship for three reasons: firstly, I was going out with her best pal, secondly, Maria didn't fancy me, and thirdly, even if she did I could never have handled the pressure of going out with Romano's sister and would have spent the rest of my life waking up every morning looking for the blood-soaked horse's head under my sheets.

So into the mix of not one but two girls I was in love with came the fact that Romano was my hero before I even met him because Rachel told me he was about to open a nightclub. I had only been to two of these in my life: Smokies in Arbroath, surely the only nightclub to be named after a fish; and Cinderella Rockefellers, the absolute definition of glamour in Edinburgh. And now I was within snogging distance of actually knowing someone who had one.

As far as I was concerned this would mean that I would effectively be Stranraer royalty. And I'd get beer, probably for free. So sex, booze and rock and roll would be mine if I could just get this guy to like me. Unfortunately I was a Hun.

I wish I could say that I went back to supporting Celtic just to shut Romano up. There would have been a nice symmetry to things then: the wee boy bullied into supporting Rangers by the thug on the school bus gets bullied into supporting Celtic by the King of Stranraer. But it was deeper than that and I know there are some who will think this is only fuelling the sectarianism that splits Scotland like a stab wound, but it was all to do with Catholicism and Ireland.

I was baptised a Catholic, hardly surprising with one grandfather from Ireland and the other from Poland. Equally unsurprising was my father falling out with our priest in

Arbroath when he decided that four kids by the age of twenty-five were quite enough for him and he'd have a vasectomy. My dad decided that, by the way, not the priest. This was 1975.

Our local church in Arbroath was St Vigeans which was Church of Scotland, or Proddy, depending on how you view these things. It was a great community church with cubs and brownies and dinner dances and whatnot all put on in the Church Hall and we went there often as a family. My mum has this theory that those times were the happiest our family had, because we were going to church regularly. Or it might have just been that my dad had a job on the rigs and managed to bring back cheap tobacco and free copies of ZX Spectrum games as part of the gargantuan black market that existed offshore at the time.

When I went to Strathallan I was confirmed in the non-denominational school church but if anybody ever asked what religion I was I always answered Catholic. I always felt like a Catholic. Maybe it's because of the depth of passion and commitment I feel the religion has, maybe it's because of the veneration of Mary the original Mother, or maybe it's because my family always used guilt as a way of getting their own way, but I was always Catholic.

When I met Maria she asked me why I didn't go to Mass at Kilgraston Convent and I had no good answer. Well I did, but I thought it was wrong to say, 'because I never wanted to pump any of the girls down there until now.'

Maria got me thinking about Catholicism. Maria got me thinking about a lot of things. So it was perfect timing when, after I'd met Romano a few times and he'd stopped slagging me off long enough to have a conversation with me he asked, 'Do you know what they sing about Catholics at Ibrox?'

'Of course not! I've never been to Ibrox in my life and to be honest in the last six years I've been a casual football fan at best concentrating instead on playing rugby and getting ten O levels at my posh school in an attempt to prove I'm as good as the other kids.' That's what I *should* have said. But I was seventeen and an arsehole.

'Yeah!' I lied, with an air of defiance.

'How can you support that team knowing that's what they sing?'

'Cos . . .' I continued, with that defiance shrinking like a post-swim ballsack.

'You don't actually know what they sing at all, do you?' said Romano, dark eyes piercing my skull like mental alien mind probes in some Cold War era sci-fi movie.

'Naw,' I murmured and shuffled.

'They sing about being up to their necks in Fenian blood. They sing songs about bouncing up and down on Catholics till they were dead. The club itself refuses to sign Catholics.'

'They don't all sing songs like that!' I said. I knew many Rangers fans at school, none of them had ever used the words 'Fenian' and 'bastard' in the same sentence. Then again this was a posh boarding school I was at. They would have probably said 'child of uncertain parentage' instead.

'They don't all sing songs like that, no,' said Romano, in what I think was the first time he'd ever agreed with anything I'd said. Then he went on to say the words that changed my life. 'But by supporting that club you're standing shoulder to shoulder with people who are fundamentally opposed to your religion, your background and your way of life.'

And that, as they say, was that.

The year I met Romano was also the year we were studying the so-called Irish Problem at school. We'd started with the Act of Union in 1801 and gone through Pitt, O'Connell, Gladstone, Disraeli, The Potato Famine, Catholic Emancipation – the whole shebang. It struck a chord in me. I had a very liberal British History teacher at school called Simon Pengelly who did nothing to dispel debate and I would regularly be standing up and banging on tables, shouting about the disgusting acts of colonial murder and oppression committed by the English throne.

(I also swore to myself then that if I ever formed a band I'd call it The Catholic Association. I actually did form a band that year, but we opted for The Erogenous Tones instead – Andy Beith on drums, Dave Thompson on guitar, me on vocals. We rehearsed three numbers (*Freebird*, *Stairway to Heaven* and *Blue Moon*) but split up due to creative differences the week before we were due to play our one and only gig at the school disco. I only say this because I always wanted to be in a band that someone wrote about one day, even if it was just me.

I don't believe you can be an intelligent person in possession of historical facts and *not* have sympathy with the appalling way the Irish Catholics have been treated by British oppression. I believed that at seventeen, I believe it today and I expect I'll believe it till the day I die.

In addition, the chip on my shoulder about being a working class boy from a council estate in one of Scotland's most exclusive schools instinctively made me feel like, and sympathise with, the underdog. You put all those things together and I was *always* going to be become a Celtic fan at this stage. And become one for whom the Irish and Catholic side of the club was always going to be as important as the football side.

'I shouldn't be a Rangers fan, should I?' I said humbly to Romano.

'Listen Dominik, all joking aside, you're obviously a good guy. It's up to you, just think about things and make your decision. But one day if you want I will take you to the Jungle and you will be transformed. You will just get it. I know that.'

I was amazed. This was a different Romano; a calm, measured, dare I say it, 'sensitive' Romano. Well, as calm, measured and sensitive as an Italian mental case gets.

'Romano,' I said, 'from this day on I am a Celtic fan.'

'Good Dominik,' he said. 'Ya former dirty Orange bastard.'

The revelation was a shock for some of my schoolmates. Johnny Ball was one of my best pals at the time. A fine piper, head boy of our house and a Rangers fan. 'What the fuck?' was his response when I told him. 'Is this just so you can get in Rachel Smith's knickers?'

'No,' though obviously it would help. 'It just feels right.'

'It just feels mental,' Johnny countered. 'You don't just slip quietly from supporting Rangers to Celtic. You just *don't*.'

He was right. I didn't slip quietly. I slipped very, very loudly. From being a casual teenage Rangers fan to a militant teenage Republican. I read voraciously about the Irish struggle, making me slightly different from all the other politicised teenagers of the time at school who tended to plump for Che Guevara or Billy Bragg. This was the time when newspapers were full of the deaths at Loughgall and of John Stalker's removal from the investigation into the British Government's apparent shoot to kill policy in Northern Ireland. It wasn't difficult for a newly-politicised teenager to find the underdog in this particular conflict.

What was great about Strathallan School was that freedom of speech and freedom of thought were encouraged. Though this was a school for the elite and wealthy, it actually allowed a socialist magazine to be published. *Turn Left*, as it was called, was created and edited by Jim Gellatly, who would go on to become Scotland's greatest ever new music DJ and included articles not just by myself, but by David Dinsmore, who became a future editor of The *Sun* in Scotland and Rikki Fulton, one of the longest-serving feature writers at the *Daily Record*.

As a result of the school's liberal attitudes I was probably the only prefect in the history of the Scottish public school system to have a poster of The Hunger Strikers on my study wall, their faces against a silhouette of Long Kesh with the Biblical quotation 'Greater love hath no man than this: that he lay down his life for his friend' printed underneath.

Admittedly it was pinned up next to a picture of Sam Fox and Bobby Sands was effectively looking out at her right nipple, but while I was republican I was still teenage and hormonal.

Mostly I was a pretty pathetic republican though, in a lot of ways more like Rik from *The Young Ones* than Gerry Adams. I was always talking about protests about this, that and the other then chickening out at the last minute. I concocted an elaborate plan to run an Irish Tricolour up the school flagpole when the then Secretary of State for Scotland Malcolm Rifkind was guest of honour on school speech day, then decided not to when I realised it would cost me the English, History and Reading competition prizes he'd be presenting me with.

But I did see one protest through to the end. Pupils were encouraged to host their own school chapel service where they picked the readings, the hymns and gave a short sermon. I got together with Chris Fehilly, the only other person who was in anyway militantly Catholic (his nickname was Fehinian) and we wrote a short play about the Irish Problem using the clumsy analogy of two boys playing in their respective gardens. The plot went thus: Boy 1 liked the look of the other boy's toys so he went over and started playing with them. Then when Boy 2 said his mum wanted him to go in for his tea Boy 1 refused to leave the garden, saying that because he'd been playing with the toys they were now equally his. The two boys argued and then in desperation Boy 2 hit Boy 1. I finished the story with the wonderfully teenage melodramatic lines.

'Did the first boy realise the error of his ways and leave the garden and the toys that did not belong to him? No. He called the second boy a terrorist and sent for his friends to invade the garden, take all the toys and beat him up.'

Then Chris pushed play on a ghetto blaster and we walked out to the strains of U2's *Sunday Bloody Sunday*. It was the highlight of my school career for me.

I began the school year as a Rangers fan. I ended it as a Public School Provo. My sympathy for the IRA waned as I grew older and more and more innocents got caught in the crossfire. I realised that while I supported their cause I could not support their methods but back then I was pretty hardcore and for me Bobby Sands and the Hunger Strikers were the bravest of the brave. It was against this religious and political backdrop that I had made my first pilgrimage to Celtic Park, so Catholicism, Irish Republicanism and Celtic were and always will be intertwined for me, as they are for so many Celtic fans. To this day I don't understand why that seems so unreasonable to some people.

So the ideology was in place. I just had to put it into practice.

# 3

## WELCOME TO THE JUNGLE

I had hoped to get into Oxford University, but failed at my first attempt. I didn't believe them when they said I was too stupid so after leaving school I took a whole year off to reapply just so they could tell me again. My second interview was particularly notable because not only did I get an essential part of the plot of King Lear incorrect, but I then proceeded to tell the notable Oxford don that it must be *he* who was mistaken.

My family had moved down to Milton Keynes so my younger brother and sister could go to stage school in London, a move that left us fairly impoverished. By the latter stages of 1987 I was desperately trying to keep what was now a long-distance relationship going with Rachel. I needed a big flashy present for her forthcoming birthday, but had no money with which to buy one so I spoke to Romano and we came up with a plan.

I would turn up as a surprise to Rachel's birthday party in Stranraer with the clincher being that Romano had tickets for us three and Maria for the next day's Old Firm match. This would be my first ever Celtic game.

With no money my only option was to hitch-hike everywhere. This involved standing at the exit of the Newport Pagnell Service Station on the M1 and trying to work out whether the guy driving the lorry had a rape face or not before I stuck my thumb up. I truly hated hitch-hiking. I was slave to a vivid imagination, a pessimistic outlook and the recent release of the Rutger Hauer movie *The Hitcher*. The fact that in that movie it was the hitch-hiker rather than the driver who was the bad guy was no consolation. I just presumed that the law of averages meant the roles would be reversed next time I leapt into the passenger seat. Even if the driver didn't gruesomely murder me I still had to sit there and endure the most tedious conversations with complete strangers which at the time felt almost as bad.

This particular time I got a tedious truck driver from Newport Pagnell to the M6 turnoff, a salesman from the M6 to Liverpool whose halitosis was so bad it almost peeled off his tax disc, another trucker who kicked me out after one stop when I said I was going to University at the end of the year, and finally an old man who had just lost his wife. By the time he dropped me off in Dumfries I suspected she might have done herself in just so she wouldn't have to listen to him anymore. From there I got a bus to Rachel's party.

The surprise worked a treat, especially when I said we were getting picked up by Romano the next day to go to the Old Firm game. I can't remember much of the rest of the night but I have just spent a pleasant half hour trying to. The next morning I drove to Celtic Park for the first time.

If I thought Romano was a scary, mad bastard in the past, nothing prepared me for Romano on Old Firm day. His car belted out 'traditional Irish tunes' at the kind of volume that wilts flowers. He looked and sounded like Pacino in the final scene of *Scarface* but instead of a big gun he had a Celtic scarf and a Golf GTi. Any driver who did not let him emerge from traffic was labelled an instant Hun and every second he would turn to me with another memory from Old Firm games of the past.

'Nineteen-seventy-fucking-nine Dominik, ten men win the league! Roy Aitken – feed the bear, feed the bear, feed the bear!'

'Frank McGarvey with four minutes to go, fuck you Peter McCloy!'

'Hampden riot by the Huns, can't get a fucking drink anymore cos of that mob!'

'Oh Hampden in the sun, Celtic 7 the Rangers 1.'

'Paul McStay, chipping in from just about the corner flag! Get! In!'

I had no idea what half of these things meant, but I was so intoxicated by the sheer pace and excitement that by the time we got to the ground my heart was battering against my chest like Keith Moon was playing it. We parked the car and walked up to the ground and it seemed that everybody knew Romano. It was like walking around with a rock star. It's a measure of how much I hero-worshipped the guy by this stage that not once did I look at my girlfriend, or her beautiful best friend. I couldn't take my eyes off Romano. I wanted to be him when I grew up.

And then I entered The Jungle.

First impressions? It was dark, then again I suppose most jungles are. It was crowded. And it was *alive*. Not only had I never been to Celtic Park before, but I'd never actually been in a packed football stand. The few games I'd been to at home in Arbroath were sparsely attended affairs where the players on the pitch were frequently closer to you than the next spectator. If you wanted to chat to the fan next to you then writing a letter or using semaphore was arguably the most efficient method. So this was the first time I'd been part of that entity that is produced when a large number of football fans cram together in a small place. It's a living, breathing organism that makes thousands of individual bodies react as one. This was not peculiar to the Jungle at Celtic Park, of course, indeed years

19

later I spent some terrifyingly wonderful afternoons in the left side of London Road with Oxford United fans in which you had no chance but to move when everybody else does.

But what you got in the Jungle on Old Firm day was this heaving throng with added hate; hate that made the individual vertebrae of this green snake jump up in fury. And there was a lot of hate at that particular game, thanks to a certain Graeme Souness deciding to try and kill Billy Stark in the second half.

I didn't see the incident, because I couldn't see anything. I was still finding my 'Jungle legs', that way of moving with the supporting snake that allowed you to rise and fall in time with the rest of the crowd. But I could hear well enough and I knew that Souness' full name was Graeme Ya Big Dirty Orange Animal Bastard Souness. I had never felt such venom from a mob before, it was frightening and infectious. It meant that within minutes I hated Souness too and I never even knew the guy.

(It's ironic that, in common with a few of the other Rangers players I 'hated' as a Celtic fan, I actually quite liked Souness when I interviewed him in the late 90s for a Channel 5 Saturday lunchtime show called *Turnstyle*. He was measured, calm, intelligent and affable, the complete opposite to what he was as a player. I didn't end up laughing and swapping dodgy gags with him, as I would later with the likes of McCoist and Graham Roberts, but I'd still have a drink with the man any day, that's not to say I've liked them all when we've crossed paths. I hated Terry Butcher, for example.)

I missed Billy Stark's match-winning goal too. I saw Mark McGhee's cross clear enough (I remember thinking how much he looked like that old Celtic key ring I had as a child), then I saw the back of someone's head, then I saw the back of lots of heads, then Romano smiling at me, which was a sight I welcomed even more than a Celtic goal.

Again, if one were to look for signs of my Celtic-supporting destiny, one could look at the life of the goal scorer himself that day. Billy Stark had, like me, flirted with the dark side by almost joining Rangers as a youngster before finally going to Celtic much later in life than he should have.

The final whistle, the walk back to the car, the journey back to Stranraer and the subsequent session at Romano's nightclub Bar Pazzarello (behind closed doors, it didn't officially open until a couple of months after that) are a blur. But the fact is that my first trip to Paradise saw us beat the Huns 1-0 and their manager getting sent off. Romano *had* to like me, if only for my talismanic properties alone.

The next morning I kissed goodbye to Rachel for what would turn out to be the last time. Another surprise trip up to another party a few months later would reveal her to have a new boyfriend, though my paths were to cross with Romano, and his sister Maria, on some very magical moments in the future. To this day Rachel Smith remains the only girl who ever dumped me, but I think I can forgive her that because if I hadn't gone out with her I'd never have been a Celtic fan.

If I needed any more proof that my conversion to Celtic was meant to be it came at the side of the A75 near Dumfries on the way back down. I had my thumb up for about ten seconds when a car screeched to a halt. Not just any old car, but a car with green and white scarves fluttering from the windows, a car that turned out to be driven by a couple of mad Tims from London who played 'traditional Irish folk songs' even louder than Romano and averaged 120mph all the way down the A75, M6 and the M1 and even dropped me off at my mum's door.

The journey up had taken twelve hours; the journey back down was over in the flash of green and white. I was now a part of the Celtic family and it felt so right.

# THE WILDERNESS YEARS

If this was one of your normal football autobiographies you'd expect this chapter to detail how I spent every weekend for the next ten years cheering on the Hoops from my regular spot on the terraces with crazy trips to away games on alternate weeks. There would be in-depth descriptions of how the Formica changed on the floor of the toilets of Dens Park over the next decade slipped in between descriptions of relationships that ended because the girl didn't understand my love of football.

You'll be disappointed then. I never saw a ball kicked at Celtic Park for the next six years. With the kind of timing that always blighted our family when I was a kid, my dad lost his job on the rigs just after we moved to England leaving us with a big rent bill and no money coming in. He tried his best to get other work but the strain put my parents' marriage into meltdown. I tried to help out by getting a job in the purchasing department of John Laing Superhomes until I went off to university, but it was a truly horrible time for all of us. Trips to Celtic Park were the last thing on my mind.

The rest of that glorious centenary double winning season passed me by. I'd get letters from Maria with breathless mentions of McStay taking Rangers apart in the 2-1 win at Ibrox, thousands of fans cramming into Celtic Park for the decisive win over Dundee and Thatcher getting booed at Hampden after some idiot thought it would be a good idea for her to present the trophy that year.

I'd read the letters and wonder A) if there was any way I could afford to head up for the next game and B) whether the fact that Rachel had dumped me meant it was acceptable for me to ask out Maria. Then I'd hear the shouting begin downstairs which meant another evening of domestic hell was about to begin and those thought bubbles would burst just like they do in cartoons.

It wasn't all bad. I managed to fall in love briefly with another club: Milton Keynes City Rugby Football Club. That big working class chip on my shoulder that made me so ridiculously competitive throughout my school years had meant I'd become a decent fly half and a guy I worked with at Laings, Pete Holmes, encouraged me to join his club. This was an eye opener, for it was men's rugby.

There I was a cocky seventeen-year-old Scottish kid lining up against thirty-five-year-old flankers who couldn't wait to kill me. I remember my first game against local rivals Olney where I was flattened and raked the first time I got the ball. I leapt up and squeaked 'fuck you!' at the offending flanker. The rhyming slang is intentional. I added my 100 yard stare that had reduced public school opponents to jelly on account of the fact that I was over six foot tall when I was sixteen.

The flanker in question just laughed at me. Then his teammates joined in. Then the whole crowd joined in. The rest of the game was a brutal lesson that I was no longer playing school rugby.

Anyway, Milton Keynes City RFC became my refuge that year; a place I could escape from all the hell breaking loose at home and be part of a different family. It wasn't Celtic Football

Club but it was another example of feeling displaced and not belonging, only to be welcomed in by a sporting fraternity. Like Romano, these were older father figures to me who took me under their wing and looked after me.

And welcome me they did. Not only was I fly half, I kicked all the points and wrote the post match reports, the start of my newspaper career. This meant that every week the *Milton Keynes Citizen* was full of the exploits of 'hotly-tipped young fly half' Dominik Diamond, written by Dominik Diamond.

One week I had a poor game, missing some half a dozen penalties in a game we only lost by a few points. I got so drunk after the game that I passed out. Our inside centre, a one-eyed teacher called Mickey Malton whom I always referred to as 'veteran centre' in my reports, much to his annoyance, got his revenge. He wrote the match report that week and the head-line on the back page of the *Citizen* was Broken Diamond Flops It.

It was the first time I'd ever read something horrible about me in the papers and I realised then the power of the man who wields the pen.

When I went off to Bristol University in September 1988 I was even further away from the east end of Glasgow than Milton Keynes and even more skint than I'd been during my year off at home. From 1988 to 1991 my idea of splashing out on dinner was buying a bit of butter to put on the pasta, otherwise I'd just have salt and pepper.

I started off doing English and Drama and the amount of work you had to do was ridiculous. I went from taking two years to study two Shakespeare texts and a Chaucer for A level to having to read half of Shakespeare's entire output in a week. It ruined Shakespeare for me. I had loved *Othello* and *King Lear* when we studied them at school, but it's only when you read all his comedies in a week that you realise they're actually as formulaic as *Who's the Boss* with Tony Danza. Some bloke is always hiding in the bushes overhearing something they shouldn't and getting the wrong idea then dressing as a woman to find out the truth.

The drama side wasn't much better; it was horribly pretentious and you weren't allowed to study any play or movie unless it was black and white, Czechoslovakian and featured wheelchair bound lesbian Marxists talking about death. All I wanted to do was write about *The Breakfast Club*.

This left about three minutes free time each week. I could have got a part-time job or I could have slept with women. So I took the sensible option of starring in as many plays at the Student Union as I could, which was always the best way to cop off. I worked during the holidays at whatever job I could find to save for the next term, which I would stretch out using a very friendly slot machine in the Princes Bar on Park Row, which for some reason always seemed to reward me when I needed it to. I was probably the only Catholic in Bristol at the time who would go to Mass on a Sunday and genuinely pray for three bars and a feature hold.

The fact I was studying drama meant I had a bunch of friends who were more interested in painting themselves purple and doing performance mime about Bolivian rainforests than football, so I had no Romano figure to further my education in footballing matters, apart from Sad Andy.

Sad Andy was a die-hard Oxford United fan. This was not why we called him Sad Andy, in spite of the version of events that were later detailed on my Radio 5 live show *Sportscall*. Oh no, Andy became Sad Andy after he went out with a girl at university who dumped him then became a lesbian.

Andy would sit in the Princes Bar and regale us with tales of 'The Yellows', but compared to Jock Stein, The Lisbon Lions and the rivalry with Rangers, hearing about Jim Smith, the Milk

Cup and rivalry with Swindon Town didn't quite set my heart a-flutter.

That did all change a few years later when I actually discovered first hand the passion, the triumphs, the local rivalries and the religious bigotry were not too dissimilar to that I would experience in Glasgow.

To be honest it was not the worst time to be AWOL as a Celtic fan. The combination of Rangers' treasure trove, our on-pitch limitations and ridiculously tight shorts did not produce many spectacles of interest to the heterosexual Celtic fan at that time. I did get a video sent down of the 1989 Scottish Cup Final which I watched until the tape wore out. It was the first time I'd realised just what a mesmerising player Paul McStay was. His passing in particular was so good it was like the ball was being moved by Olympian Gods using set squares and protractors.

My other memories of that game included wee Joe Miller tormenting the Rangers defence, the crazy amount of horrible challenges, Davie Cooper coming on and being in a different class and how guilty I felt at wanting a feather-cut like Ian Ferguson. In fact I thought the Rangers team's hair at that stage was just outstanding. In hair terms alone they were Duran Duran, with the obvious exception of Richard Gough who sported what I call The Ginger Prefect look.

By contrast Celtic were Dexy's Midnight Runners. If you were to write a book about the Celtic team at that time you could call it Barely Contained Perms; they all had that hairstyle peculiar to the late 80s where it was like a perm had been rammed into a space just slightly too tight for it. It was as if the hair gel was attempting to cage the curly beast, leading to different degrees of curl, even if in Joe Miller's case it was only in the bottom centimetre of his mullet and Mark McGee was more what you would call a 'perm waiting to happen'. The only people in that team who did not have so much as a potential trace of perm were Anton Rogan and Pat Bonner, whose straight bowl cuts were the kind mum's gave you in Oor Wullie cartoons.

I was still jealous of the fact that Rachel had obviously fancied Derek Whyte more than she ever fancied me so I will refuse to acknowledge his man-of-the-match performance or the brilliance of his goal-line clearance from Mark Walters and will instead just refer to his hair as 'poofy'.

It was obvious that Rangers were so flush in those days and that it wasn't just transfer fees and pre-season training camps that Murray's millions were being splurged on. A significant amount was being punted in the direction of hair styling and product and I feel this may have been Souness's major contribution to the Scottish game.

The reader may have inferred that at this stage of my life my hair was hugely important to me. The reader would be correct, but the reader cannot imagine how fantastic my hair was back then, looking as it did like Morten Harket's from Aha. If I'd known how much I would lose this hair over the next decade I'd have had it preserved in formaldehyde instead of simply Boots Mousse.

The only other incident that sticks in my head from that game was Tommy Burns getting a ball booted into his face and the commentator going on and on about how potentially dangerous this was because he wore contact lenses. He made it sound like this could kill him, how or why he did not say. Perhaps the force of the football would ram the contacts through the eyeball into the brain? The combination of those two events meant that, when I got the job on *Gamesmaster* and the producer asked me if I wanted to swap my glasses for contact lenses to look 'cooler', I declined. No way, I said. I remembered how they'd almost killed Tommy Burns.

I'd always had a deep fear of contact lenses since my Auntie

Wanda became the first person in Arbroath to get a pair (I think there might have even been a civic ceremony to recognise the fact). The next Hogmanay party at our house was ruined when one of the lenses slipped round the back of her eye and an army of drunken adults argued for an hour as to what was the best way to retrieve it. At one point I remember two uncles holding her head still while my Dad descended on her retina with a pair of tweezers. I have no idea whether this worked, but Auntie Wanda still has both her eyes today, more through luck than anything else I imagine. I now know that it's impossible for a contact lens to slip around the back of an eye, but it wasn't obvious to a load of drunken adults on Hogmanay.

Celtic won that cup final 1-0, ruining Souness's dreams of a treble, but that game was the last clear moment for me as a Celtic fan for a number of years, not surprising when you consider how barren they were for the club. When following them from afar, snatching details of progress through the English newspapers, with the odd paragraph on a Sunday detailing how Rangers, Aberdeen, Motherwell and even St Mirren were going to Celtic Park and leaving with wins, it ceased to be about the vibrancy and passion of that Old Firm game with Romano, and became just a series of numbers in black and white.

There was that horrible league table at the end of the 1989/90 season. Celtic in fifth place, only ten wins in the league and a goal difference of zero. Third in 90/91, same again the next two years. Down to fourth for the two years after. Dire times for the club with Rangers starting their nine-in-a-row reign. For the fans up the road I can't imagine how demoralising and heartbreaking it was to be in Glasgow at the time. To spend your hard-earned cash week in week out going to see that and having defeat rubbed in your face every Monday at work.

For me though, as a guy trying to get a degree, do plays and persuade female cast members to let me sleep with them and still have change from a student grant, it was just numbers on a page after a while. Numbers, numbers, numbers. While the true Celtic fans were up in Glasgow organising demos and trying to sack the board, I just slowly stopped caring. After all, by that stage I was on the telly and the radio!

# 5

## UNLEASHING THE MONSTER

'Radio is a really intimate medium. You need to imagine you're speaking to one individual listening out there. And just like you were meeting them in the pub and having a chat over a beer, you need to tell them little bits about yourself as the conversation progresses. What's the first thing two guys talk about when they meet?' asked Eddie, the Radio 5 producer.

'Judge Dredd?' I immediately replied. I had always been a big 2000AD fan, now with the wage packets I was getting from my new TV show *Gamesmaster* I was spending a fortune on comics.

'What else?' he continued.

'Who can pee the furthest?' I offered. What can I say; I had always liked to pee. And I was very competitive.

'Football,' replied Eddie, as he continued his speech about How to Be a Radio Presenter. It was August 1993 and I was about to start my first show at Radio 5, a sports quiz show called *Sportscall*. It's interesting that in a career that was to be dominated by me walking out of jobs, that I got my first radio show because of another guy doing the most famous 'walkout' in radio history – Dave Lee Travis.

The Big Hairy Cornflake had quit his Radio 1 show live on air earlier that month, saying that 'changes were afoot' that he just couldn't tolerate. Nicky Campbell was parachuted into his Radio 1 weekend slot meaning he couldn't do his Radio 5 Saturday lunchtime show any more. We had the same agent, Tony Fox, which is how I got the audition and how I ended up getting this crash course in radio a few minutes before going on air.

'So,' continued Eddie, unaware that he was about to begin the most ridiculously insane chain of events over the next fifteen years, 'as soon as you can, mention what football team you support, then the listeners will know you're one of them.'

And so it came to pass that during what was my very first show for that most venerable of institutions, the BBC, I was running through the pick of the fixtures that weekend to try and establish my sporting credentials (remember up till now I was just the guy who said funny stuff about *Super Mario*). Remembering what Eddie had suggested, I slipped in my football allegiance in what I thought was a casual manner.

'And in Scotland my team Celtic are playing Dundee Utd and the Huns have got Aberdeen.'

And that was it. In the space of a dozen words I'd done what Scottish broadcasters never did; declare an allegiance to one half of the Old Firm. I didn't know at the time that you were supposed to pretend you really supported St Mirren, how could I? I had walked out of university straight into filming a TV show with three million viewers and a flat in Notting Hill. I hadn't even been back up to Scotland in years, let alone been briefed on the code of McMedia Omerta that existed with regards to Old Firm allegiance.

'How was that?' I asked Eddie at the end of the show.

'Great. Really good show. Some guy phoned up and called you a Fenian Bastard but apart from that the feedback from the listeners was great.'

Little did I know that this sentence would be one that summed up my entire radio career, outbreaks of great listener feedback with intermittent showers of religious abuse.

So the next week I mentioned Celtic again. And I mentioned who 'the Huns' were playing. And I got a couple of people complaining. Eddie, my producer, had no idea how controversial that three-letter-word was. To be honest neither did I. I still hadn't been back up to Celtic Park since that Old Firm game with Romano. From the moment *Gamesmaster* first aired in January 1992 my life went absolutely silly. The show went straight into Channel 4's Top Ten and every day was devoted to riding the wave it threw up. I had that poor working class kid mentality of *never* turning down work so I was taking every personal appearance this phenomenon offered so I could help out myself and my family. The video games boom was in full swing so I was doing two or three of these appearances a week. Kerching!

So to me 'Hun' was just a word Rangers fans were called. They were Huns, we were Tims. End of story. To this day every Rangers fan I know refers to themselves as a Hun. Even Rangers players I've come to know refer to themselves as Huns. Not on the air, though, but I guess that's what made me special.

As far as Eddie my producer was concerned, if people were phoning up to complain that meant they were listening to the show, so he wasn't bothered. And sure enough the show went on to become one of Radio 5's biggest successes of the 1990s.

But *Sportscall* wasn't the problem, because it was a sports quiz show. There were different quiz rounds during which listeners could win different sports prizes: 5 Nations Rugby tickets, books about horse racing, signed football shirts – that kind of thing. It wasn't a show on which to express controversial football opinion and take the Mickey out of rival teams.

However *Fantasy Football* was.

This was the radio version of the football TV show presented by Frank Skinner and David Baddiel. Again it was on BBC Radio 5, (now renamed Radio 5 live) and again someone else presented it before me but left for some reason, though this time I'm pretty sure it did not involve Dave Lee Travis.

I had actually known Frank Skinner when I was still at Bristol University when his manager had seen my stand-up act and booked me to do a few support slots with him and Phill Jupitus in the Midlands. To see Frank doing stand-up back then was incredible. He would go on stage in the roughest of Birmingham pubs and just seize control of a room. I would go on and try to do political comedy as a fresh-faced nineteen-year-old with Harry Potter glasses. 'Hands up who hates Maggie Thatcher?' I used to ask. 'Fuck off you little twat!', the hard-bitten audience would reply.

I remember one nightmare gig in particular during which nothing had gone right. The microphone wasn't working properly, someone told me to fuck off early on, I told him to fuck off back, my timing was all over the place and I rushed the whole set just so I could get off. Which I did. To a chorus of boos.

I was sitting in the bar afterwards feeling borderline suicidal when Frank (who had followed me and, it goes without saying, tore the house down) approached. Once again I was in one of those situations where I needed that father figure to put a comforting arm around my shoulder and tell me that I was doing OK and not to worry.

'You were fucking shit tonight, mate!' Frank said instead. And he laughed that high-pitched laugh of his. 'Absolutely fucking shit!'

I looked around for the nearest razor to open my wrists with. *Then* he put his arm on my shoulder and proceeded to go through my whole act and tell me step by step where I went wrong. It was the most incredible dissection of humour and how to work a live audience. Where I went wrong, he said, was in alienating my audience. 'You can challenge an audience, sure, but don't ever tell them they're cunts. You have to keep 80% of an audience on board to have any chance of success.'

So I went on the next night in a place called The Kings Head and totally stormed the place. But with the exception of that night I never learned a damned thing from Frank. Instead, I took the country of my birth and pissed off 50% of them.

Which brings me back to the *Fantasy Football* radio show. The show involved me and a mix of celebrities and listeners who managed teams in our own Fantasy League. Each week two managers would be in the studio with me and we'd discuss how their teams had done for about twenty four seconds then just have general light-hearted banter about football for the rest of the hour. This was 1994 and, though Fergus McCann had just taken over, Celtic were still in that horrible fallow period which became a regular stick for the other panellists to beat me over the head with. But given that it was a love of the underdog that led me to Celtic in the first place, this was not a problem.

Other managers included Nick Hancock, Paul Hawksbee and Clare Grogan and it was during this show that I started to get a little bit over-exuberant with my support, slagging off Rangers more and more. I thought it was only fair, not just because I was a Celtic fan but because they were the big-money dominant club in Scotland. They were The Man. And I was a rebel. And rebels have to stick it to The Man. I was Robin Hood with a microphone instead of a bow and arrow. I was taking the pish from the rich to give laughs back to the poor.

Celtic fans would get in touch and say how wonderful it was and it made me feel like I belonged in their gang. And at that time I really needed to feel like I belonged to something. My dad had finally walked out on us when I was in my last year at university, which nearly destroyed my poor mum. I refused to have anything to do with him as a result, so that traditional family unit had gone. There was nothing to seek solace or comfort in there.

The speed and size of the success of *Gamesmaster* had disorientated me, making me feel something of a fraud. It had all seemed a bit too easy, I hadn't paid my dues. I was in my final year at Bristol when I auditioned for the Channel 4 show *The Word*, which held a nationwide search for a new unknown presenter. I got down to the final fifteen before Katie Puckrick got the job. The producers of *Gamesmaster* knew they'd had 15,000 applications so asked if there was anyone they could recommend. Someone recommended me. I auditioned for *Gamesmaster* three months after I left Bristol and got the job. I was at university one minute and then I was on the telly with three million viewers the next. Jammy bastard!

There were friends of mine from Bristol who were much more talented than I was – David Walliams and Simon Pegg for example, who were both in this comedy troupe I ran called David Icke and the Orphans of Jesus – who were now trawling comedy clubs for a few quid a time while I was sipping champagne in London nightclubs.

If you think Simon Pegg is a comedy God now, you should have seen him back in 1991 when he was doing comic poetry in the character of this public swimming pool lifeguard. He was genius. Sheer genius. You have simply never seen a human being with such an innate grasp of comic timing and delivery. We both opted for a Comedy Tutorial Course in our final year and we'd analyse why certain things were funny and why certain things weren't. At times I wanted to just write 'Simon Pegg' as the answer.

Anyway it has become obvious over the years that with regards to Simon and David Walliams, the Success Gods have more than restored the karmic success balance to this talent deficit!

So I didn't feel I belonged to a biological family, I didn't feel I belonged to this media family I was now part of, I had never felt I belonged in Arbroath and as much as they tried to include me I never felt worthy of belonging to Strathallan School. But there was something that connected with me about Celtic, even from a distance, even though at this stage I'd still only been to one live match. Every time I mentioned supporting them on the radio it felt like an extra rope had fastened me to the club and, more importantly, to the supporting family.

But I was also twenty four years old, drunk on success and really not thinking before I opened my mouth. Someone would mention Rangers and I would say – 'ah yes, Rangers, the scum of the earth' without thinking. Imagine for a second someone like Chick Young saying that on Radio Scotland (obviously a stretch of the imagination for many reasons), he'd be stabbed before he got home that night.

But I was in London, in a big comfortable, indestructible showbiz bubble, taxied from doorstep to doorstep, surrounded by friends, without a care in the world. And it was such fun! It was such fun being naughty and controversial and saying things that I knew were going to result in steam pouring out of red, white and blue ears. Because every complaining email or letter I got from them made me feel closer to the Celtic support.

Here is a quote from a letter I received in 1993. I won't say the gentleman's name but he was from Ayr and he wanted me sacked for the following outburst with a caller to the show.

*He made it clear that his hatred for Rangers had a longstanding foundation and then went on to glory in the fact with comments like 'wasn't it great, wasn't it wonderful that Rangers had been defeated in Europe in midweek.' . . . and the presenter went on to clarify his position and assure him that he would 'rather have cut off or have cut off his testicles than be thought of as a Rangers supporter.*

I know those were silly, inflammatory things to say, and things that nearly got me killed years later, but at the time I used to absolutely hose myself laughing when I received these missives.

I was trying to make up for not being able to shout from the terraces by shouting twice as loud on the radio. The radio shows were at the weekend so I could never get up to a game, but I did go out and buy the biggest *Subutteo* set Hamleys had to offer, with stadia, floodlights, the whole shebang. I'd come in at night from some film premiere or video games party (there were a ridiculous amount of video games parties back then) and I'd sit like an eight-year-old and re-enact the last weekend's Celtic game if they'd won.

That *Subutteo* set did not get a whole lot of use in the early 90s. The Celtic team fared much better in *Sensible Soccer*. The game was out in 1992 and myself and Sad Andy became ridiculously obsessive about it. We would edit the teams so that Oxford United and Celtic were as up to date as possible, then we'd play fixtures between the two for up to six hours at a time.

Lou Macari's Celtic team of 1993/1994 may now be considered one of the worst in living memory, winning only fifteen league games that season, but on the Amiga, with a green bug joystick in my expert hands, the likes of Lee Martin, Brian McLaughlin and Gerry Creaney were world beaters. Well they beat Sad Andy's Oxford Utd anyway.

When *Sensible World of Soccer* came out in 1994 I was asked to supply a team for the list of Miscellaneous Teams they had. The choice was simple. It was Famous Catholics. Off the top of my head I remember it included JFK, Torquemada, Wolfe Tone, Pope John Paul II (in goals, of course) and myself (up front, of course).

The next actual live Celtic match I got to was a bizarre mix of the amazing, the pitiful, the explicable and the sad. It was Ian Rush's testimonial on 6 December 1994. A bunch of guys from Ocean Software had a box for it and invited me up. It was to be a great night of firsts: my first trip to the great football cathedral of Anfield; my first experience of Liverpool women; the first time I'd ever seen Kenny Dalglish in a Celtic top and the first time I'd experienced sectarianism up close. Really close.

But first I met Duncan Ferguson.

I was staying in the Moat House hotel in Liverpool and entered the lift to go down for a drink with the rest of the guys. Duncan Ferguson, recently signed by Everton from Rangers, was inside. Just my luck. Not just bumping into an ex Rangers player, but an ex Rangers player who'd done time for assault and was just about the biggest guy I'd ever seen in my life. I stared at him. He stared at me. The following transcript of the conversation is indicative of the kind of tongue-tied doofus I always seem to be in those situations.

'Are you coming in?' he asked.

'Er . . . yeah OK,' I replied.

'Where are you going?'

'Er nowhere. Well to a pub, probably.'

'No. What floor?'

'Oh, any one.'

'Eh?'

'Ground, sorry. Ground.'

Still, this was nothing compared to my all-time classic 'dumb conversation with a famous person' which had taken place a year earlier. It was the first ever T in the Park, and there was a big after show in the Hilton Hotel in Glasgow. I'd gone there with a bunch of friends and wives and bumped into Robbie Williams, who had attended as part of his post-Take That indie-cred-gathering stimulus package. Robbie was slightly hammered and came over to lambast me for saying I'd slept with his mum in *Smash Hits*. This wasn't even close to the truth, but I steered Robbie away from defcon 5 by reminding him of how he won the *Gamesmaster* Golden Joystick when Take That were on *Gamesmaster* a couple of years before.

Not only did Robbie go round every single wife in our group and give them a big kiss, but he invited me to come and meet Noel Gallagher. Too good a moment to pass up. I got my mate David Wells to come along as well. David was in that classic 1980s Scottish pop outfit H20 and now runs a fine indie record label called Neon Tetra from a glorious shed in Glasgow.

Noel was bored. Noel just wanted to get away from all the fawning acolytes and get up to his hotel room. Noel did not really want to meet anyone else.

'Noel this is Dominik Diamond from *Gamesmaster* and *Smash Hits*!' Robbie announced excitedly. Tumbleweed blew slowly across Noel's eyes. He shook my hand without a word. I was desperate to think of a killer line to impress him. I was a fan, David Wells was a fan – if I could just be amusing and interesting I would end up getting invited up to Noel's hotel room with Robbie and a million women and it would be the night of our lives. So here goes.

'Hi Noel. This is my friend David,' I paused. 'He plays guitar too.'

Needless to say David and I never saw the party Noel was having in his room. It took me years and another meeting with Noel to get over this humiliation.

Back in Liverpool the Ian Rush testimonial showed how poor the Celtic team now was, getting humped 6-0. I know it was just a testimonial but the gulf in class was as huge as the gulf between Pete Hooton from The Farm's vocals and the actual tune of Altogether Now when they played at half time.

Still, I got to see Dalglish in a Celtic top. Live. So much of my Celtic supporting at that time was making up for lost time by getting videos and books of all the greats who had played before. Now, from up high at Anfield you could see the Dalglish's immense football brain at work still, even at forty three years of age. His touch and turning skills were undimmed; using a few steps he would get into the kind of space other players would have to run twenty yards to achieve. Rush himself was asked if he regretted not linking up with Maradona when Napoli tried to sign them both in 1984 and he replied that you really couldn't top playing with Kenny Dalglish. Now I could see why. And I could now chalk another thing off that list I had called Things I Really Should Have Done If I'd Been A Proper Celtic Supporter All My Life Instead of a Twat.

Even more amazing than seeing Dalglish that night though was seeing the Celtic fans. It is not without reason that they are such a popular choice for testimonials, and no surprise that they've won accolades for being The Greatest Fans In The World. They sang their hearts out, drowning out the Liverpool fans. But notice I said 'they' not 'we'. I did not belong to that crowd yet. I didn't feel I had earned the right.

Which is why I was stunned when walking the streets around Anfield to have Celtic fans coming up to me and throw their arms around me. 'Dominik ya legend!', 'Haw Dominik, you're a good Tim!', 'See when you get it up they Huns on the radio? I pure love that!'

I was embarrassed, because I didn't agree with them. I wasn't one of them. I hadn't been to the games they'd been to. I hadn't paid the money they'd paid. I hadn't made that emotional investment in the club they had. I felt guilty. I felt a fraud.

Towards the end of the night we ended up in The Continental nightclub. Some of the Liverpool players were in there and I got chatting with them. There was Phil Babb, Stan Collymore, Steve McManaman, Jason McAteer, Rob Jones and Jamie Redknapp:

all great guys I was to have a few laughs with over the next year. And one who later tried to sue me for calling him a selfish scumbag on Radio 5 live. Then again that's the same one who battered his girlfriend in a French pub during the 1998 World Cup so I think I called that one correctly in the end.

I was waiting outside for my mates at the end and got talking to this Celtic fan. He hit me with the same comments I'd heard all night, but by this stage I'd had enough.

'Listen mate, I'm not a real fan. Not like you guys.'

'Course you are, Dominik, course you are.'

'No I'm not. I've only been to Celtic Park once.'

'So what?'

'You guys are there week in week out. You travel hundreds of miles to go and see them play. I don't.'

'Yeah Dominik, but you wear a Celtic top on the telly. You go on the radio and say you support us. We don't know anybody else who does that. You do that week in, week out. And I tell you, seeing the shite the club's been in the last few year, that's counted for a hell of a lot. *That's* why you're one of us.'

'Really?'

'Oh yes. And what's more . . .'

And I really should have guessed what was coming next.

'. . . you really, really, REALLY get it up they Huns.'

And then, with a timing that was impeccable, and yet another of those moments that always made me feel a higher power was controlling all this, a bunch of lads shouted over from the other side of the street.

'Hey Gamesmaster?'

'Yeah?'

'You fucking Fenian bastard!'

Things were never going to be the same ever again.

# 6

# INTERNATIONAL FENIAN BASTARD

On 27 May 1995 I did one of the daftest things in my life to date. I watched a game from the Rangers end. Technically it was the Airdrie end at Hampden, because it was they who were playing Celtic in that Scottish Cup Final, but it was amazing how much the Airdrie tops looked like Rangers ones that day, right down to the letters R, F and C on the chest.

A mate of mine called Graham had a brother who was something to do with Airdrie and could get me a pair of tickets for their end, with the caveat that on my head be it.

'You're joking, right? It's Airdrie we're playing against, not Rangers.' I professed.

'How naïve are you?' asked Graham. 'You wait till you get there. Seriously, you need to go in disguise.'

I decided to go with my best pal Kirk. I'd met him at *Gamesmaster Live* where he asked me to present an investigative documentary with him for STV about how Glasgow was the epicentre of videogames piracy at the time. Making the documentary was an intense investigative week of getting drunk and stoned in Glasgow and occasionally filming me outside the Barras. It was immense and by the end of the week Kirk and I became best friends. He liked the Celtic, but more importantly he was bigger and slower than me. Whenever I was swimming in hot climes I always liked to make sure someone who looked like Kirk was a bit further out than I was, working on the basis that a shark can only eat one human being at a time. I felt the same rules would apply to the Huns Den at Hampden.

I thought long and hard about what Graham had meant as 'going in disguise'. One of those old men masks perchance? Subtle rhinoplasty? In the end I spent the four weeks leading up to the game growing a beard. On telly up to this time I'd always been clean shaven. In addition I had a hooded top and sunglasses. And a black scarf wrapped around my mouth and nose. The irony that I was going to be sitting amongst a bunch of hardline Rangers fans looking for all the world like a Provo was not lost on me. In retrospect with my full, shaggy beard and glasses I looked like Gerry Adams. Again, not the smartest move.

In spite of the fact that Kirk lived on the south side of Glasgow, a mere ten minutes walk from Hampden Park, we were late getting into the ground. I cannot remember what the reason was but it may have involved beer, marijuana and some freshly baked meat and pastry goods from Greggs, almost certainly in that order.

In what was the first in a series of games I went to but missed crucial Celtic goals because I was late or pished or going for a pish, Kirk and I shambled up the steps just as the ball left Pierre van Hooijdonk's head and into the Airdrie goal.

The stadium erupted, apart from the section we were in. I started to shout. 'Ya beauty!' and tried to leap into the air but something was holding me down. That something was actually two things – Kirk's hands, on my shoulders. 'Don't fucking celebrate!' he hissed. 'The place is full of Huns!' Luckily he said this just as the 'ya beauty' was only halfway out my mouth and I managed to change it to 'ya bastard!'

Kirk was right. The place was full of guys wearing Rangers tops. What followed was the most uncomfortable eighty one minutes of my life. The mood was horrible, full of violence and menace. There was hardly a sentence that wasn't uttered by one of my 'fellow' spectators that didn't have the words 'Fenian' and 'Bastard' in it. I had to sit there amidst the hatred and the bigotry, the Billy Boys and The Sash, wondering what the hell I'd let myself into? What kind of world was this? This was not the nice cosy BBC Radio studio where I'd happily slag off the Rangers and have a giggle when they complained. These were the people I was offending: faces twisted and contorted into violent hate, Red Hand tattoos on arms stretched taut by clenched fists.

Every time Brian McLaughlin went on a mazy run I had to sit on my hands. Every time Peter Grant came in with a crunching tackle I had to stick my fist in my mouth to stop from crying out my support. And all the time I was waiting for that moment when somebody would fix their gaze a little too intently on my face and say 'Do I know you, pal?'

'Hey! Do I know you, pal?'

Shit! This was not my imagination or a skunk-induced hallucination; this was a guy walking past me, a mountain of a man with Rangers top stretched to breaking point over his belly, looking me right in the eyes. I panicked. Actually I did more than panic, I went cockney.

'Dahn't fink sow, mayte!' I drawled, thanking the Lord for three years living in London. One of the reasons I'd opted for TV presenting instead of acting was because I was so bad at accents when I was a drama student, with an American one during a performance as Chris in Arthur Miller's *All My Sons* at Bristol Student Union in 1990 being the nadir. Now we'd see if I had improved at all.

'You Australian, pal?' his eyebrows furrowed in confusion.

Now I faced a terrifying choice. Did I try to switch to an Australian accent, knowing fine well that nobody outside of Australia can actually do one?

'Nah, mayte. Lahndan mate. Chelsea, mayte. Australian muvver, tho! Mayte.'

'Mate' was one word I knew I could convincingly say in cockney, having travelled in about a thousand taxis since I moved to London. I felt I could just 'mate' this guy into believing me.

Luckily Peter Grant saved my life. He went in for another tackle, quite possibly the yellow card side of fair and the section I was in rose in violent disgust.

'Haw pal?' assorted spectators said to my 'mate'. 'Gonnae get out the fuckin' way?' And off he shuffled.

Other details of the match are sketchy, what with the four-teen stone lump of trembling paranoid fear I'd now been reduced to. That said, I've asked many Celtic fans over the years what they remember about that final and it's the same. Big Pierre's goal, Peter Grant immense, shitey game of football, but Paul McStay finally got to lift a trophy as Celtic captain.

The final whistle went and again I felt Kirk's hands on me, but this time I was more than aware of the situation we were in so I just sat there and buried my head in my hands, looking as if I was crestfallen, but inside my heart was doing cartwheels. Not only was this Celtic's first trophy since that Joe Miller Cup Final I'd worn out watching on VHS back in 1990, but it was the first game I'd been to in Scotland since we'd beaten Rangers in that Old Firm game. I felt I was a talisman for the team, that their run of bad form had coincided in some way with the fact that I hadn't supported them enough.

Luckily our section emptied within seconds and I was able to finally stand up, throw off the hat, unwrap the scarf from around my neck and take off my coat to reveal a Celtic top underneath. I ran down to the front of the seating section and went absolutely mental. Jumping up and down like a loon. When the team did their walkabout round the perimeter I'd like to think that Paul McStay looked me directly in the eye and said, 'G'wan yersel Big Man!'

Though that probably was not the case.

Kirk and I celebrated that night by going from bar to bar with the kind of indestructibility you feel when your team has just won its first trophy in five years and you really don't have a clue just how dangerous it is to walk about Glasgow as a high profile Celtic fan. At one point we had emerged from the Clockwork in Cathcart, a once phenomenal Glasgow pub that had the honour of being the only pub in the world that brewed its own Hazy Daze Ginger lager on site. David Wells used to hold court in there of a Tuesday and it became our regular drinking hole, then it changed hands, they stopped the ginger and I haven't been back there for years. Anyway on the night in question Kirk and I emerged with only the most passing relationship with reality to be met by a guy with a Rangers top on.

'Oh fuck,' I thought. 'This is it. I'm going to die.' Then a strange thing happened. The guy in the Rangers top smiled at me. And shook me by the hand.

'Aw Dominik, I just wanted to say I pure love that *Gamesmaster*. How are ye?'

'Alright my friend,' I replied, more through relief than anything.

'A word of advice though, get the fuck out of here. This is Hun Central ya mad bastard.'

So the hoody went back up, the sunglasses went back on and I staggered off into the night.

That win not only stopped the trophyless streak, but also got Celtic into the next season's Cup Winners Cup, which was the next leg on my big Celtic adventure.

By that time I was playing Sunday League Football in London for a team we called Diss United which consisted of myself, Sad Andy, some of Sad Andy's other mates and guys I'd met in the video games industry. We were terrible. Actually that's unfair. On the days when we had eleven players turn up we were OK, but we were such a bunch of caners and pissheads those days were few and far between. Most Sundays we'd have around nine players, many of whom were still flying from the night before.

I was never that bothered about this, because the team was the subject of a monthly column I had in *FHM* magazine at the time called *Parklife* and our substance-fuelled awfulness on and off the pitch meant the column really did write itself. I actually got my first ever award nomination that year for this diary, though I was beaten by someone from *Knitting Monthly*.

The shoddy state of the team, however, would infuriate the rare 'proper' players we were able to attract, the most proper of whom was Berna. Berna worked for the video games company Infogames of *Alone in the Dark* fame and he was our Cantona, because he was French and he was brilliant. He was also furious with us every single Sunday.

'I cannot stand zees!' he would march about screaming at half-time. 'Ow can we expect to ween a game, weeth you all zo drunk all ze time? And zee smoking during zee game – why? Why? Zut alors!'

Berna had a mate who worked for Paris St Germain and when Celtic drew them in the Cup Winners Cup we made a deal. He would sort out tickets and accommodation for us in Paris for the away leg; I'd do the same for Glasgow.

Paris was amazing. It was my first European away trip to see the Celtic, my first time seeing how loved our fans were in foreign cities and how desperately unlucky our team was when it came to away European games, losing as we did 1-0 to a

Djorkaeff goal when big Pierre missed a sitter that would have given us a deserved draw.

Berna had laid on all manner of classy treats in Paris: we got a tour of the stadium after the match, and he took me out for a beautiful dinner on the Champs Elysees afterwards. Nice food, nice wine, all very civilised.

Two weeks later Berna came to Glasgow and got a pie and a pint. Actually he got more than a pint. He got many, many pints in the legendary Rab Ha's in Glasgow's Merchant City. I remember him staggering out to spew at one point, screaming about the fug of cigarette smoke that clogged the air of the bar like fog in a Jack the Ripper movie.

The game itself was a nightmare for Celtic, but another part of my education as a fan. We were played off the park by a team that was as much in a different class as Berna was when he played Sunday league with us. The Parisian passes pinged about the park, all lovely one touch stuff. It made us look like cloggers in comparison, even though this was a Tommy Burns Celtic team who played the Celtic way. Two of the goals were scored by Patrice Loko who had been through a horrible time leading up to the game with his baby dying then him getting arrested and flashing a female policeman. The guy deserved a break by then, so fair play to Gordon Marshall for being such a charitable soul that night.

What was amazing that night was that the Celtic fans never stopped singing, never stopped cheering and most amazingly gave Paris St Germain a standing ovation at the end. 'That is a team full of honour,' Berna said in summation. Not surprising considering who our manager was at the time.

Coincidentally, the line-up that night of Marshall, Boyd, McKinlay, Vata, Hughes, Grant, O'Donnell, McStay, Van Hooijdonk, Thom and Collins was the best I ever played with in *Sensible Soccer*.

That game was at night, obviously. I only point that out because next time I went to Celtic Park was in broad daylight and things were a little bit different.

About a month after the Scottish Cup Final that year Kirk and I had started a TV show together called *Dom & Kirk's Night O Plenty* on the Paramount channel. Though only on cable, with a tiny audience, it was without doubt the greatest TV show I ever did. And here's why.

It consisted of Kirk and me basically talking pish in between assorted US sitcoms. Our brief was so wide-ranging and open it was visible from space. The boss at Paramount, a lovely big beardy bloke called Tony Orsten, was a big fan and encouraged me to do what the hell I liked.

I would sit and write the script during the week. My best pal would come down; we'd get bladdered, then go on live TV and have a laugh. On each show we would have a special guest in what we called The Totty Slotty, which may give some indication as to the kind of guest we wanted. Women. Attractive Famous Women. Attractive Famous Women who we were then given a whacking great Guest Expenses Budget to take out on the town in London.

By all that's unholy you cannot imagine what a tear up that was. I could give you details, but there would be arrests. It was that wild. Davina McCall, Tracy Shaw and Angela Griffin from Coronation Street, Sian Lloyd and any girl who happened to be on the front cover of *Loaded* that month all came, saw and got absolutely destroyed with us afterwards. Apart from Davina McCall, who was in recovery at the time, but by God she was the biggest laugh in the world.

I felt sorry for Kirk, because he actually had a proper job. He worked for a video games company in Dundee called VIS and would effectively fly down, do the show, stay out all night on the razz, then catch a flight back up the road at 7am the next morning for a full days work designing video games, while I at least had the luxury of being able to lie in bed for the next twenty four hours coughing up blood. Oh the glamour . . .

The best thing of all for me was that Kirk was married to the most beautiful woman in Scotland, so while he was an admirable wingman, chipping in with the gags and the drinks and whatnot, the path was left wide open for me to try and cop off. There was no chance of what, in modern guy parlance, is referred to as a cockblock here.

The fact that we were ostensibly allowed to do what we like meant that when I decided one day to do a show from Glasgow, no-one cared that this was just a chance for me to go up there and have a laugh in what I dearly wanted one day to be my adopted home town.

We decided to do *Dom & Kirk's Guide To Glasgow* which would include us filming what we thought would be a few guys arriving for that Saturday's game at Celtic Park.

Well Kirk and I were late, again. For the same reasons we were always late and by the time we got there the London Road was heaving. And I literally couldn't move. I was, for want of a better word, mobbed. More than in Liverpool, where it was random bands of Celtic fans. This was mobbed in the sense that Davy Crockett was mobbed at The Alamo. But these guys were killing me with kindness.

'Dominik ya legend!'

'Dominik, gonnae get it right up they fuckin Huns on the telly!'

'Dominik, yer a good Tim!'

And, following a recent front page tabloid story about my love life, 'Dominik, what was it like shagging Kirsty Young?'

I wasn't prepared for this. Sure, *Gamesmaster* was a big show in its day and there would be crowds when I opened up a games shop, but I was never the kind of guy that used to get mobbed in the street. Until now. Part of it is that Scottish thing whereby people are so loyal above and beyond the call of duty to any Scottish person in the media. This is why there's always a rubbish act from Scotland doing well on a TV talent show. And it's also why I was held in far bigger esteem north of the border than my talent and success deserved.

But it was also a Celtic thing. I guess it was like that guy had said in Liverpool. This was a club that had the crap kicked out of it over the last ten years and I was still willing to go on telly and radio and say I supported them. By coming up and shaking my hand these guys were saying that meant something to them.

It felt terrifying. I wasn't aware of this level of recognition, I certainly hadn't asked for it and deep down I still didn't feel I deserved it. Mind you, it wasn't just on the radio I'd been papping my Papedom. In the picture for the *FHM* Sunday League column I was holding a beer, smoking a fag and proudly wearing a Celtic top. I took this to more extremes in the column I had in *90 Minutes* at the time.

My standard picture was of me in the hoops. But the deal was that whenever Celtic lost to Rangers they used a photo of me in a Rangers top instead. What with me being a madman back then I didn't just wear a Rangers top in those photos. I would pull faces as if I was in pain; in others I held my nose, in one I was even setting fire to it. These are the kind of images that seep long into people's memories, the daft incendiary fool that I was.

'Now do you understand the power of the media?' Kirk asked. I did, and it was freaking me out. I didn't want that responsibility. I was just a guy farting around in the media and saying stuff to get a laugh.

Actually the funniest moment of the day concerned a comment one of the Tims said to Kirk, and showed how doing the

Paramount show and appearing regularly on *Gamesmaster* had increased Kirk's level of recognition too. A guy walked past, looked at me and went.

'Fucksake man – it's Dominik Diamond! How are you big man?'

Then he looked at Kirk, and a big smile broke out on his face as he exclaimed.

'And there's the other cunt an aw!'

We couldn't film the links until after the game had kicked off. The crowds were such that it was impossible to get a shot of more than a few seconds without me getting crowded by green and white shirts. We didn't have a ticket for the game because we had to carry on filming that afternoon, but I stood outside the ground as the crew were packing up and heard the roars and songs from inside. It was amazing and frustrating to have connected with these supporters but now still realise there was a literal and metaphorical wall separating me from them. It was like being adopted by a family, getting a big hug, then having to sit in the kitchen on your own while they opened their Xmas presents.

Sadly though, the day would not pass without more sectarian abuse, but this time it became even more sinister.

I'd gone to buy some DVDs after we wrapped while the crew packed up the van. I was walking down a side street called Mitchell Lane to meet up with them and passing the glass windows of a pub called Ross's when I heard banging on the glass. I looked round to see a gang of guys, casually dressed, only one of them with a Rangers top on, giving me what appeared to be Nazi salutes.

'What the fuck?' I thought. This was surreal. I'd had no experience of this particular extreme section of the Rangers support and it was . . . weird. My brain tried to compute why supporters of a Scottish team would be making a sign synonymous with

52

the biggest evil that has ever stalked this planet. Not just that but an evil that was responsible for raining down bombs on their own city of Glasgow during World War II, bombs that landed a stones throw from their beloved Ibrox. Did they think I was Jewish or something? Was that it?

What was worse about these guys is their faces were not twisted in hate like the ones in the Airdrie end at Hampden. These guys were smiling and laughing. How can you smile when you're doing a Nazi salute? What moral depths do you have to sink to? What emptiness must you have where your soul is supposed to be?

In retrospect blessing them with the sign of the cross was not the cleverest thing to do but I knew two things by then. Firstly, this would wind them up, and secondly, I could run fast. Thankfully the crew car was waiting for me on Mitchell Street with the engine running.

The incident remained more surreal than disturbing, but on my next trip up I was treated to another example of the Nazi element of the Rangers support, this time without the benefit of a glass window between me and the threat, or a car full of colleagues with the engine running.

We were out on another bender in Glasgow. Kirk was there, so was David Wells, and three or four other guys. We'd ended up in The Variety Bar on Sauchiehall Street and a bunch of young lads had started chatting to me while I was getting a round in at the bar.

They announced they were Rangers fans which made my pals slightly cagey. But it seemed like good-natured banter so when my pals said they were off to get something to eat at the Chinese next door I said I'd catch them up, after all I had half a pint left and these guys seemed alright. Silly boy.

I finished up, said my goodbyes and headed into the Chinese. None of my pals were there. They'd decided to go Indian instead,

I later found out, but for now I just got some chicken chow mein and sat down in a corner of the restaurant to eat it, away from prying eyes.

But not all eyes, unfortunately. I was looking down at my food so I didn't see the guys from the bar approach until they'd sat down around me, hemming me into the corner. The atmosphere was now a tad strange.

'Right Dominik, are you familiar with Combat 18?'

'No,' I said. I'd genuinely never heard of them.

'Well you should be, because this is official notice that you're on our target list.'

What the fuck was this now? I think because they were young lads and because I had no idea what Combat 18 was, I felt strangely calm. So I just said. 'Why?'

The leader, a chubby-faced boy, explained. 'Well firstly because of the nigger-loving shit you write in your paper, and secondly because you're a Fenian Bastard who likes to be cheeky.'

This was not long after the death of black teenager Stephen Lawrence and I'd written numerous articles in my *Daily Star* column about what a disgrace his murder and the subsequent investigation had been. I'd had a couple of racist letters in response, but this was the first time I'd been taken to task face to face.

'What do you mean; I'm on your target list?' I asked, trying to compute the information through Stella and stir-fry.

'It means you watch your fucking back, you dirty Taig.' And with that they stood up and left. I stayed there and finished my chow mein, my mind racing. Who the fuck were Combat 18? And where the hell were my pals? I phoned David. They'd jumped in a cab home, leaving me in the city centre. It was the one and only time they ever did that.

Sauchiehall Street on a Saturday night at chucking out time was busy enough for me to not feel too worried about the guys jumping me, so I walked out, hailed a cab and headed back to David's on the south side.

If I'd known more about Combat 18; that their name was a numerical representation of Hitler's initials, that they were about to start a letter bomb campaign targeting mixed-race marriages in the next twelve months in the UK and that they were murdering non-whites all over Europe, I'd have been more worried. But ignorance in this case was bliss. Needless to say I went straight on the internet to find out more. Then shat myself.

David said to me that night, 'Your problem Dominik is you can never put that genie back in the box now. That's it. You're a Tim. Up here that means for half the people you can never be one of them. And a fraction of those people are headcases. It's the worst thing you could have possibly done in terms of your media career in Scotland.'

I wasn't giving a damn about my career. I was more worried about my life.

Kirk's view was slightly more reassuring. 'Don't be daft. It doesn't matter how much they hate you. This is Scotland; we don't stab one of our own if they're on the telly. It means an English guy would get their job.'

Sadly it wasn't just in Scotland I was getting this kind of abuse. Though the weekend radio shows meant I couldn't get up to Celtic games at the weekend, they left me just enough time to drive up to The Manor Ground to see Oxford United with Sad Andy.

Ian Davis was the box office manager and a fan of *Sportscall*. He'd heard me mention Sad Andy my Oxford-daft mate many times so he invited us to come up to a game and have a drink in the players lounge afterwards. I got Andy and all his mates in and we had a great time. After that I spent most of the 1995-1996 season following them. They had some good wee players at the time; Paul Moody and Nigel Jemson were a good pair of strikers, Matt Elliott who Martin O'Neill signed for Leicester (and who infamously got sent off for Scotland against the Faroe Islands in that woeful draw in 1999) was then the best central defender in division two and Bobby Ford was a mercurial midfielder in the Paul McStay mould.

The irony is not lost on me that these days Oxford is where a number of Rangers youngsters get sent out on loan and their hated rivals Swindon Town have taken the likes of Simon Ferry from Celtic.

But the main thing I loved about Oxford then was that it was another club, like Celtic and like Milton Keynes City Rugby Club, that took me in and made me feel I belonged somewhere. Apart from one guy.

Sad Andy and I had gone up to Nottingham to see Oxford take on Forest in the FA Cup. (1-1, Paul Moody equalising from a corner flicked on at the near post by Matt Elliott right in front of us.) At half-time we were getting some chips when I heard this shout in an Oxford accent, 'Oy you, ya fucking Fenian bastard.'

I know. Once again those two words I kept getting called. It made me wonder if I'd got really drunk one night and changed my name by deed poll without realising. The words were spoken by the kind of guy you just know is trouble. Wiry and sinewy, skinhead, tattoos, piercing eyes and giving off the kind of energy that tells you he needs to get into a fight every day just to let off enough steam to sleep at night. He hit me with a machine gun volley of words, spoken in such a way I'm sure some form of amphetamine was aiding the delivery.

'Yeah it is you, innit? Ya fucking Fenian Bastard. What the fuck are you doing supporting my fucking club you fucking Fenian Bastard. Stick to your own fucking Fenian club.' Basically take those words, repeat them and keep rearranging the words and you pretty much have the gist of the next few minutes of my life.

This time I really had had enough.

'What is your fucking problem?' I asked, but more desperate-sounding than aggressive.

'Walk away!' hissed Sad Andy.

'What you fucking saying to me?' speeding Skinhead asked.

'I said . . .'

'WALK AWAY!' Andy grabbed me.

'WHAT YOU FUCKING SAYING TO ME YOU FUCKING FENIAN BASTARD!' The stewards grabbed him. He started knocking hell out of the stewards. Seriously. This guy was hardcore. Andy pulled me back to the steps leading up to our seats.

'That guy is BAD news!' he said. 'I'm not kidding. I have seen him take on four policemen outside the Manor. He's a legendary Oxford hard nut. And he's National Front as well.'

Oh great. More fascists after me. Perhaps I could have asked them to form an orderly line. Maybe installed one of those numbered ticketing systems you get at the supermarket deli counter. 'Number 43? Number 43? Ah yes, National Front. Please take a seat, Mr Diamond will be with you in a minute, he's just having the shit kicked out of him by Blood and Honour.'

Sure enough a few months later my phone rang. It was Sad Andy. 'Have you seen the *Mirror* today?'

Inside was a spread on the UK's most notorious football hooligans. Right in the middle was my mate from half-time at Forest, who'd just been banned from every ground in the UK. I may have been cut off from reality in London, safely ensconced in this media bubble, but it was becoming very clear that the minute I stepped outside it life was anything but safe.

# THE SPICE BOYS

Sometimes there were nights as a Famous Celtic Fan where there was no downside. There were some nights when I didn't get called a Fenian Bastard once, and these are nights I look back on and thank God that in spite of all the stress, insomnia, depression and therapy that my choice of career ultimately led to, there were some moments where it just entered the realms of fantasy. Like the night I got £20 million of talent to sign for Celtic.

I'd kept in touch with Phil Babb after Ian Rush's testimonial and he invited me and Sad Andy up to the Liverpool – Coventry game on 14 October 1995 to see the game then go along with him and the rest of The Spice Boys to the nightclub Cream's birthday.

The Spice Boys was the term that had now been given to that Liverpool team. David James and Jamie Redknapp had done some Armani modelling, Robbie Fowler was rumoured to be going out with Emma Bunton, McManaman and Babb regularly appeared in the likes of *Loaded* magazine and all those things contributed to the nickname. They ended up taking a lot of flak for these things, with the feeling being that as a generation of supremely talented Liverpool players they underachieved.

I'm not so sure. It was to be injuries that ultimately robbed Redknapp and Fowler of more success, McAteer got to score that winner for the Republic against Holland in 2001 *and* got name checked by Bono live on stage for doing so. Babbsy went on to have a good career in Portugal, David James *did* turn out to be a legend when he stopped playing *Tomb Raider* long enough to concentrate and Macca, the most talented of all of them, was just one of those players who is so supremely individually gifted they can never fit into a team of ten other players with rigid positions (see also McGeady, Aiden).

What they did do, however, is get a load of people interested in football, and specifically that Liverpool team, that otherwise would not have cared. They helped football cross over into other cultures and were a hell of a lot more interesting than 99% of their colleagues. They were the Rodney Marsh and Stan Bowles of their generation. And what's wrong with that? OK. What's wrong with that *apart* from the pink suits they all wore to the 1996 FA Cup Final?

The problem is that Liverpool, like Celtic, is a team that demands success and when they *do* have talented players and success doesn't come then the press know that it's easy to stoke the fire by coming up with an angle of discontent that can then strike a chord with the fans. After that it becomes a mutual feeding frenzy betwixt fans and tabloids.

Anyway, they were great guys to hang around with. Actually they were amazing guys to hang around with because they were the Kings of Liverpool and to go out in that city with them in the 90s was like going out with Sinatra and The Rat Pack in 1960s Las Vegas.

But it is maybe telling that on this day the game was a totally forgettable 0-0 draw. Like I cared! Because Phil Babb came and got Sad Andy and I from outside the ground. He walked us in across the actual Anfield pitch, took us up *that* tunnel with *that*

This Is Anfield sign. And yes, of *course* we touched it. To not have touched that sign would have been like walking past Kylie Minogue at a party for *Face* magazine and *not* touching her bum, which I also did at around the same time.

This was also the time when the continental influence started hitting UK training grounds and there was much debate about refuelling properly before, during and after games. One person in particular in the Players Bar at Anfield that day knocked this idea into touch. Neil Ruddock, another very funny guy, was actually serving as the barman, and while the likes of Robbie Fowler and Jamie Redknapp were rehydrating with pints of Lucozade, Ruddock was pouring me a pint of Carling, drinking half of it himself in one gulp, then topping it up and handing it to me.

Sad Andy, Babbsy, David James, Macca, Jamie Redknapp AKA Red Stripe, Stan Collymore and myself then went on a crawl of what were some cracking Liverpool bars. Mello Mello, The Baa Bar, The Magnet, The Cavern (which they went to because I begged them to take me to it like the total tourist I was). It remains the greatest night Sad Andy and I ever had, possibly topped only by the night Oxford Utd got promoted to the Second Division and we gatecrashed a series of posh Oxford University balls with our faces painted yellow and blue.

But if you'd have been able to overhear the conversations that night you'd have been very disappointed. Mostly it was me, Babbsy, Collymore and David James talking about video games and Sad Andy talking to Jamie Redknapp and Steve McManaman about obscure times when their career trajectory had taken them within a hundred miles of Oxford Utd.

Sad Andy is a walking encyclopaedia. I swear he's one of those guys who genuinely does know everything about every-thing and never forgets it. Not just Oxford United and football in general, but tropical diseases, ancient civilisations, space travel and The Yorkshire Ripper, the last of which was to hold us in great stead at the end of 1999 when we interviewed Martin O'Neill and were instrumental in him taking the Celtic manager's job. Kind of.

The funniest part of Sad Andy's inner encyclopaedia was his ability to take any football player and somehow relate them to Oxford United in a Six Degrees of Separation way.

For example, one night we ate at a new Gordon Ramsay restaurant in London, The Boxwood Café. Following the most incredible rib of beef I have ever tasted in my life Ramsay came out and 'worked the tables'. When he came to ours the combination of the phenomenal meat and the fact that he knew who I was made me so excited I could hardly speak. Unfortunately this meant that Sad Andy got to open the conversational gambit with the fact that he was an Oxford United fan and Gordon had played for the Oxford United youth team in the early 1980s. Andy sat there and bombarded him with names and places from back then and that was that. My chance to discuss just how Ramsay had got the jus flavoured in such a way (reduced veal stock? Marrowbone? A secret blend of the Colonel's herbs and spices?) gone forever.

Spices. Spices? Oh yes. Back to the Spice Boys of Liverpool.

We had ended up in the VIP room in Cream, and we'd all had a bit to drink. I went round all of the players there and got them to sign a bit of paper. I said it was for a mate of mine who was a big Liverpool fan, but in reality it was folded in half. On the bottom half were the signatures of Babb, McManaman, Redknapp, James and Collymore. On the top half, unbeknown to them, I had written. 'We the undersigned hereby agree to sign for Celtic FC this year for £20 each.'

I'm no legal expert, and I'm not sure if it would have stood up in a court of law, though it's arguably a lot less dodgy than when we signed Du Wei. One can only imagine what Celtic could have achieved that year with McManaman and Redknapp joining McStay and Di Canio in midfield feeding Cadete, Van Hoojdonk and Collymore up front. We'd have hardly needed to rely on Babb, McNamara and Stubbs in defence, nor big David James in goal. We'd have won everything. And it would have meant Steve McManaman could not have scored that heart-breaking wonder goal against us in the UEFA Cup in 1997.

But unfortunately I went off to meet up with a police sergeant called Paula whom I'd snogged at the Ian Rush testimonial and who I had in the interim months fallen desperately in love with. At the end of the night I finally swapped telephone numbers with her. I realised to my horror the next morning that the piece of paper I'd written my number on and given to her was the same piece of paper I'd signed The Spice Boys on for Celtic.

# 8

# LIVE AND A BIT TOO DANGEROUS

1997 was the year it all changed, for Celtic and for me. 1997 saw Rangers getting nine in a row to complete Celtic's dark period, but also saw Fergus McCann's plans start to come to fruition and the dual arrivals of Wim Jansen and Henrik Larsson, which all combined to make sure they didn't get the ten. For me it represented the last year of video game telly. The success of *Sportscall* and *Fantasy Football*, coupled with the *90 Minutes* column had meant I was starting to be taken seriously as a sports presenter. This was a relief because, as much as I loved *Gamesmaster* and was very proud of what the team and I had done with that show, it was an albatross around my neck.

People like to pigeonhole you in TV. No matter how hilarious his general observation columns are, Jeremy Clarkson will always be the car guy. Kim and Aggie could come up with a cure for cancer tomorrow but I guarantee TV chiefs would get them to say they discovered it while cleaning the back of some bloke's sofa. So I was 'the videogames guy'. It didn't matter how much I liked sport, or how knowledgeable I was, I was not 'the sports guy'. With music it was even more frustrating. Music was, is and always will be my greatest passion. When I had a video games column in *Smash Hits* back in 1991 I mainly used it to tell their readers about this amazing band Manic

Street Preachers that I adored. As a result after a year I finally persuaded the editor to let me interview them. It was their first interview outside of the *NME/Melody Maker*. But it took me another fifteen years before I finally got that music radio show I'd dreamed of.

For now though I was just happy to get away from Patrick Moore. The best thing I could do to obliterate the *Gamesmaster* image was to make a big controversial impression on a new sports show. It's just a pity that this show was in the middle of the night on a channel half the country couldn't pick up.

And it's also a pity that I was so desperately trying to be dangerous and controversial on it I pissed off a lot of what was a tiny audience to begin with and, more importantly, the people in charge too. I watched an episode of *Live and Dangerous* recently and I cringed. You have never seen a presenter more deluded about his importance in the world. Actually maybe you have. Maybe you did that night. Congratulations on being one of the few.

It was a mistake I made throughout my career. I was swayed by the people who would come up to you and say how they loved the mental stuff I said, the dangerous stuff, the stuff no-one else would. So every time the little voice in my head said 'do not say what you're about to say' the other voice would say 'go on! Those guys on the London Road will think you're brilliant!' And the second voice would always win.

I only lasted a year on *Live and Dangerous* before I quit but it was not a total waste. I worked with a great team behind the scenes, had a lot of fun with Shelley Webb and Helen Chamberlain and managed to interview some sporting greats, including Celtic ones like Danny McGrain, Roy Aitken, Frank MacAvennie and Charlie Nicholas. Or good guy, good guy, good guy, wank as they'd be known if this was *Chewin The Fat*.

It's not that Charlie Nicholas was unpleasant, it's more that he just really, really, really fancied himself. Mr McGrain and Roy were just solid men of honour and integrity. There was just something class about them. You know when you're little, and one of your pals has always got a dad that just seems so straight and true that you kind of wish he was your dad? That was what Mr McGrain and Roy were like. I wanted them to be my dad.

I just wanted Frank MacAvennie to be my pal! You got the impression from Frank that he couldn't believe his luck at the hand life had dealt him and he had made the most of every second of it. Sometimes even on the field as well as in the bars. He was hilarious.

But Charlie was a bit 'look at me', a bit arrogant. The kind of guy who in spite of what he achieved still thought he was a bit better than all of it. In other words, a bit too much like me. I'm sure if I met him now we'd get on fine, what with me not being a total wanker any more. Honestly, ask my wife or my mum.

It wasn't just former Hoops that we had on. Channel 5 had the rights to cover Chelsea in Europe so we had a conveyor belt of former Rangers players with Chelsea connections on: Ray Wilkins; Nigel Spackman; Mark Hateley. To be honest though, my moments with them passed without incident. Well the law of averages state that there had to be *some* moments without incident in my life.

But then there was Terry Butcher. Oh yes. Terry Butcher. I cannot remember for the life of me what Terry Butcher was on the show to talk about. I cannot remember anything that I asked him about on air. All I can remember was one interchange and one interchange alone that shook me to the core.

We were in the Green Room where the guests could relax before going on air, or at least that's the official reason for it. The real reason is so that guests can have enough to drink so that they relax and say something they would normally be too guarded to say.

I never liked to meet guests before shows. By the time they'd arrive I'd have worked so hard at preparing the interview that I didn't want to waste any conversation off air. There is nothing worse than speaking to a guest off air and something really funny is said and you know you can't repeat it on air, because it will sound faked. Which doesn't stop hundreds of presenters doing this, but I think it shows.

But I still made a token effort to be polite, although in Butcher's case I wish I hadn't. I shook his hand and there was something a little too firm about the grip. I said 'pleased to meet you' and there was something a little too fixed in his smile, something a little dead behind the eyes. I had heard that whereas the likes of Wilkins and Spackman had been footballers who had happened to play for Rangers, Terry Butcher *was* a Rangers man through and through. So I just assumed he hated me for being a Celtic fan.

We were standing by the side of the set, about to go on and Terry said very softly so only I could hear, the words I had prayed no-one would ever say to me in the media.

'I hear you were a Rangers fan.'

'What?' I did my usual of feigning deafness until my brain could catch up.

'You were a Rangers fan, weren't you?' he repeated, with a smile. The kind of smile I had last seen on the face of the Child Catcher in *Chitty Chitty Bang Bang*.

'Who told you that?' I sputtered as the floor manager shouted. 'Three minutes to on air, Dominik and Terry take your seats please.'

'That's just what I've heard.'

'Nah, you must be mistaken, Terry,' I said, trying to finally see if I had, as I always dreamed, been given Jedi Mind Control powers that could make people believe me if I just said the words in a meaningful yet slightly fey way.

'Maybe we should talk about it on the show, then?'

The fucker. The utter fucker.

And then we were on air. Like I say, I have no recollection what the interview was about. I cannot remember so much as one question asked and answered. I just tried to get through the questions I'd prepared while my mind was racing. What the hell would I say if he came out live on air with the fact I had been a teenage Rangers fan? Should I confess? Deny? Explain about the big boy on the bus and how I'd never even been to a Rangers game in that time so it didn't really count? Every time Butcher opened his mouth I thought he was about to give the game away.

But he didn't. Why didn't he? Was it because he was enjoying seeing me squirm too much? Possibly. Or more likely he thought it was too risqué a thing to get into on air, especially as I'd denied it. We'd be live and bit too dangerous, and no-one really took those kinds of risks on the box. No one apart from the idiot writing this book.

Can you imagine what I'd have been like if it had been the other way around? If I'd heard that Terry Butcher had been a childhood Celtic fan? I'd have come right out with it as the first question, presented him with a Celtic top complete with his name and number on the back and whistled Boys of the Old Brigade as he was answering questions.

Maybe, and this is the hardest thing to think, maybe he just took pity on me. Whatever the reason, when the interview ended I had to stay on set to do the next section. I shook his hand as quickly as I could, again he gripped it a little too tightly, and then he left.

People often asked me 'do you get nervous doing live telly?' And I would reply 'no'. From this point on if they asked me I would reply. 'No, unless Terry Butcher is there.' And then start to cry.

I was presenting another sports show on Channel 5 at the time, an effervescent Day-Glo Saturday morning sports magazine show that broadcast from Southampton called *Turnstyle*, alongside Gail McKenna. She was a Scouser. She was smart. She was funny. And she was a former Page Three girl. I was in heaven.

When I say that I didn't have time to get up the road to see Celtic during these days, let me put this workload into perspective. I would be doing *Live and Dangerous* four nights a week. I'd prep the interviews during the day, watch hours of footage from whatever sports had happened in the last twenty four hours, be it football, rugby, cricket or synchronised swimming, then get to the studio for about 9pm, do the show and get home by 2am then be so pumped on adrenaline I'd stay up till dawn playing *Final Fantasy VII* on the Playstation. On Friday I'd scoot down to Southampton to rehearse *Turnstyle*, then as soon as that was off the air I'd get the train back to London to prepare for *Sportscall* on Radio 5 live which had now moved to Sundays. Such were the demands on the young media bawbag about town in those days.

Graeme Souness was manager of Southampton at the time I was doing *Turnstyle* so it was just a matter of time before I bumped into him. On live telly. I actually liked Souness. I know I'm not supposed to. I'm supposed to think that the likes of him, Ally McCoist, Graham Roberts and Alex McLeish drown kittens in sacks at high tide. But they are all Huns I've liked. In fact that's how Ally would often introduce himself when we met. 'Hey Dominik, it's the one Hun you really like!' he would say with relish.

Souness was a bit more reserved, a bit more detached. Dare I say it, Souness was *cool*. He was one of those people for whom movement of any kind seemed effortless. I am one of those physically clumsy people: if I go to shake your hand chances are I'll knock your pint over and catch my ring in your wife's dress too. There are many like me, in fact the whole series of Carry On films wouldn't exist if we didn't.

Souness seemed to glide across the room. When he went to shake your hand his hand was just *there* as if he didn't even have to lift it from his sides. And his voice had the same effect as the one that snake has in *The Jungle Book*. He would start telling you something in those soft tones and you'd just get sucked in. He'd have made a great hypnotherapist.

I had real problems equating this Souness I met with the hard-tackling psycho in the dark blue Rangers shirt. But the voice in my head didn't. Oh no. The voice in my head was desperate to make trouble. This time it was sounding like my old friend Romano. And every time I went to say something to Souness, Romano's voice would go chime, 'Call him a Hun. On air. G'wan. Just say Souness ya big dirty orange bastard. G'wan. You'll be a Celtic legend.'

What didn't help was that I had my hair dyed orange that day, as a result of losing an on-air bet with Southampton full-back Jason Dodd. It was a pretty abject season as far as The Saints were concerned, in spite of the fact that Souness had brought in Egil Ostendstadt and Celtic . . . er . . . legend Eyal Berkovic. In fact it was at Southampton that Berkovic nailed his colours to the mast as a class player, with two goals and three assists in Southampton's famous win over Manchester United that season. This was back when he was still incredibly gifted on the ball, as opposed to his time at Celtic when he was an incredibly gifted bawbag.

In spite of the talents of that team (who still had Le Tissier) they were down at the bottom of the table and in serious danger of relegation. I made a bet with Doddsy that if Southampton stayed up then I would dye my hair ginger.

Which is why I ended up talking to Graeme Souness with orange hair. The irony was not lost on Souness. We began the interview with the chat about my hair, and Souness said, 'You're a Celtic fan aren't you?'

For a fleeting second I was terrified he was about to continue, 'That Terry Butcher tells me you were once a Rangers fan, though.'

But instead he said that he'd worn a blue shirt just for me.

This was May 1997 and so I had to ask through gritted teeth how much he felt he'd been responsible for Rangers' nine in a row. And then had to endure a caller asking if Graeme thought Rangers would get ten in a row. He thought they would.

'What colour will your hair be then, Dominik?' he asked.

'Grey,' I replied.

I asked if he thought Celtic would be able to lure the likes of a Bobby Robson or Joe Kinnear, who were two of the fron-trunners to replace Barnes at that time. He said they needed to get someone in who was experienced and ideally Scottish as well, being more used to the passion and the aggravation that goes with managing Celtic and Rangers.

I knew someone who fitted all those criteria, so here was my chance to get the headline of the decade. 'You wouldn't take the Celtic job, would you, Graeme?' Either way he answered would give us the kind of back page headlines a tiny show like ours was crying out for. His answer was diplomacy rendered verbal.

'Football wise it *would* be managing a big club, but for me, where would I live?'

Like I said, this guy was cool. This was a very reflective Souness by this stage, who said during the interview that he now realised there were more important things than football. He said some really wise things, the kind of things he might say to Ralph Macchio if Souness had a white beard and a fence that needed painting in a film called *The Football Kid*.

'I tell my players that when they were 2 foot 6 high they started kicking a ball because they enjoyed it. Then they become professionals and they get paid a lot of money for kicking a ball and it seems to become a burden to them. I preach to them – enjoy the game of football like you did back then.'

It's the kind of advice I should have heeded many times in my presenting career, but I ended up quitting *Turnstyle* because once again I had an executive in charge whom I thought was a tube. Luckily at the same time the BBC had said they were moving *Sportscall* back to Saturday and offered me the chance to produce it with my own production company. For a megalomaniacal, control-freak, madman like myself this was a dream.

It was also a good lesson in how horrible the media can be. I had told this executive producer I was leaving the show but I was happy to serve out my notice. We parted on good terms. Then I got a call from my agent during the week to say I was not to do any more *Turnstyle* shows. The next show went ahead without any mention of what had happened to its main presenter.

Now that's a dishonourable thing to do. And in the head of a madman like me it can only lead to bitterness and recrimination. So for the first few weeks of the new *Sportscall* series I spent a considerable amount of time saying how awful *Turnstyle* was. Until the head of Channel 5 Dawn Airey sent a letter to the head of *Live and Dangerous* saying I'd be binned by Channel 5 if I didn't stop.

She used words like 'perverse, naive and unprofessional' to describe me, which pretty much describes my entire career. I was exciting and my attacks were fun but I wasn't winning any friends. Substitute the word 'trophies' for 'friends' and you've got Tommy Burns' Celtic managerial career and poor Tommy left Celtic at the same time as I left Southampton.

And then there was Wim. Celtic had decided not to follow

the sage advice Graeme Souness dished out on *Turnstyle*, possibly because like everybody else in Britain, they weren't watching.

Wim started winning things. It's amazing when you think of how many players he brought in: not just Henrik, but Regi Blinker, Craig Burley, Stephane Mahe, Darren Jackson, Jonathon Gould, Marc Rieper, Paul Lambert and of course Harald Brattbakk, who was going to bring the good times back, back, back. I can't think of any football club that bought so many players who became important first team players *that same year*. That's half a squad of newcomers the Hair Bear Magician moulded into shape along with the likes of Boyd, Wieghorst, McNamara, Stubbs and Donnelly.

It's also worth pointing out that with Henrik, Wim, Sid and Darren Jackson we finally had some players who had hair worthy of a rock band.

One game I did get up to see that season convinced me not to go back again. In fact Danny McGrain point blank *told* me to stay away.

Like I've mentioned before, Mr McGrain was an absolute gent. He wrote a letter after his appearance on *Live & Dangerous* saying how much he'd enjoyed the interview. We used to let them run for half an hour and Danny said it really helped to have the time to relax into it. He also said that if I ever wanted a ticket for a Celtic game to give him a call.

It took me about a month to pluck up the courage. Even though I'd interviewed him, and he'd written to me, I *still* felt intimidated by who the man was. When I called him up he was in the middle of his tea and I felt so embarrassed as Danny McGrain tried to arrange a date with me in between mouthfuls of fish and chips.

It was arranged that I'd come up for the game against Dundee Utd on 15 March 1998. It was a Sunday so I'd flown up to Glasgow after *Sportscall* on the Saturday, gone out with Kirk, got hammered, woke up at 2am with an ear infection, got a taxi down to the Victoria Hospital and sat among the stab victims for an hour or so facing in towards the wall so I wouldn't be recognised. My eardrum burst while I was in the waiting room and I had yellow gunk expelling from it for the next few days. Oh yes, it was to be one of *those* weekends.

I was to meet Mr McGrain inside the main club entrance. We had learned from our previous experience, so to avoid being recognised this time Kirk and I dressed in full gorilla suits with masks, or maybe we just walked faster. Like I said, it was one of those weekends.

Mr McGrain was standing in his suit, next to Tosh McKinlay, who was out injured at the time, and once again that device that rendered me incapable of meeting famous people without being a Muppet got switched on.

'Hello Dominik!' said Mr McGrain.

'Hello Mr McGrain,' said I.

'How do you do Dominik, you're a legend,' said Tosh with a smile.

'Thanks Todd, but you're the legend, not me,' I replied.

Todd? *Todd*? Who the hell is Todd? Oh yeah, you're such a legend that I can't even get your name right. So I did that thing that people do when they realise they've got someone's name wrong. I tried to cram in his correct name as many times as I could.

'How's the leg Tosh?' I asked. 'Hell of a shame you can't be out there today Tosh. Must be infuriating for you, eh Tosho? Tosheroony? Oh yes, tis a shame I cannot see the Toshmeister in action today.'

And then I felt wetness running down the right side of my neck, wetness coming from the direction of my ear. Oh that was just fantastic! In the posh foyer of Celtic Park, with Danny McGrain, getting Tosh McKinlay's name wrong and now yellow pus running out of my infected ear. So I turned my fetid ear away from Tosh with the effect that I had now turned a full ninety degrees away from him as sharply as if I was on a military parade ground. Now this looked a bit strange, but there was no way I wanted him to see my manky ear. Nor did I want to appear rude, so I affected that thing Gordon Strachan used to do when being interviewed after a game. I call it the Off Camera 90 Degree Flickaround.

Basically someone asks you the question and you look away from them for the most part as you reply, but now and again you flick your head back round to show that you're still interested in what they're saying. Loads of footballers and managers do it. More so in England when they're looking around for an exit to run into during one of those long pauses in the middle of a Garth Crooks question. So this style of dialogue would not be completely inexplicable to Tosh and Mr McGrain. Many football people spoke in this fashion.

Not when they've got pus dripping from their ear they didn't. Because when you've got pus dripping from your ear and you flick your head then the pus comes off your ear and flies through the air.

No. Don't worry. It didn't hit Tosh. Or Mr McGrain. But a bit of my ear sputum did hit a serious looking bloke in a suit as he headed past me. He was probably one of the board, so fair enough.

I wrapped up the conversation with a final 'Tosh!' grabbed the tickets from Mr McGrain's hand and headed off. Tosh McKinlay is a true Celtic fan and I have seen him a few times since, sat in the middle of us fans at Ibrox. I have hidden my head in shame each time in case he ever saw me.

This was a significant day for many reasons; including two I didn't know yet. Kirk and my seats, high up in what was then the East Stand Upper, later renamed The Lisbon Lions Stand, were about a coin's throw from where I finally sat when I got season tickets four years later and fulfilled the dream. And a 15 March in the future would see my one and only controversial appearance on Celtic TV. But for now there were two things that mattered in the present. Rangers had lost to Motherwell the day before so if we won this we would go seven points ahead of them with a huge chance of stopping them getting ten in a row. And it was my first chance to see Henrik Larsson in the flesh over ninety minutes.

Neither events worked out well. Henrik should have had a hat trick in that game and when he missed a sitter of a header from a few yards out I turned to Kirk and actually said, 'This guy's pish! Not a patch on Brattbakk.'

Can you believe I made my living as a football pundit at the time? In my defence Brattbakk had a fantastic game. Linking beautifully with Henrik and Simon Donnelly and having a few shots saved and a cracking volley from outside the box that just floated over the bar. We had a stonewall penalty denied after the United keeper Sieb Dykstra fouled Simon Donnelly but the referee, a certain Mike McCurry didn't award it.

'That ref's a Hun in disguise,' I said to Kirk. 'Bet you any money.'

Did I ever mention I was a brilliant pundit at the time? With fifteen minutes to go we were still leading 1-0 from Sid Donnelly's first half goal but had missed so many chances you got the feeling it was not to be Celtic's day, given how important the game was, and how much my ever paranoid mind was messing me up.

'You know they're going to lose, don't you? Because you didn't pay for your ticket!' the voice in my head said. 'Oh yes, call yourself a real fan? Don't make me laugh, ya freeloading ex-Hun celebrity wanker!'

And then Dundee Utd equalised with about fifteen minutes

to go through Kjell Olafsson, whose tally of scoring against Celtic almost matched the total his name would get you in Scrabble. And that was that. You can say all you want about how much Jonathon Gould should have saved it or how much our defence should have tackled him or how our midfield should have held onto the ball in that last quarter hour or how we should have been eight or nine up by that stage, but I knew differently.

I knew it was my fault. I knew it was God punishing Celtic and all their proper fans because I was a rubbish media fan who once supported Rangers and had spent the last decade getting pissed in London nightclubs and being a slave to the media when I should have been in the Jungle. I probably should have realised this was the moment in my life I started to go a bit mad. I popped back in to say thank you to Mr McGrain.

'First game you've been to in a fair while, eh Dominik?' He said, luring me in.

'Yes, Mr McGrain,' I replied, looking down at my feet.

'Aye well don't come back again this season will you, we need to stop ten in a row and you're a bloody jinx!' And he laughed.

But I didn't laugh. I vomited inside.

*Live and Dangerous* went the way of most of my TV and radio shows. I started off really enjoying it, but it was only a matter of time before someone in a suit started making decisions about the show I didn't agree with and my inability to play the media game resulted in me telling them to shove their job up their arse.

The irony about this departure was that it came about after I was told by the head of Channel 5 Sport Robert Charles that I had to stop being so dangerous. On a show called *Live and Dangerous*. My head exploded with the irony.

Still, that was only one media company I had completely

alienated and there were others out there, including the BBC, who were giving me a lot of love and new commissions. Roger Mosey was a great controller of 5 live. One of that rare breed of boss I encountered in my career who liked what I did, gave me the freedom to do it and was a big enough name to back me when the flak hit without worrying about his own career. The bosses I got on best with were always the ones who realised I was a ridiculously immature but vaguely gifted man-child who needed to be fathered in the media sense. In return, although I said some dangerous things, I worked my proverbial backside off for the guy. He commissioned my company's first documentary *A Drowning Of Sorrows*, the story of Scotland's World Cup woes told from the point of view of the Tartan Army.

My producer Jo Treharne had set up a load of interviews north of the border and it just so happened that they were congregating around Saturday, 9 May 1998, the last day of the SPL season. Celtic should have wrapped up the league by then but a 2-0 defeat to Rangers (with one of the goals, naturally, coming from Jörg Albertz) and a heartbreaking draw at Dunfermline meant it was all down to the final game at home against St Johnstone.

I then made one the most difficult decisions of my Celtic-supporting life. A random listener had called up *Sportscall* and offered me a ticket to the game. I worked out that if I flew up straight after the show I could have got to Celtic Park at around 3.30pm. But I remembered the Dundee Utd game. I remembered the words of Mr McGrain and I remembered the voice in my head telling me that draw had been my fault. Superstition has never worn such a comfortable cloak as my psyche. So I turned it down and Jo and I went up on the train instead.

But not before we'd had a bit more mischief on *Sportscall* that day after I said on air that I'd gone round the entire BBC and taken a straw poll and everyone, from the cleaners right up to

77

Terry Wogan, wanted to wish Celtic all the best that day in their efforts to stop Rangers getting ten in a row. It was not the kind of thing they did often, I said, being a politically impartial state public broadcaster, but on this day the danger was so great the BBC were happy to say they were backing Celtic. Yes it was madness, but it was a beautiful kind of madness sometimes.

One of our many prizes on the show at that time was these little 5 live branded radios. They were jammed so that the only frequencies you could get were 909 or 693 MW. And they were pretty cheap. So we sat, with beer, on a train listening to the crackly medium wave signal of 5 live giving updates from the Celtic game and Rangers game against Dundee United.

People who were at Celtic Park that day will remember that Henrik Larsson scored after two minutes, by our train time-frame, however, he will always have scored 'just outside Lichfield Trent Valley'.

Unfortunately Rangers scored 'just outside Stafford' and 'just outside Warrington Bank Quay'. So we still knew that any slip up, like the one that had happened at Dunfermline the weekend before, or against Dundee Utd at the game I ruined for them and it would be over. Ten in a row would be Rangers.

More beer. More crisps. A pitiful attempt at a bacon sandwich. Then something happened. Only we weren't quite sure what.

Have you ever tried to listen to a radio on a train? Especially on medium wave? It's a complete nightmare. The commentators all become like Norman Collier, with every third syllable disappearing into the ether. So when we were just coming into Preston we heard the Sport on 5 announcer say they were going to Celtic Park, and we heard the following.

'McNamara xxzzzxx crackle spit fizz right hand side zzjjdnbe Brattb zxxxsssd . . .'

Then the radio went silent. What had happened?

'Have they scored?' Jo looked at me with a mouthful of crisps having heard the same intergalactic muffle.

'I don't know?' I screamed, to the alarm of the rest of the carriage.

'All I heard was Brattbakk,' she continued, crisps now flying out her mouth.

'That means it must have been a miss,' I decided.

And we sat there, in much the same way I imagine they sat in NASA as Neil Armstrong was descending to the moon's surface, desperate for any kind of aural confirmation that everything was alright. Except their tables probably weren't covered with cans of Stella and empty packets of Walkers Salt and Vinegar. The roof of Preston Station was blocking out the radio signal completely. If I thought it would have helped I would have got out and pushed the train into an uncovered area. Instead we had to just sit there.

Eventually the train moved out of the station. Still static. Then finally Roddy Forsyth's voice came on and confirmed that Celtic were 2-0 up. That was the moment we could celebrate. Jo and I leapt up, hugged each other and started running up and down the carriage because at a time like that you really need to run around.

We sat there with big smiles on our faces and got a strong enough signal leaving Oxenholme to hear Roddy Forsyth sum up the atmosphere after the final whistle. 'Perhaps the best tribute should be paid by simply listening to the Celtic fans singing their beloved anthem'. Then the Celtic fans started singing 'You'll Never Walk Alone' while the train headed into the mountains of the Lake District and the signal went the way of Rangers' Ten In A Row hopes.

We went absolutely mental that night in Glasgow. The evening was the proverbial blur with starring roles and guest appearance from a lot of booze, a lot of this, that and the other: Jinty

79

McGinty's, The Ubiquitous Chip, Ashton Lane awash with Celtic fans, Big Shade Munro, former Scotland lock and the biggest guy I'd ever seen in my life, back to David Wells's where Jo met her future husband and I had the room next to them in the Malmaison Hotel. What was worse was that her future husband was one of my best pals Riff. You don't want to hear your pal in that situation, league title win or not. I threw a load of pillows over my head and then I blacked out.

The next day saw me with the worst hangover of my life. We had to drive to Kilmarnock to interview one of the Tartan Army foot soldiers for the documentary, but a quick look at the *Sunday Mail* over roll and sausage with Irn Bru convinced me there was other work to do because it had one of those wrap-around covers as a tribute to Celtic.

'Let's go to Ibrox!' I announced to Jo.

'No way, we've got to get to Kilmarnock in an hour!'

'Who pays your wages?'

Poor Jo. A young girl, also suffering the worst hangover of her life, emotions all over the place having met Riff, forced by me to drive us into the lion's den on the morning the lion would be extremely grouchy. Hey! It was character building!

Part of the problem was that Jo was always up for the naughtiness. I had given her the job as producer because she'd made what, up till then, had been the greatest documentary ever made about football in the history of the world, *Orient: Club for a Fiver.*

This classic slice of Channel 4 Factual Programming told the story of when Barry Hearn bought Leyton Orient for the princely sum of £5, but actually became a study in car crash reality TV as the cameras followed the breakdown of former Orient player John Sitton, as he crashed and burned as Hearn's managerial appointment.

Things came to a head when on 7 February 1995 Orient went in at half-time 1-0 down to Blackpool and Sitton let rip about the lack of heart his team were displaying. It included the following excerpt, a motivational speech which, in my opinion, deserves to stand shoulder to shoulder with anything Henry said before Agincourt.

*You, you little cunt, when I tell you to do something, and you, you fucking big cunt, when I tell you to do something, do it. And if you come back at me, we'll have a fucking right sort-out in here. Alright? And you can pair up if you like, and you can fucking pick someone else to help you, and you can bring your fucking dinner. 'Cos by the time I've finished with you, you'll fucking need it.*

John Sitton became a legend. I knew that Jo, by osmosis, was a legend also. So she was *always* going to be talked into some Ibrox-related mischief.

Jo drove us to Govan and we parked right in front of the Ibrox Gates. I ran out of the car and held that morning's *Sunday Mail* like a banner in my hands, as Jo snapped away. Then out of the corner of my eye I saw movement. People from the flats across the road were stirring from their slumber. Heads were poking out of windows; the odd figure was walking slowly towards us. It was like a scene from a zombie movie.

'I think we should probably go,' I said to Jo. We leapt into the car as more and more figures seemed to appear. We actually had to swerve past one guy on the road.

We laughed solidly for an hour. So much so that we took the wrong turning on the M8 and headed away from Kilmarnock with the net result being that we were two hours late to interview the Tartan Army guy, who had dressed up in full Highland regalia and amassed about twenty of his pals for his big interview. Quite how he thought this would translate on the radio I do not know.

We rushed through the interview and somehow made it to Duck Bay on the side of Loch Lomond, where we promptly exited the car, threw our guts up, then slept by the shores of Loch Lomond for an hour.

By the time we got back down to London, Wim Jansen the saviour had already left the club. He appeared to have been having the same problem with 'the suits' in his job as I was having in mine. His career at Celtic lasted as long as my career at Channel 5, but he will always be The Man as far as I'm concerned and the only manager since Stein to have a truly spotless Celtic managerial legacy.

There was still time for one final bit of naughtiness to cap the season. As soon as we got back to London I got Jo to write a letter to a Mr Martin Bain, Commercial Director of Rangers Football Club, to see if he'd like to donate some tickets to *Sportscall* as a prize giveaway.

Funnily enough they were the only club in the English or Scottish top flight to ever refuse our request, but I did get a very nice letter from the Rangers FC Public Relations department which read 'on behalf of the players and staff at Rangers Football Club I would like to wish you well with your show and hope it goes from strength to strength.'

Which was very nice of them and showed a lot of dignity.

# BREAKING BREAD
# WITH FUTURE LEGENDS

Life should have been pretty good for Celtic and me. They'd just stopped ten in a row; I was in tight with the BBC, with my own production company, making my own shows with total control and nobody really telling me what to do. What's more, they were shows I loved.

But I was as successful at running a production company as Dr Jo and then John Barnes were at running the Celtic squad. Like Dr Jo I made some good signings (many of the youngsters I employed at the time have now gone onto pretty good positions in the BBC and ITV – they are my Moravciks), like John Barnes I produced some attractive stuff, but, like them both, I was out of my depth.

Hiring staff, doing budgets, pitching shows to BBC management, payroll and, most importantly, taking all the staff out and getting blind drunk, was not what I should have been spending my time doing. I was a presenter, not a businessman or a boss. I should have been writing stuff, reading it out and getting paid, like all the other presenters. Or rather turning up and reading out stuff other people had written and getting paid, like all the other presenters.

But I was a control freak. I had an idea in my head of how

all these shows should be and I was obsessed with getting them right. Sixteen hours a day, seven days a week and without a holiday for three solid years. That was 1998, 1999 and 2000.

So once again I was forced to follow the progress of the Celtic through the London edition of the *Daily Record* and VHS tapes sent down by pals. But I did cross paths with four men who were to become huge rival forces in the future of both sides of the Old Firm.

Take that time on the Trivia Machine for example. When *Sportscall* was transmitted from Broadcasting House in the centre of London the production team would retire to a pub around the corner, the name of which escapes me except I know it wasn't The Yorkshire Gray because that was where all the 'proper' BBC people like Barry Cryer used to go. And we thought we were rebels.

Actually it was around this time that we turned up at a BBC Christmas party at Chelsea FC all wearing *Star Wars* masks and refused to take them off. I'm sure it sounded hilarious at the time, and in our own heads we thought this was us making a statement that we were crazily independent and different, but I bet all the other Radio 5 live people were standing around thinking, 'Why are Dominik Diamond and his team wearing masks? Have they come back from a future of H1N1?'

Anyway Jo and I used to spend a ridiculous amount of time playing the Trivia Machine in there, heedless of the fact that the more we drank the less money we would win. One Saturday Jo had gone up to get what was our sixth or seventh pint and when she had returned what she referred to on air the next week as 'some big Ginger bloke' was standing chatting to me.

We were in the middle of a game so Jo kept suggesting the right answers while I was simultaneously trying to push the right buttons and keep a conversation going with 'some big

Ginger bloke'. As a result, my performance diminished and we lost a few quid.

Eventually, having the lager rage within her and having worked with me long enough to not stand on ceremony, Jo slurred. 'I'm not being funny mate, but either help us to play the game, or fuck off, right? We're losing money here.'

At which point I remembered my manners and said. 'I'm so sorry, mate; this is my producer Jo Treharne. Jo? This is Alex McLeish.'

And we spent the next three hours playing that machine with the future Rangers manager (and officially the most successful Scotland manager of all time) and getting hammered with the guy.

Alex was another one of those guys whom I seemed to keep randomly bumping into: in a hotel in Manchester after a Prince Naseem Hamed fight was another great night we had. He was a lovely guy, no matter what kind of company he kept later. I often wondered if we would have shared quite so many beers if we'd crossed paths when he was Rangers manager. I like to think so. Perhaps we might even have swapped the odd near-the-knuckle joke about the situation. Like Ally McCoist and I used to do.

Coisty is without doubt one of the funniest men I ever had the pleasure to meet in my line of work. And equally exasperating. I can understand why he had more slaps from Walter Smith than any other player.

I remember the first time we tried to get him to appear on *Sportscall*. It was a charity round we did – simple questions on a sporting celebrity's own life, with a tenner for each correct answer going to the charity of their choice. Jo had got in touch with Ally's agent, Ally had given the OK and Jo was told to wait for further instructions about dates.

We heard nothing more. Jo sent more emails. She phoned

various numbers. But nothing happened. And literally months passed. One night, actually two in the morning, and her mobile phone rang, waking her up.

This is the way Jo remembers the dialogue going.

'Is that Jo?'

'Yes, and who the FUCK is this?'

'Oh God Jo I'm so sorry I've got you out of your kip!'

'Who are you and what do you bloody well want?'

'I'm so sorry Jo, it's Ally McCoist!'

'Ally! Great to hear from you! Asleep? Nah! Just dozing, still OK to come on the show?'

He was great but he was so unreliable back then. His media career was just taking off and I remember Jo going off with a portable recorder to get Ally talking about something for another documentary where she basically had to follow him around all day while he filmed *A Question of Sport* because she knew if she let him out of her sight it might be months before he called again. In the middle of the night, no doubt.

He was funny though. When we first met face to face he walked into the studio singing 'Follow Follow', big smile on his face, hand outstretched. 'Haw Dominik! It's your favourite Hun! How're you doing, pal?'

*110%* started off as a BBC Choice in-house show I presented, then became the name of what was effectively a chat show made by my company. One half hour with just me and a famous sporting figure, the show featured guests like Brian Lara, Francois Pienaar, Seb Coe, David Campese, Colin McRae, Graham Taylor, Martin Offiah and Gareth Edwards. As a sports fan it was a dream, but sadly for me and my career once again this stuff was being broadcast to one man and his dog.

Ally's *110%* interview was a classic. It was on the 2 June 1999 and it was a measure of how much this particular game hurt Rangers that even though they had won the 1998-99 title, the

5-1 win at Celtic Park that season (AKA The Lubo Moravcik Show) still smarted and it was this game we spoke about off-screen, more than even the notorious Hugh Dallas game of a month before with which Rangers clinched the title.

I think it's the nature of the Old Firm that the bad defeats are more memorable than the great triumphs for either set of fans.

I opened the interview with a quote from the *Telegraph* about how Ally's record in football showed remarkable consistency in so far as all his managers had hit him.

I asked, 'Why did Graeme Souness take an instant dislike to you?'

Ally replied, 'Because it saved time.'

Half the interview was about the run-ins he'd had with Souness, Jock Wallace and Walter Smith, or Walter as he's known by Scottish journalists. Just one name. Like Pele. If trivia fans are wondering, according to Ally it was Jock Wallace who packed the best punch.

He told a great story about getting back five minutes late into the team hotel in 1984. He was sharing a room with Cammy Fraser who was sitting in bed watching the Los Angeles Olympics and smoking a big cigar. Jock Wallace banged on the door. 'Don't worry son, I'll sort it out,' said Cammy to the young McCoist as he got up, stubbed out his cigar and headed for the door. At which point he turned right and locked himself in the toilet just before Jock Wallace kicked in the door and lamped Ally square in the pus.

Listening to Ally talking about the relationship he had with these managers, I was struck by how much the manager-player relationship in football was one of a father and son. It seems obvious now, as someone who always viewed Celtic as a family I wanted to belong to, this was just another example of football fulfilling that kind of role for someone.

We also spoke about the Old Firm cauldron and the pressure of living inside it. Ally had just started playing for Kilmarnock and was loving the relative lack of pressure. He acknowledged that the Old Firm world was madness, but he still missed that madness. And he also felt lucky that he always seemed to have an OK rapport with the majority of Celtic fans so he never felt threatened by that madness off the pitch, which is how it should be. And how I wished it had been for me when I finally fell into that cauldron in a few years from then.

I kept crossing paths with Ally over the years and one such time speaks volumes for the man. In 2003 he'd split up with his wife and the media were hounding him, and one day virtually barricaded his car in when he was picking up his wee boys from school.

I wrote a piece about it my column in the *Star* saying this was out of order. The guy had made a big mistake with infidelity but it was breaking up his family and that was surely punishment enough for the guy. The press were acting like he'd killed someone and they should give him a break: they certainly should not be chasing him when he was with his kids.

The day the column appeared my mobile phone rang. When I answered a familiar voice rang out. It was Ally.

'Hello Dominik!' he said. 'It's the greatest striker in the history of the Old Firm here.'

'Oh my God!' I screamed in mock hysterics. 'Henrik! How did you get this number?'

He had just wanted to call and say thanks for the support during what was a really difficult time for him and his family. He didn't have to do that. But he's class. I don't care what colour of shirt he wore or what horrible team he now assistant manages.

Speaking of managers, it was at the end of that year I got Martin O'Neill to sign for Celtic. Kind of.

Same show, same setup, except this time Sad Andy was the director and we headed up to Leicester for the interview.

Dr Jo had come and gone. Ish. He was no longer manager but was instead officially known as European Technical Advisor while Kenny Dalglish was Director of Football Operations and John Barnes was Head Coach. On paper this should have worked. Dr Jo had found Moravcik, Mjallby, Riseth and Viduka so he knew how to spot a player, even if one of those was mentally a few shots short of a hat trick. And a shitebag. John Barnes was such an intelligent, skilful player that surely under the tutelage of King Kenny he would be amazing.

Then again *on paper* having my own production company full of talented young people making shows for the BBC with full control should have worked too. Neither did.

But at least I did get Martin O'Neill to sign for Celtic. Have I mentioned that yet?

Martin's name had been in the frame the last two times the Celtic manager's job became vacant and by the time I stepped into his office at Leicester it was obvious that Barnes and his 4-2-2-2 Brazilian tactics were not going to work. So I had a mission.

Martin is one of those men whose intelligence would be quite intimidating and smothering if it weren't delivered in that warm Kilrea brogue, like the kind of Professor you'd want in university. He was a great interview subject. His footballing credo was simple, even back then. 'I like guys that can cross the ball and guys who know what do with a cross ball,' he said that day. Ring any bells? Any future UEFA Cup Final-making Celtic teams come to mind?

I wasn't stuck for things to talk about. This was a guy who, as a player, had not only won the European Cup but had also achieved the greatest double imaginable: played alongside George Best and played under Brian Clough.

He had a great George Best story. It was 1976 and before they played Holland in a World Cup qualifier, Danny Blanchflower had decided to take his Northern Ireland team, complete with the ageing George Best and the young Martin O'Neill, and have a training session in Luton. Blanchflower had a plan on how to deal with the Dutch from the start. As Martin told it.

'We would kick off and George would pass to Trevor Anderson and Trevor would pass to Chris McGrath and so on until we had these five intricate moves. He spent about five or ten minutes drilling this into us then we kicked off. And George Best just dribbled round everyone until he lost the ball.'

Then, according to Martin, Danny Blanchflower turned round and said to him. 'That boy never listens.'

But as Martin put it, 'George didn't have to listen. He was the best player we had. Even when he didn't turn up.'

It was obvious though that as much as he respected Brian Clough, his treatment at the hands of Ol Big Head had hurt Martin. At that time, as you would expect from a team that won the European Cup two years in a row, they had some immensely skilful players like John Robertson, Archie Gemmill, Peter Withe, Tony Woodcock and Trevor Francis.

Martin was consigned to the role of right-sided midfield ball-winner, the fetcher and carrier. He told me that Cloughie had once told him his sole job in that Forest team was to get the ball to John Robertson, even if it meant crossing the entire pitch to do so.

Another time they had been playing Leeds Utd and Martin was playing just in front of Viv Anderson, a hugely talented right back but a superstitious one as well. Viv used to insist that his first touch in a match was a tackle rather than a ball rolled out by Peter Shilton in goals. As a result Martin barely touched the ball in the entire first half, as any time Shilton had it he'd be forced to roll it out away from Anderson to the left, which was John Robertson's side.

At half time Cloughie approached Martin and said 'Eh son, you've gotta get into this game.' Martin tried to explain.

'There's only one ball. And it's been down Robbo's side all game.' To which Clough replied.

'And so it should be, son. And so it should be. He's the genius, you're the hod carrier.'

As Martin added, 'John was lapping that up, he was getting great praise and I'd get one bit of praise every seven months.'

Martin is so modest when it comes to his own ability I think it hides just how much Clough's attitude hurt him. Once again it goes back to this father-son relationship between a manager and a player. John Robertson was Clough's favourite son and I think that's why Martin was so loyal to Neil Lennon throughout his playing career. Compared to a Moravcik or a McGeady, Lennon too was a 'hod carrier'.

That didn't stop me having Lennon 18 on the back of my shirt each season, partly because of his importance to the team, partly because he was the only person I could think of whom Rangers fans hated more than me.

By the time I interviewed Martin the show had been rebranded from *110%* to *Dominik Diamond meets . . .* partly as a reformatting and partly as a study in my monumental arrogance at the time. As part of the reformatting I had *Dominik's Magic Bag O Questions* – general fun bits I'd throw in at the end.

Not with Martin.

A simple question about travel aspirations led to him revealing that he'd taken a three day trip to Dallas to investigate the Kennedy assassination. He had all the photos and looked at all the angles of all the supposed shooters, at one point nearly getting knocked down by a car in the middle of Deeley Plaza as he was working out some angle or other.

'Do you think there was a conspiracy?' I asked.

'Absolutely. Stone cold certain. He was shot from the front.'

This was brilliant, normally when interviewing people in the world of football it was hard to get them to commit on whether they thought their team had a chance of winning the league or not. Here was Martin O'Neill taking the biggest mystery in the history of America and nailing his colours to the mast. He went on,

'Listen, I've not been able to resolve that particular crime but in my opinion it was a conspiracy.'

I had never heard anybody speak with such conviction about anything in their life! It was not the only murder Martin was interested in. I think mine was the first interview in which he revealed that, as a keen student of law and criminology, he had sat in the public gallery during the trial of the Yorkshire Ripper Peter Sutcliffe, bizarrely bumping into legendary Republic of Ireland keeper Pat Jennings while there.

What made this revelation even more bizarre is that Peter Sutcliffe also happened to be someone my mate and director that day Sad Andy was obsessed with. Martin very kindly kept the club canteen open for us and he joined Andy and I for what had to be the most gargantuan portions of roast meat I had ever seen in my life. And the most surreal conversation.

I saw a new side to Sad Andy that lunchtime. As I've mentioned before, any time we met anybody remotely involved in football he would work out how they related to Oxford Utd and talk of nothing else. I expected this would be a big day for him because Martin had just signed Matt Elliott and Phil Gilchrist from Oxford. Well this day he spoke about that *and* the UK's most notorious serial killer. He and Martin were like excited wee boys. I just sat and listened.

The only interview that ever topped that for Sad Andy was when we did John Aldridge. Not only had Aldo played for

Oxford, he had won the Milk Cup with them in 1986 and, with a goal every game and a half, was their best striker. Me? I was more interested in his story about him pouring Stella Artois into his brand new snooker table and getting a mate to tip it while he supped it from the bottom corner pocket.

Andy went into the toilet after the meal with Martin and it was now I had my chance. I said, 'Martin I know you must have been approached the last two times the Celtic job's been open. Why did you say no?'

Martin was the ultimate professional. 'Now Dominik you know that even if I had been approached by Celtic, and I'm not saying that I was, I couldn't be discussing it with you.'

Great! He'd been more than happy to talk about the JFK assassination and the Yorkshire Ripper, why be coy now? But Martin is a man of honour and integrity.

I, on the other hand, had no honour, or pride. I got down on my knees, right in front of him. In the canteen.

'Martin O'Neill. I beg you with all my heart and with all my soul. If they ever offer you the Celtic manager's job again, please, please, please tell me you will take it.'

'Now Dominik, you know that even if I . . .'

'I know you can't actually promise me. But please, just take it. You'll be amazing in that job, and you'll love it.'

'OK Dominik, what I will say is that there are certain clubs as a manager you would always love to manage at some point in your career. And I can tell you that Celtic is one of those clubs.'

I got off my knees just before Andy returned from the toilet. Martin was offered the job six months later and took it, and was renamed St Martin a few years later. All because of me.

At least that's what I'm telling myself in my tiny deluded Zelig mind. Martin probably doesn't even remember the interview. In that way I'm no different than the fan who thinks the team won because he wore certain socks. But who knows . . .

I never asked Gordon Strachan to be Celtic manager, but I interviewed him for the same show a few months later and, as with Martin, there were insights into the man that became interesting when you look at his career as Celtic manager.

Take my first question. 'Gordon, you've been doing the management thing for a few years now, what have you learned?'

His reply? 'That I don't like it.'

And I think that was Gordon's problem. I think he felt it was a great honour to manage Celtic and, in spite of how much he seemed dismissive of them at times, I think he did love the fans. But I don't think he was ever happy in the Celtic hot seat, for two reasons he spoke about at length in the interview that day.

The first was to do with the difference between coaching and managing. As he said, 'I enjoy the coaching bit because I can be close to people . . . a special breed of people. With the management . . . it becomes a business . . . I have to be with people I didn't join the game to be with.'

By the time Gordon was Celtic manager the club had become a plc for customers rather than a club for fans, with a board obsessed with clearing debt rather than winning trophies. I can only imagine how frustrating this must have been for the man who sat opposite me as the Coventry boss that day.

The second area of discussion was even more enlightening. In the 1997/1998 season Coventry had escaped relegation on the very last day in what was only Strachan's second season as a manager, and his last as a player. I asked him how winning that game against Tottenham to stay up that day had compared to winning the European Cup Winners' Cup with Aberdeen or the FA Cup win with Man Utd.

Very different, he said. When you're winning something you're on a roll and it's just fun. Relegation battles however are four months of torture. To win on that final day, 'it's like being in a car crash. You have that initial half hour of exultation and relief. Then you get ten minutes up the road and you just start to shake.'

As an Old Firm manager you are constantly in a relegation dogfight, only in this case relegation means finishing second in the SPL. I have a theory that all of Gordon's tenure as Celtic manager consisted of half hour pockets of 'exultation and relief' but mostly spent sitting and shaking. I don't think it was fun. And I think that showed as he got more and more chippy with the press during his tenure at Celtic.

The chippiness was in evidence that day as well. If I had thought Brian Clough had hurt Martin O'Neill as his manager, this was nothing compared to what Sir Alex Ferguson had done to Strachan.

Ferguson had just brought out an autobiography in which he had spoken of how he didn't trust the now Coventry manager. 'Don't turn your back on Gordon Strachan!' were more or less the words. Gordon wasn't the only one to be targeted: Fergie had been pretty nasty about Jim Leighton too and damned his assistant of ten years Brian Kidd as being fraught with mental insecurities.

Within seconds Gordon had made his first unprompted dig at Sir Alex. While talking about how he hated people who were obsessed with winning, he labelled Fergie as the kind of guy who would want to beat his kids at *Monopoly*.

While talking about the great Aberdeen side of the 1980s Gordon was quick to say how close he and his team-mates were, how they were men the same age, with kids the same age whose families used to be close to each other and that was part of the reason for the success. But even when acknowledging Ferguson's part he used words like 'manipulate' rather than 'inspire'. He said. 'We were young and he could make us do anything, run through hoops for him. Hoops of fire even.'

These things were not said bitterly, rather with a lot of humour. Gordon was smiling as he related how Fergie told him in 1986 at the World Cup that he would leave Aberdeen for one of two clubs: Barcelona or Man Utd. Gordon was praying the Barcelona manager would get sacked, but Big Ron got the hoof first, so Gordon was stuck with Fergie again.

All this time he was denying he had a problem with Ferguson. He denied he left Man Utd under a cloud. 'I'm no like that. I was so happy about winning the Championship . . . I don't hold any grudges,' he said, unconvincingly.

I asked him about the things Ferguson had written in his book. Did they hurt? Gordon looked down as he said. 'His book should have been a celebration of what he's done in life. I've got the greatest respect for him but it hurt a few people. When you hurt someone . . . you're actually hurting the family of the people. If you say Brian Kidd is a backstabber then that hurts Brian Kidd's mum. His eighty-year-old mum thinks I've brought up a backstabber.'

Have you ever noticed that whenever people start a sentence with the words 'I've got the greatest respect for him but . . .' they then go on to say something that makes you realise that actually they don't have any respect for that person at all?

Gordon and Martin were psychologically more similar than one might imagine. Both were funny and intelligent but obviously very sensitive. If they were both affected by what they felt were personal attacks on them by Ferguson and Clough, how would they cope in the goldfish bowl of Old Firm management?

Gordon also said that one of his reasons for moving away from Aberdeen was that the Celtic and Rangers games were getting nasty and it was doing his head in. It was stopping him enjoying this football. If you put all those things together you can see how he was never going to be truly happy at Celtic.

He stayed as long as he did because he was winning everything.

In the interests of full disclosure the funniest story Gordon told that day was about the last big bender he ever went on, unsurprisingly with Bryan Robson, which ended up with him in the boot of Robson's car. When he was dropped off home his wife opened the door with the words. 'You the next George Best, aye?' And that was the last time he got blootered.

He spent his honeymoon on the Wembley pitch with his wife, best man and the Tartan Army after the England Scotland game in 1977. A policeman said to him 'you might as well go on son, everyone else is.'

His favourite toy as a kid was a Johnny 7 gun he got for Xmas and broke the same day as he tried a complicated move throwing it in the air as he jumped over the sofa. Finally, when I watched him play five-a-sides with the Coventry squad that day he was still the best player on the pitch by a country mile.

I had no idea at the time how much a part Big Eck and Super Ally and St Martin and Wee Gordon were to play in the next eight years of Celtic. I had no idea that I would actually end up seeing so much of that period up close and personal as a fan in the stands.

By that time I had no real idea about anything, because I was about to have a life-changing moment. Or 'mental breakdown' as they call it in some circles.

# 10

# THE WILDERNESS YEARS – PART 2

It wasn't all fun and games at this time. Of course it was amazing to hang around with Martin and Gordon and Big Eck and Super Ally but I did start to go mad in 1999. Seriously.

I don't mean mad in terms of 'Oh see that guy, he's pure mad so he is, he once ate a goldfish for a bet.' I mean mad in the genuine 'honestly, I should have been institutionalised' sense of the word.

I had my own production company in London making my own radio and TV shows for the BBC. I filled it with the funniest, brightest people in the world to work for me; my mum was the office manager and I had met the woman who would become my wife. It should have been the most incredible time of my life. But then I had a child.

On 19 September 1998 Molly Teresa Stephanie Diamond was born after a slightly problematic labour in Chelsea which was promptly translated by the *Scottish Sun*'s Matt Bendoris in his usual responsible, unexaggerated way with the headline Ma Bairn Was Deid So She Was. Or something like that. Matt started off in newspapers at around the same time I was starting off in telly, and I've done a few interviews with him over the years. Ours is a classic love/hate relationship: he's loved taking what I've said to him and twisting it into the most ridiculously sensationalist tabloid pap and I've hated myself after reading it every time.

In spite of the arduous nature of the birth, when Molly was born I did not cry. I was so disappointed at this. I thought that was a guaranteed thing. I screwed my eyes up hard, but couldn't even squeeze out a tear. Instead I just looked down at this thing in my hand with a head stretched out of shape so much she looked like Ridley Scott's Alien and I just thought. 'That is one ugly wee thing! What do I do now?'

I knew I was going to get her one of those Celtic bibs that said 'Celtic's best dribbler' but apart from that I was unprepared. The lack of tears were a harbinger of what turned out to be the biggest anti-climax of my life.

I think all new dads feel this. When you have your first child there are no choirs of angels doing Busby Berkeley routines down the clouds outside your house; there are no fireworks going off in your head; the world is still exactly the same shade of magnolia it was before. You have gone from being a man into a dad; the greatest shift you will ever make in your entire male life and it feels, well, just like before. You are no different. You don't suddenly feel wiser or more mature. You don't automatically grow ear-hair and a pipe. What's more, nobody treats you any differently. Because you're just the dad.

You haven't even gone through childbirth. The *mum* is the one who's gone through all the blood and poop and painkillers to produce the next generation. You have just been attached to the event through sheer coincidence. You're like a substitute who doesn't get on during the Scottish Cup Final but whose team still wins. The visiting dignitary gives you the winner's medal, but he does it grudgingly. You can see it in his regal eyes, smell it in the fetid breath seeping from the fake smile and feel it in his soft handshake. He's wondering why you're getting a medal for doing nothing. Nothing but sitting and watching the game. Like the visiting dignitary did. Why should *you* get any praise or recognition for that?

When it comes to newborns, dads are useless, in the truest sense of the word. You have nothing to give the baby because you don't have breasts. Your baby would plump for Eva Braun before you, because even though she may have been the lover of choice for the leader of the Third Reich and most evil man that ever lived, Hitler's lover could lactate.

Here's a way to test this theory. Take your top off and hold your baby. What does it do? Does it gaze into your eyes trying to connect what it feels on a subconscious level with what it is breathing in from this powerful alpha male? Does it grab your fingers knowing innately that you are its provider and protector? No. It tries to suck your tits. Admittedly in my case the confusion was acceptable because of their size.

If you don't have lactating jubblies you might as well not be there for the first six months. So I wasn't. Actually for the first two years of my daughter's life I was in my office or a studio, building up my production company, getting commissions from the BBC, being a total slave-driver to anybody who worked for me and, in case that wasn't enough to make me a complete arsehole, I held many of our creative meetings in the pub after work. If you are already starting to suffer from depression it doesn't take a lot of drink and recreational drugs to send you into a really bad space.

You know how they say that cocaine makes you aggressive and paranoid. Have you ever wondered if there's scientific proof of that? Here are a few quotes from an interview I gave at the time to the *Glasgow Herald* that might give an indication.

On my recent departure from Channel 5 . . .

'I left Channel 5 because [the Head of Sport] Robert Charles was an arse!'

On getting into trouble for calling my Radio 5 live colleague John Inverdale a posh twat.

'John Inverdale *is* a posh twat.'

On television presenting . . .

'It's a job that requires no talent whatsoever. Anthea Turner, Ian Wright . . . I mean Jesus Christ!'

On why a recent TV show proposal of mine had not been commissioned.

'One or two people in the upper echelons of BBC Sport like me and the rest of them stick pins in me. Gary Glitter would get a better reception.'

And on why I wasn't doing bigger and better shows than I was doing . . .

'If I think someone is an arsehole, I will say they are an arsehole.'

This last quote is particularly ironic, given that the biggest arsehole at that time was me – and nobody dared tell me. Actually my mum tried to. So I sacked her. She had the audacity to suggest to me that my production company had just become a place for me to surround myself with funny people to go out on booze and cocaine binges with. Of course she was spot on. So she had to go. Without my mum, or anyone to tell me to rein things in, what followed was a fairly spectacular career implosion.

To put it into perspective, my life was not like the final reel of *Goodfellas*. Cocaine was never something I did to get me through the day while I stirred tomato pasta sauce thinking the FBI were after me, it was reserved for times when I was going out and I was going to be drinking a lot.

But I 'went out and drank a lot' a lot, to help deal with the total mind warp of being a dad. I had sailed through life with nothing stopping me, until I became a dad. Through the grace of God I'd gone to a great school, got my qualifications, got my degree and got a big TV show by the age of twenty-one. Even when I left that show I'd walked straight into the BBC.

I thought I was indestructible. I thought I was brilliant. I thought I had this big destiny that was all prepared and it would always be good. Then for the first time I encountered something I couldn't do well straight off the bat – be a dad.

This wee baby girl was the first thing in my life that I didn't seem to be able to control: I couldn't make her sleep, couldn't stop her crying and couldn't feed her. It was an existential nightmare: how could something that I had made from part of me be something that I couldn't get to work properly? Did this mean I was going to be bad dad? Did this mean I was going to eventually walk out on my kids like my own father had? Was this curse lying in my genes? This wasn't how my life was supposed to be, unless this was a sign that this blessed life was not quite as blessed as I thought it was.

This is why I drank, to stop those thoughts going round and round in my head. But I also hated the sluggishness a certain amount of drink gave me, so if there was any coke around (and this was the late 1990s in London, it was everywhere) I'd take a line, just so I could drink some more. As a result, the doubt turned into full blown paranoia and rage. And depression is just rage turned in against yourself. But initially the rage was directed at anyone who tried to tell me what to do.

Stuart Murphy was head of BBC Choice at the time and had commissioned a load of shows. We had a great relationship which had led to him being on the brink of rubber stamping the biggest commission my company would have had to date. An arts series, filmed all around the world, taking ordinary punters to things like The Bolshoi Ballet and whatnot to see if it connected. It was worth something like three quarters of a million pounds to my company, and could have taken me out of Sport and into the Arts for the next stage of my career.

We shook hands on the deal and I'd submitted budgets. He called me on a Sunday on his way to LA on a buying trip. There had been a rescheduling of the next year's budget. He was still commissioning the series, but it would have to wait a year.

'Fuck off,' I said.

'What?' he responded, not unreasonably.

'Fuck off, Stuart. I've got a load of staff I've told are going to work on that show this year.'

'Dominik I'm still going to commission it. It will still happen, just next year instead of this.'

'Fuck you,' I shouted. 'You will commission it this year or you can fuck off.'

'Dominik, you don't speak to the Head of a Channel like that.'

'I fucking do. Fuck off then.' And I hung up Stuart. And three quarters of a million quid.

At the same time Bob Shennan, who had been my original senior producer on *Sportscall* at Radio 5 live, had just been made boss of the station. He called me into a meeting to say he wasn't recommissioning my latest offering *The All New Dominik Diamond Radio Show* because it wasn't the kind of show he wanted in his vision for Radio 5 live. Which I can understand now, consisting as it did of me getting all the people who had been my heroes as a child (Brian Jacks, Floella Benjamin, Limahl, Dr Robert) and getting them to review records, movies and the week's events. As an example of taking public money and converting it into pure self-indulgence it's up there with that palace of Saddam Hussein which was in the shape of his signature and visible from space.

I can understand that *now*, because now I am a man of reason and wisdom and maturity. In 2000, though, I was Cocaine Man! Able to leap entire careers in just a single sentence.

'Well you can fuck off, then, Bob!' I said, interrupting him in mid flow. Bob carried on, probably because we'd known each other for a long time and he knew by this stage I was an idiot.

'What I was going to say, Dominik, is that you can move on to Sport on 5 instead, or we can talk about knocking off your rougher edges and turning you into a daily news show presenter.'

'Fuck off Bob!'

'You know, Dominik, I was talking to someone in the BBC yesterday and they said you really could be the best radio presenter in the country if you just learned to grow up a bit.'

'Bollocks.'

I'm not kidding. That was the conversation. With the head of Radio 5 live. And I walked out of his office, out of London and effectively out of a promising career. I was probably the only person in the history of broadcasting to tell two BBC bosses *in the same month* to fuck off when they were actually offering me jobs.

So I walked out on London and my career and into the Lake District. Oh. Not quite. First I took what money the company had left in the bank and hired one of those gigantic buses that rock bands use to go on tour, filled it with beer and drove the whole company to Belgium to play minigolf and eat lobster. For a laugh. We left from the BBC in Shepherd's Bush straight after what would turn out to be my last ever Radio 5 live show and if memory serves me correctly I think we nearly kidnapped Limahl and took him with us.

Now that *was* good fun! So why did I move from London to the Lake District? Oh jeez, this is getting silly now. Well . . . have I mentioned the cocaine? The cocaine paranoia had another effect on my life that will seem hilarious to people now, but about which at the time I was deadly serious. I thought that the Millennium Bug was going to destroy civilisation as we know it.

Seriously, in the rare minutes when I wasn't burying myself in work to hide from my responsibilities as a father, I was dragging Phoebe and baby Molly all over rural England looking for a place to hide from the forthcoming apocalypse. Devon, Cornwall, Dorset, Somerset, Norfolk, Suffolk, the Peak District – all were scoured on Sundays to look for a suitable house far away from the cities, which I was convinced would became seething hotbeds of rape and pillage at a minute past midnight on 1 January 2000.

As this imagined Doomsday Clock was ticking ever closer to its end, we finally found a house in the Lake District that ticked all the boxes. It was remote and isolated, but with a couple of neighbours nearby if we needed them for guns and whatnot.

We rushed the purchase through within a month and moved in at the beginning of December 1999. That left me just enough time to buy camping stoves, candles, tools, tins of fruit and veg and baseball bats and assemble a handful of my best friends, whom I suspect may have not come up for sundry 'end of civilisation as we know it' reasons; rather because 31 December 1999 also happened to be my thirtieth birthday.

None of this is a joke, by the way. What *was* a joke though was the moment on my birthday when I happened to be looking at a map of the Lake District, no doubt to try and find fresh water supplies and an escape route if needed, I saw a thing called Sellafield. It was less than twenty miles away as the crow flies.

'That's not *the* Sellafield, is it?' I asked Sad Andy.

'Of course it is.'

'The nuclear reactor?'

'The very one.'

'So that would be one of the worst things to be beside when the Millennium Bug occurs.'

'Oh yeah,' said Andy with a huge grin on his face. 'You're fucked here!'

Lo and behold midnight passed and the world was still there. Unconvinced I forced Sad Andy to sit up with me until dawn as I consumed single malt whisky with cocaine chasers. At first light we walked up to the top of the nearest hill to check for signs of Armageddon only to find that the sole danger facing us was a heart attack.

So it made sense that having told everyone in the London media to go take a running jump that I would use the opportunity of this farmhouse in the Lake District to sit in quiet reflection and forge a new pastoral life. One where I could relax, get my priorities straight, spend quality time with my wife and get to know this wonderful child I had hidden from through work.

Or I could take my cocaine addiction with me and lock myself in a shed posting on *Popbitch* all day and writing what I thought was going to be the most hilariously satirical novel about the media ever written by man or beast but what in reality was just a nasty pile of angry words and thinly veiled attacks on everyone I had ever worked for who hadn't kissed my backside.

The scary thing is how close that book came to being published when I sent out the first few chapters. I've still got 120 pages of it festering on a hard drive. Occasionally my finger hovers over the file, wondering if it really could have been as bad as I imagined it. My brain teases me, tries to goad me into opening it. But I don't. It's like catching your mum and dad having sex. You know it happened but you really don't want to see it ever again.

It's one thing taking cocaine in London's finest nightclubs in a whirl of champagne and celebrity. It's quite different when you're taking it on a dark Tuesday in Cockermouth during quiz night at the Black Bull, then going home and sitting in a shed on your own playing *Championship Manager* on the PC till dawn.

My wife had no idea, but that's the insidious secretive world of the addict. Anyway, it ruined the Lake District for me. A beautiful part of the world, full of lovely people and for two years one messed-up angry tube.

If you take one thing from this book, please take that. It may not change your views on Celtic, on me, on Catholicism, on sectarianism, on Ireland one bit. I don't care. But my God if this book stops just one person doing coke, then it's the greatest thing I've achieved in my life.

My mate Jonny Ffinch, former *Gamesmaster* producer and former party animal himself, describes it best. The only thing cocaine does . . . is make you want more cocaine.

Unfortunately I went on wanting more cocaine for another four years. And it was responsible for my skankiest experience at a Celtic match. The AC Milan toilets, 29 September, 2004. I know I'm jumping ahead in the timeline a bit, but this really is a cautionary tale to anybody who thinks dabbling in drugs is glamorous.

Drug addiction is all about psychological triggers. They could be mood triggers (I am stressed therefore I will have a cigarette), social triggers (I am going to be going out with a bunch of people I don't know so therefore I will have a drink) or even daft things like smell triggers (oh my God the smell of this toilet reminds me of doing cocaine in it.)

Seriously, when I finally decided I'd tooted my last line there were about fourteen bars in Glasgow I could not go into for the first year, because the smell of the toilets would give me an instant flashback.

I'd never really done coke on football occasions. To be honest I'd never really drunk at football occasions either. I was never one for sinking half a dozen pints before the match, but I think this probably stretches back to that deep-seated fear of piss-freeze in public toilets than anything else. There was no way I wanted to risk The Freeze, especially if I had a bladder full of beer that medically had to be dispelled. Better to not let the bladder fill up in the first place.

Going to see Celtic was quite a pure thing for me. I think by the time I'd finally become a card-carrying season ticket holder

I was so proud I could hold my head high as a proper fan I didn't want to infect it with booze or drugs, which infected most of the rest of the week. But in Milan I broke the rule. I think it's because it was the first European away trip of that time that didn't involve my wife, so I was determined to make up for past good behaviour by behaving very, very badly indeed. It was to be a proper 'lads away trip'.

I'd flown over with Mark and Jer who, can I state for their wives benefit, in no way shared any powder-based indiscretions that day, and we'd hit Milan early after the standard issue travelling pints at Prestwick Airport. Bang! Straight into a pizzeria. Bang! Straight on the Italian beer till I hit the magic four pint mark (I never did coke on less than four pints.) Bang! Straight on the ching chang.

What I had forgotten though, was that I had arranged to do a phone-in on Real Radio with Ewen Cameron and Alan Rough on their *Real Phone In*. So I'm sitting with the Mark and Jer in the middle of the Piazza del Duomo, in the shadow of one of the most beautiful monuments to the Catholic religion ever created, and I am bombed off my nut on booze and coke. And my mobile rings. At first I thought it was going to be my wife, but it was even worse.

'Dominik? Ewen Cameron here. You ready to talk to us?'

What. The. Fuck? Ready to talk? Are you kidding? I'd done a dozen lines of Charlie and it wasn't even teatime yet, I could talk forever. But it would not make any sense and the words would come out very, very fast.

What did I talk about? No idea. I remember mentioning how beautiful the women of Milan were. That is all. That may have indeed been all I talked about, I was too embarrassed to ask when I returned.

But this was nothing compared to the experience in the Milan Stadium toilets. The cubicle was about the size of a small bedroom, with a hole in the corner, and guys had just taken it upon themselves to crap everywhere. Still think drugs are glamorous, kids? Try balancing between two steaming jobbies in a football stadium toilet tapping out coke on the back of your hand when you know you've battered so much of the stuff that day you will need another one in twenty minutes. Horrible.

The place was crawling with armed Italian police as well. We were sitting right up at the top of one seating section and at one point as I was twitching away and rubbing my nose furiously I felt a thick leather glove touching me on the shoulder.

Oh shit, I thought, here it comes. I'm going to be busted for being a cokehead in Italy. They're going to put me in a cell for years like they did in *Midnight Express*. I know that was Turkey but that's *exactly* how paranoid coke makes you.

He pointed to the back of my T Shirt. It was one of those brilliant football shirts the Philosophy Football company make, where they take a philosopher, or a political figure, or a writer or a famous footballer and stick his name and number on the back, with a cool football-based quote on the front.

The one I was wearing on this day had the quote 'Football without fans is nothing' on the front, and the name and the number of the man who'd uttered those words. Stein. 4.

'Stein,' the policeman said. 'Lisbon Lions, si?'

'Aye. Si. Lisbon Lions.'

'Great, great manager.'

'Aye. Si. Great, great manager.'

But at this stage that was all the chat he was going to get out of me. I was scared to deviate from repeating what he was saying incase I inadvertently gave something away about the gram of coke I still had in my pocket. You know, incase I said something like, 'Yes officer Jock Stein was a fine manager and did you know I HAVE GOT A BIT OF CHARLIE IN MA POCKET YA DANCER!'

What was worse was that here was a policeman in a foreign land for whom that team of 1967 meant something, something he admired and respected, and their manager's name was stuck on the fat sweaty back of a cokehead.

Of course we lost the game. Of course it looked like we might snatch a draw after big Stan Varga had cancelled out Kaka and Shevchenko's raping of our defence in the first ten minutes. Of course Henri Camara should have had a hat trick. Of course Shevchenko's class showed again and of course we then suffered another deflected free kick to make it 3-1. Of course it was all I deserved. And of course it was all my fault because, believe me, on days when I used to do coke, it was all about me.

If I hadn't disgraced the memory of Stein with my squalid jobby-surrounded addict actions would the Gods have smiled more favourably on Celtic that night? Of course not. But that's the way a crazy mind works. It ruined that night, and many nights for me.

It wasn't the only thing. I know now that I had a breakdown in London at some point during 1999 or 2000, but the sheer amount of work had covered it up. I've always been lucky in that no matter how depressed or manic or crazy I've felt, if you tell me I've got to interview Brian Lara the next day then the work takes over and everything else disconnects, but it really is like driving a car with worn brake pads, sooner or later you get down to the metal and things get broken. When I closed down the company and 'retired' from broadcasting, this distraction of work was gone. I woke up one morning in the Lake District around September 2000 with nothing between me and staring into my own mental abyss.

I spent the next year in the blackest pits of depression. The irony being that Martin O'Neill had not only taken over at Celtic by this stage but was busy winning the treble in his first season. It passed me by. Not literally, because I remember one of the few bright spots was being able to pick up *Scotsport* in the Lake District. I saw arguably more footage of Celtic games that season than I had at any point in my life.

I can't remember one bit of it. The 6-0 rout of Kilmarnock at New Year? No memory. Larsson's getting the better of Bob Malcolm in the League Cup semi final as he knocked the ball over Stefan Klos while Big Bad Bob lay prone on the ground? Sorry, you got me there. The 3-0 win at Ibrox with Henrik getting his fiftieth goal of the season and Lubo getting a pair? Nope. Total blank.

Depression is a horrible thing. It crushes the life out of you and shrinks the world to a tiny space about an inch in front of your eyes, the rest is blackness. I would sit for hours on my own in my garden, looking out at the most beautiful mountain scenery without registering a thing.

Months passed. Or did they? According to the calendar they did but I wasn't really sure. I tried to do things to fill the void; golf, walking up mountains, cooking. Cooking was the only thing that worked because it was the only thing that provided the intensity and adrenaline that broadcasting had – or at least it did the way I cooked. I did Angry Cooking. A teaspoon of salt and a tablespoon of shouting.

I was ridiculously methodical, following recipes to the letter in a way that bordered on obsessive compulsive. My first recipe book was Anthony Worral Thompson's *ABC of AWT*. I started working my way through the recipes. Alphabetically. It seemed to make sense at the time. If a recipe suggested slicing vegetables to the width of a pound coin I would line up a pound coin to use as a measure. If I got a slice over or under this width it went in the bin.

I became obsessed with cooking because it was something I could do where I could see the results and get instant feedback and gratification. I would spend hours every day preparing our dinner. Reduction of this, ceviche of that, chicken stuffed with this, that and the other. The kitchen would be a war zone. Phoebe and Molly knew that the hours between three and six each afternoon were a good time to go out with our farmer neighbour Bill on his tractor to look at his lambs.

As aggressive and controlling as my cooking was, it did at least give me something to focus on, which rescued me from the inactivity of depression and was more productive than sitting in a shed at 2am chopping up lines of Charlie and playing computer games. Just as well because at this time I was asked to be a panellist on *The Wright Stuff*, a new Channel 5 show being broadcast from Norwich. Matthew Wright had been a long-time fan of my *Daily Star* columns. I hadn't done any broadcasting in a year but I went down there, did a couple of shows and loved it.

I came back energised. The media career that had sent me mad had stepped in to save me in the nick of time. Although it had resulted in my booze and coke habit, doing TV and radio had actually kept it in some form of check, because I never drank or took drugs if I was on the telly or radio the next day. So time for round two. Start at the bottom again, not making the same mistakes.

London had too many bad memories, though, too many triggers to fall back into the old ways. I needed somewhere to make another fresh start, somewhere I could draw a line under the misdeeds of the past and start anew, with wisdom and serenity, somewhere I wouldn't be under the same pressure, where I could go about my business in a quiet manner away from intense scrutiny.

So we moved to Glasgow, into the cauldron.

# INTO THE CAULDRON

I had wanted to live in Glasgow since I was seventeen and not just for Celtic-orientated reasons. When I left Strathallan School in 1986 I had spent a few glorious summer weeks there with a couple of school pals, Al Lenman and Gavin Clark, just crashing in their flat in Woodlands. Glasgow was so exciting and vibrant. Edinburgh was great for an under-age pint and was full of kids I knew from school, but there was something a bit more authentic about Glasgow.

It seemed to just have the most amazing pubs – The Rock Garden, The Granary, Escobar, Bar Luxembourg, Henry Africa's – and, in Change at Jamaica's, the most phenomenal twenty-four-hour café in which we could while away the wee small hours.

I remember one evening out with Gav and Al heading to some pub or other when I had ended up about thirty yards ahead of them; I am the most ridiculously fast walker and have thought many times over the years that I could, even today, make a decent fist of it in an Olympic event. I'm not saying I would win, but I wouldn't come last, and I can't help but feel that the fact that I'd be walking normally, instead of lolling my body around like an Edwardian boxer with crabs, would get me a certain cache, possibly even a sponsorship deal from a loafer company.

I was standing waiting for them to catch up, when a bloke sidled up to me from the outside of the pub.

'Awright big man. How's it gaun?'

'Er . . . what's going?'

'Whit?'

'What's going . . . er . . . how's it?'

'What the fuck kinda patter is this pish?'

'I was just wondering why you were talking to me.'

By this time Gav and Al had caught up and looked quizzically. I started to explain that I was about to be mugged or raped by a madman but before I could open my mouth the guy tapped his finger to his head and said to my friends.

'See that pal o' yours? Pure mental so he is!' and walked back into the pub.

'What did you do?' asked Al.

'Nothing!' I exclaimed. 'That weirdo just started talking to me. Asking how it was going. Was he trying to sell me drugs or something?'

'No,' said Gav. 'It's Glasgow. People just come up and talk to you in this city. It's called being friendly.'

My only worry was that my wife might encounter some abuse up there, being as she is posh and English. Not one negative comment in all the time we were there. The Glaswegians loved her. I just wish I could say the same about me.

It was December 2001 and I'd only been living on the south side for about a fortnight when I had the first of many Kebabshop Kerfuffles. I had attended one of David Wells' regular Wednesday night men sessions at the Clockwork on Cathcart Road. Having consumed more pints of Hazy Daze Ginger Lager than was strictly safe, I proceeded in a northerly direction to Mr V's Takeaway on Battlefield Road. Upon entering I ordered a king size mixed kebab and awaited it's cooking to optimum tastiness.

Within moments a man I can only describe as 'a pissed up mental jakey' entered said takeaway and set about me with words of one syllable. These words were aggressive in nature but cushioned by slurs. Through the fountain of saliva I could just about make out the facts according to Mental Man: firstly that I did not belong in this city because I wasn't a Glaswegian and secondly that I was a Fenian bastard. By analysing the differing shades of redness in his face I could assume the second part was worse than the first. I tried to reason with the man but upon realising we were two men separated by a common language I picked up my kebab and wandered off into the night.

I was lucky. He was too drunk to fight me, but the warning shot had been fired over my bows. I would always be on my guard at that time of night on the south side.

The odd kebab shop skirmish aside, it was great to finally live in Glasgow, for many reasons. We had a load of great friends and we lucked out living in Strathbungo in a street full of families. Molly was able to start going to kindergarten in the same street, I started talking to BBC Scotland and STV about shows and I was finally able to go and see Martin O'Neill's Celtic.

I started off going on my own, picking up home tickets through the club shop whenever any became available and slipping into the stadium incognito with cap and scarf covering my face. I was still reeling from my mental disintegration in the Lake District and could not handle getting recognised by my own family, let alone people I didn't know. I managed to get in five home games before the season ended, including both the 5-0 wins against Dunfermline. The timing was impeccable. This was a team coming to the peak of its powers. Hartson was getting a goal a game, Sutton was showing he was almost as good a defender as he was an attacker. The spine of the team from Mjallby through Lennon, Lambert and Lubo up to Henrik was peerless.

They were big as well. What I refer to as the 'casual tickets' were always in the south corner of the Lisbon Lions stand and for many games I ended up about four rows from the front, rubbish for watching the other end but great if they happened to score four goals in the first half, like they did in one of the Dunfermline games.

I'd never seen Celtic players up close like this. Hartson was huge, like a big obelisk with a ginger top, but even he was dwarfed by Bobo Balde, who was at that point the most powerful looking human being I'd seen outside of porn.

I couldn't get a ticket for the Livingston game though, the one in which that team clinched the championship. I was gutted, but by that point I'd been offered TV shows on BBC1 and STV as well as a radio series on Radio Scotland and I'd pretty much stopped the cocaine. Surely even I, the master of chaos, couldn't destroy our new life in Glasgow with a start like this, at least not for a few years? So I felt it was safe enough to stick my name on the waiting list for two season tickets, one in my name and one in the wife's. All I had to do now was try to get her interested in football.

Unfortunately, just as things looked to be going well I was hit squarely in the face by the thing that messed up my life more than anything else. More than depression, more than drugs and drink, more even than trying to complete *Final Fantasy VII*. That thing was insomnia.

It was amazing that I'd come up to Glasgow and managed to get work, but all this work came at the same time. Though it was no tougher than the workload I'd managed in London, I'd walked out on that career, so to me this was my last chance and the stakes were doubled. This time I had to make it work. I know the exact moment this anxiety morphed into insomnia. It was the night before we filmed the first *Caledonia MacBrains*.

I had been a guest on the first series of the BBC Scotland topical comedy quiz show when Rob MacLean had been the host and it had got slaughtered in the press, mostly because Rob, a fine straight sports presenter, was out of his depth when it came to delivering comedy. I had been offered the job presenting the second series, probably because no other presenter wanted to take the poisoned chalice.

I worked hard on it, harder than I had ever worked on a TV show before: writing the script and getting to know team captains Fred MacAuley and Karen Dunbar so we had a rapport. I knew I could do it. It was the kind of TV show I'd always wanted, right from the moment I'd done audience warm-up for the first *Have I Got News For You*. I wasn't as funny as the likes of Karen or panellists like Frankie Boyle, but I could hold my own as long as my brain was sharp.

Which it would be, as long as I wasn't tired. As long as I had slept the night before. And that was it. Like a junction switch on a train track, something shifted in my head. From sleep to insomnia. Just like that. I lay there and got anxious about not sleeping. The more anxious I got about not sleeping the less I was able to sleep.

And I'm not talking about lying there tossing and turning for a few hours then falling asleep and feeling a bit tired the next day. I'm talking about staying awake all night with a heart that revs up and down like a motorcycle engine. I'm talking about sitting there, being so tired you can't keep your eyes open then the second you put your head on a pillow and close your eyes you get a panic attack like an electric shock.

As the cameras rolled the next evening on the most difficult challenge of my broadcasting career, I had been awake for thirty-six hours. Luckily the adrenaline kicked in to carry me through it. And I slept that night, like a baby. Because I drank till I passed out.

Between the first and second weeks of recording though, there had been an exceptionally nasty piece in the *Daily Record* from someone who'd been to see a recording of the show and didn't like it.

For me it meant the pressure was then doubled for the second show. I worked twice as hard that week but was twice as anxious the night before and, again, not a wink of sleep. But again the adrenaline managed to get me through. I realised that I could do the show with no sleep as long as I made sure that the gags were all written the day before the show. What then happened was I would get anxious *the night before* the night before the show and couldn't sleep then. So by the fourth or fifth week I was doing the show having been awake for sixty hours.

To make matters worse, I started recording a BBC Radio Scotland quiz series *The Time Of Your Life* in the days between *Caledonia MacBrains*, so I would be sleeping three nights out of seven on a weekly basis, my own personal record being three nights in a row without sleep. I used to pride myself on the fact that I always refused to use autocue, that system where the words appear on the TV screen in front of you, because I thought it was cheating. It was bad enough that some presenters didn't write the words they spoke, but I thought they could at least get their fingers out of their backsides long enough to learn the words. But I thanked the Lord God for autocue in this period.

That was it for me when it came to sleep and TV. From that point on in 2002 I never slept more than an hour or two before any TV appearance and, as result, my brain was only functioning at about 10% of its ability. That's why I restricted myself either to those Top 100 Gay Cop War Movies shows where I could write everything in advance and memorise it so I didn't have to think on my feet or *Richard and Judy*, where it was nice and gentle.

Whenever I did appear on panel shows, such as Rob Bryden's *Annually Retentive*, I got my ass handed to me on a plate. I just couldn't compete. I'd lost that sharpness of thought you need. I was like a carpenter trying to cut wood with a brick (and I am convinced to this day that is why Sarah Heaney beat me in the final of that celebrity charity edition of STV's *Postcode Challenge* in 2008. Oh alright, technically to be working for Talk 107 and living in Edinburgh at the time and not remember that the big boat in Leith Docks was The Royal Yacht *Britannia* was stupidity, not exhaustion).

Finally I managed to convince the doctor to give me sleeping tablets and Zopiclone 7.5mg saved my life. I was taking them on and off for the next five years, though they did nearly kill me when I was doing the *Xfm Breakfast Show*.

People really don't understand insomnia. Like depression it's only now starting to be accepted as the major illness that it is. It is not simply having difficulty sleeping; it's a painful and tortuous experience.

Sometimes the panic heart rush would physically lift me off the bed with its intensity. You know those bits in *The Road Runner* cartoons where Wile E Coyote electrocutes himself and he's a foot off the ground surrounded by jaggy red and orange lines? That was me, with a smaller nose.

People think they're helping when they say: 'Have you tried Ovaltine?' Ovaltine? Of course I tried Ovaltine. And warm milk, cold milk, warm baths, hot baths, steam baths, exercise in the morning, exercise at night, lettuce, cucumber, cheese, valerian root, camomile, carbohydrates, cold rooms, warm rooms, headphones, white noise, gentle music, sex, lavender, mantras, visualisations, hypnotherapy, nutmeg and, of course, booze. Lots and lots of booze.

Sometimes I tried half of that list in the same night.

But the mind is the most terrifyingly powerful thing in the world. It can be trained to make your body feel no pain under torture and adrenaline in the battlefield can make soldiers run for a hundred yards with broken legs. By contrast, stopping you from sleeping is a doddle.

I got to the end of the *Caledonia MacBrains* run and the next week went straight into filming God knows how many shows of *Boiling Point* for STV. The good news was that this was not a live studio show; the bad news was that we had to film four episodes a day over the course of a week or so. I didn't have to just get my brain working for an hour, but for a whole day of 'humorous off the cuff banter' on no sleep.

Again I didn't do my best work, but by this stage I was fighting the mental equivalent of the Vietnam War in my head and I just wanted to get to the finish line and never do TV again.

Don't get me wrong, it wasn't all relentless horror. Although *Boiling Point* was a derivative quiz tacked onto a thinly veiled *Can't Cook Won't Cook* rip-off, it did give me the chance to meet and work with John Quigley. Not only is he a fellow Tim, but he gave me almost as many cooking tips as he did wonderfully lurid tales from his days as a tour chef for Guns'n'Roses. Evenings at his Quigley's, then Red Onion restaurants remain some of my fondest non-kebab culinary memories of Glasgow.

And *Caledonia MacBrains* allowed to me to meet and work with two legends of Scottish comedy: Rikki Brown and Frankie Boyle.

Rikki is a Hun. I only wrote it like that because it will make him laugh. Rikki is also responsible for the best *Sun* front page splash ever. One night way back in the mists of time Rikki had been on Sauchiehall Street, making a call from a phone box. Rikki is old enough to remember when such things existed.

Some neds started battering the phone box next to the one he was using, as neds do when they're not in their natural environment of a jail.

Rikki, having consumed a few Budweisers that night, decided to do his Christian bit by reasoning with the young lads, so leaned out of his phone box and said.

'Haw. Cuntos! I'm trying to make a fucking phone call here!'

At which point they recognised him from his picture in his column and responded with, 'Hey! You're that Cafflic cunt that works for the *Sun* who's always slagging off Rangers!' At which point Rikki noticed the ink work on their arm, the bright red of an Ulster hand, the red, white and blue of a Union Jack.

Rikki did slag off Rangers. And Celtic. And pretty much everything. He is and has always been an equal opportunities slagger. Once Rikki was chased down that same Sauchiehall Street by Ian Durrant, Gordon Durie and Stuart McCall who had taken umbrage at something he had written. Rikki claims he incensed the then injured McCall by shouting 'run Forrest run!' as McCall limped after him on crutches. But Rikki was not and has never been a Catholic. I need to point that out in case his family are reading this – the shock might kill them.

'Whit?' protested Rikki. 'Ah'm a Proddie!'

'Well yer a fuckin' traitor then!' they cried, and beat him up. The headline on the front page? As Rolf Harris would say, 'Can you see what it is yet?'

ORANGE THUGS BATTER BROWN BLACK AND BLUE.

Say what you like about the tabloids, but that headline is up there with any Shakespearian wordplay.

The nation knows to a man that Frankie Boyle is a master of words now. But back in the *Caledonia MacBrains* days he was a relatively fledgling stand-up and one of the show's gag writers, alongside Rikki, The Comedy Unit's Noddy Davidson and myself.

That was my favourite part of the job. Sitting in the Writers Room with those three and watching them play fast and loose with topics, like jazz comedians. I would just sit there, awestruck by how quick and sharp they were, and now and again if I could chip in with the odd punch line I felt like I'd won the 100m on school sports day.

They each had three different attitudes to a joke. Noddy would come at it from a technically clever angle, using joke theory and rules. Rikki would try and make the punch line something to do with boabies. And Frankie was just dark and surreal. I don't know if it was just because of the insomnia-fuelled exhaustion (which actually creates a feeling not too dissimilar to being stoned) but everything Frankie said made me dissolve in giggles.

It didn't matter what the story was: SNP's policy regarding North Sea oil, falling education standards on the West Coast, the result of the last Old Firm game or that year's Up Helly Aa Fire Festival in the Shetlands, Frankie would just sit there and quietly pipe up with the following punch lines:

'And most bizarrely, The Minotaur.'

'Genetically altered Mermen.'

'Jesus! You're back!'

'And then he fucked a fox.'

Rikki would get so frustrated at what he regarded as 'aw this surreal minotaur pish!' and would often leave the room for a fag only to have the last laugh when his 'boaby' punch lines got the best reaction from that week's audience. But it was obvious that Frankie was on a different level. He is simply the funniest guy I've ever been in a room with, bar none, and we had tons of laughs, though you always worry in showbiz whether the other people actually like you. However, Frankie wrote in *Metro* magazine after I interviewed him on Xfm in 2006, 'It was good to see him again. Dominik has grown a worrying beard that makes him look like a 1990s acid-rapper or Belgian paedophile, depending on your frame of reference.' I think this passes as a compliment from Frankie.

Frankie was a Tim as well and I came across this great tale on a *Celtic Forum* once in which Frankie was on stage somewhere in Scotland one night Rangers had won the CIS Cup. He asked for questions from the audience as part of his act, so some wag shouted out 'Who won the CIS Cup?' To which Frankie allegedly replied, 'Do I Francis Martin Patrick Boyle give a fuck?'

I had some fantastic nights out thanks to *Caledonia MacBrains*. We would finish filming then head off with the crew and the guests down to Groucho St Judes on Bath Street. I did this for two reasons. Firstly, if I drank enough I would finally fall asleep and secondly; it meant I got to spend a summer getting pissed with Fish, Kelly Dalglish and Hamish Clarke from *Monarch of the Glen*.

It was also the scene of my most humiliating 'meeting a celebrity' situation since I told Noel Gallagher my mate David played guitar after that first T in the Park. We were sitting in one corner of Groucho's when I saw Ewan McGregor sitting at a table on the other side of the room. He was in Glasgow filming *Young Adam* at the time and I thought it would be a real coup to get him on *Caledonia MacBrains*. Mike Tough was the Groucho bar manager at the time, a lovely fella, cocktail-making genius and Tim.

I was pished and tired so I could think of nothing else to do but send Mr McGregor a drink over, like people did in movies like *Goodfellas* and *The Godfather*. But this was not New York of the fifties and sixties, this was Glasgow in 2002, and Mike told me Ewan was off the booze.

'Send him a big bottle of Diet Coke in an ice bucket then,' I ordered.

Twat.

I watched from our corner as Mike took over a big bottle of

pop in a bucket. Ewan looked completely confused. Mike pointed over at me and Ewan's face brightened momentarily, possibly because he recognised Fish. At this point Mike obviously said, 'No, not him, the bloke next to him: fat bald guy with glasses? Used to do that videogames thing years ago?'

I could see Ewan shaking his head. He gave a half-hearted wave as an embarrassed way of saying thanks. But that wasn't the way I read it then in my tired, drunken stupor. Oh no, to me that meant Ewan was my friend. Oh yes. *Trainspotting*'s Renton was my buddy! Obi Wan Kenobi himself was asking me to come over and join him. So join them I did.

Eventually, after I had taken about four hours to traverse the room in a zigzag fashion.

'Heeeeeeyyyyyy! Eeeeeewwwwwaaaaaan!' I cried, like a drunken man making no effort not to sound drunk. 'Dominik Diamond!' I stuck out my hand.

He took it, politely and said. 'How do you do? Thank you for the . . . er . . . diet coke.'

'No problem Obi Wan!' I said. 'No problem at all.' I looked round the table and said. 'Hi guys!' To no great reaction.

Then there was a silence. One of those awkward ones you could fly a B52 through. Then they started talking again. To each other, with me standing there on the fringes, desperate for a way to ingratiate myself to the young Jedi so I could get him to come on my show. There was half an arseworth of space on one side of their table, so I plumped myself down there. Right on the edge. Technically outside of their circle of friendship but clinging onto the outside like a drowning man to a lifeboat. It was a different league of celebrity than mine. There was Ewan and Kelly MacDonald with her husband Dougie Payne from Travis and others all looking impossibly rich and cool. I was once again witnessing that sheen of true celebrity that makes movement effortless and unclumsy.

By contrast I was the fat pisshead insomniac chancer on the end, waiting for his opportunity, for a setup line in the conversation that would allow him to leap in with a punch line that would make this crowd guffaw and open their inner circle just a crack.

None came.

Eventually I realised I was looking like a complete lemon, and more importantly Fish and Kelly Dalglish were over the other side and they were my real pals. So I stood up and announced.

'I'm off guys.'

No reaction.

'Alright guys, I'M OFF!' I said louder, although bearing in mind how drunk I was this may have actually been a *Ride of the Valkyrie* decibel level scary shriek. Whatever, it got their attention.

'Nice to meet youse. Anyway, I'm doing this show *Caledonia MacBrains* and it's dead funny, like, see over there that's Fish Marillion – he's done it, see? So we'd love to have you on as a guest Ewan.' I looked round the rest of the table. 'And we'd love to have you on Kelly.' She smiled, I turned to her husband. The guy from Travis. What was his name again? 'And we'd love to have you on . . . er . . .' FUCK! WHAT WAS THE GUY'S NAME AGAIN? 'You . . . er . . . Travis.'

Everybody's heads dropped.

'Goodnight!' I said triumphantly and turned round – right into a waitress carrying some drinks.

Neither Ewan McGregor, Kelly MacDonald nor Dougie Payne ever appeared on *Caledonia MacBrains*. I did interview Dougie with the rest of Travis when I was at Xfm and walked into the room with a full apology for my behaviour that night. It goes without saying that Dougie had no recollection of it.

If I wasn't quite clicking with the world of celebrity the 2002/2003 season was when things really started to click with me and the

Celtic family. I was still on the waiting list for season tickets, so was still scouring the website a fortnight before every home game to pick up any spare tickets that were going. These tended to be for the smaller games, I don't think I missed a single game against Dunfermline at that time! But I also got to see some other teams get trounced by St Martin's Magnificent Men including the 5-0 win against Dundee Utd and 4-0 against Thistle the weekend after we'd knocked Blackburn out of the UEFA Cup.

The balance of the team just got better and better. Henrik up front with either Big Bad John or The Evil Genius Chris Sutton; that virtually flawless midfield of Stan Petrov, Lenny, Lambert and Thommo with Didier and whoever else Martin fancied that day at full back and Joos and Bobo or Mjallby in the centre, with the likes of Jackie Mac, Shaun Maloney, Bobby Petta, Jamie Smith and Mo Mo Mo Mo Mo Mo Mo Mo Mo Mo Mo Momo Sylla ready to come on in cameo roles.

It had the perfect mix of flair and strength. Oh alright maybe a bit more strength than flair. Oh alright maybe a lot more strength than flair when compared to other Celtic teams that played 'the Celtic way'. But Tommy Burns and John Barnes had tried that and failed. Martin O'Neill's brand of old-fashioned balls down the flanks and crosses into the box was working wonders.

Like Martin had said when I interviewed him at Leicester. 'I like guys who can cross a ball and guys who know what to do with a crossed ball.' That was this team personified. Not just in terms of flank men and big powerful strikers, but also midfielders who could follow up from the contact the strikers got on those crosses to score for themselves.

I said it was almost a perfect team. And notice I didn't mention a goalkeeper. Because Rab Douglas was gash. I trusted him as much as I trusted my chance of eking out a long term career in the media.

It was frustrating missing out on the big games. Rangers, Hearts, Aberdeen and the like, but I just had to be patient and wait to get the hallowed season ticket. I knew I could have jumped the season ticket queue if I'd played the Famous Fan card, but I refused to do that.

I was offered one freebie at Celtic Park that year. None of the shows I did that summer got recommissioned but they did get me a fab new agent in London, Mike Leigh, who in turn got me on the gravy train of all those *Talking Head* clip shows and *Richard and Judy* appearances which I could fit around my insomnia with judicious use of sleeping tablets.

Mike was also looking after Clare Grogan, who had contributed a song 'Her Hooped Dream' to *The Ultimate Celtic Album*. The CD was out at the end of November and Clare was going to be singing before the Celta Vigo UEFA Cup game. My agent asked if I wanted to share Clare's box. I didn't know if there would be room for me and all my innuendoes but when he mentioned that Clare was doing the half-time draw and did I want to do it with her I genuinely nearly wet myself on the spot.

On the pitch at Celtic Park! Half-time draw! On Clare Grogan's dance card! In some cultures this would mean we'd be legally married!

I was late, obviously, so I missed Clare singing but met my agent Mike in the same foyer I'd met Danny McGrain and Todd, sorry Tosh, McKinlay years before. I had never been past the front bit though, and up the lifts into one of the boxes. It was a different world, a cosy world with a bar and sandwiches and beer you could sneak into the box as long as you hid it down out of sight.

I hated it, the box experience. I think it once again tapped into this guilt I felt about not being one of the proper Celtic fans who'd stood in the Jungle all those years. Separated by a wall of glass from this family I just wanted to disappear into and become one with, wearing a suit instead of a top with Lennon 18 written on the back, it did not feel good. So I got slaughtered.

In what was to be a horrible harbinger of the climax of that season's European adventure, we had a stinking referee that night. Offsides were given where none existed, legitimate corners became goal kicks and I still don't know how Mr Columbo, a ref as shambolic as his detective namesake, escaped without a smack in the pus from Big Bad John, Stan Petrov or Martin O'Neill himself who were all raging at decisions he made, or didn't.

I didn't give a hoot. I was going onto the pitch at half-time; it was all I could think about. Even when Didier Agathe humped a sitter over the bar I was thinking about that walk onto the hallowed turf.

Finally we got the nod to go down to the touchline. I waited nervously beside Clare. I bent down, touched the hallowed grass with my right hand, brought it up to my mouth and kissed it. I had originally wanted to prostrate myself and kiss the turf, but in my state I knew there was a chance I wouldn't get up again. I can't remember exactly what the announcer said, but I remember there was a horrible long gap after he said '. . . please welcome Clare Grogan!' and then, almost as if someone next to him had said 'Baw'heid's with her an aw,' he finally said, 'and presenter and Celtic diehard Dominik Diamond.'

The cheer was probably a normal one, but with my inner ego amplifiers turned up to full it sounded as deafening as any roar gone up to Jimmy Johnstone or Kenny Dalglish. I walked on, waving, scarf in my fist . . . right into one of the biggest regrets of my Celtic-supporting life.

I was walking respectfully behind Clare, for she was the main event, and as we got about half the distance to the centre circle this ball seemed to appear, about ten feet away from me. Just sitting there. In my minds eye I saw myself running up to that ball and battering it first time with my left peg right into the empty goal under the Lisbon Lions stand or flicking it up and juggling it all the way to the centre circle.

I had seen someone do this before. Not at Celtic Park, but at Wembley when I played in a celebrity match before the Auto Windscreens Shield Final in 1995 – Birmingham City v Carlisle and there were over 45,000 people there to see me, Chris Evans, Angus Deayton, Stan Boardman and David Baddiel take on Todd Carty and Jim Rosenthal. There were others too, otherwise that wouldn't have been fair. I only remember those two because I nutmegged Jim Rosenthal down the left wing at one point before Todd Carty took my legs away from me. Then Stan Boardman screamed at me for not passing to him – the Fokker! Anyway I walked onto the pitch for that game behind baby-faced actor John Alford, who was in *London's Burning* at the time. I swear he walked from the edge of the pitch all the way to the centre circle doing keepy-ups, then flicked it up and caught it on the back of his neck.

Now this was my chance to do the same. At Celtic Park. On a European Night in front of nearly 60,000 people.

I made a slight move towards the ball and immediately stumbled. I was barely sober enough to walk, let alone become Ronaldinho. I decided that it was not worth the risk, so I carried on walking. Then simply stood beside Clare grinning like a loon as she picked the tickets, then walked back, still grinning like a loon. But a loon that was thinking, 'You idiot! Why didn't you try to at least kick the ball?'

There have been two moments in my life I look back on and wonder what would have happened if I had done things slightly differently. There was that night, and then there was a certain

Easter Friday at the foot of a cross in the Philippines. *That's* how much being on the Celtic pitch meant to me.

So I went back to the box and got more blitzed and watched Henrik head home from a Steve Guppy corner knocked on by Bobo to win the game. So all in all, it wasn't a bad night. And now the bad news.

All the TV appearances meant that the chance of a quiet life in Glasgow was impossible. I never went into the media because I wanted to be famous, I neither understand nor trust anybody who wants that in life and it saddens to me to see former friends and colleagues get seduced by the lure of it over the years and focus on that part of it rather than the work they're producing. But I accept that recognition is part of the job. But there was a sinister part of this recognition in Glasgow. It began with an S and ended with ECTARIANISM.

I first heard about it from my pal Irvine Hunter. He was in charge of my columns at *The Star*. He was a dyed in the wool Bluenose and one of the greatest men I've ever met. Over the years he became like a dad to me, teaching me all the ins and outs of writing a tabloid column and surviving in the news-paper world. I lost count of the number of times he would phone me up and say. 'Look I'm going to recommend you take this bit out of your lead piece because I think if the Editor sees it you'll be out on your arse.'

He called me up one day to say that there were members of a certain Rangers forum who were giving me a right going over. I'm not going to give it the oxygen of publicity in this book but this was really nasty, violent stuff. The problem with the internet is that you never know who is making these threats. Are they fourteen-year-old kids or grown men with Neo Nazi connections? And these threats were not restricted to the internet.

I couldn't get tickets for that season's League Cup Final on

16 March so I invited what I call 'a mixed bag' round to the house to watch it. This involved Rikki Brown, Irvine and his pal Tam in the Blue corner with my neighbour Archie, my mates Lorraine and Mark and Frankie Boyle in the green corner. Yes, it was tipped towards the Celtic side, but my house – my rules.

It was a great atmosphere in the house, fuelled by what was one of the most incident-packed Old Firm games ever. Joos Valgaeren cleared off the line after Rab Douglas came out with all the speed of a tractor and got chipped by Lovenkrands. Lennon got sent off after pushing Ricksen right under Kenny Clarke's nose then following it up with a body check on Michael Mols fit to grace any WWF ring. Hartson had a perfectly good goal chalked off for an offside even though he was onside by the length of a Mitsubishi Shogun. Bobo Balde singlehandedly tried to murder any Rangers player that dared to invade his personal space that day, including a full throttle on Lovenkrands in the Celtic box, again missed by Clarke. There were about three good chances missed by each side and John Hartson missed *that* penalty, ironically enough after Bobo had gone down in the Rangers box after a part of Amoruso's shorts brushed against him. I know Lorenzo was supposed to be a big boy, but that was ridiculous.

And I haven't even got to the goals.

Rangers won 2-1 after a goal that Rab Douglas should have strangled at birth plus what seemed like Peter Lovenkrand's five millionth goal against us. A peach of an inswinging corner from Thommo was met by a glancing bullet header at the near post in return. Some might think that 'glancing' and 'bullet' is a contradiction in terms when it comes to heading a football. Not when the head belonged to Henrik Larsson it wasn't.

I have never seen a living room full of people more exhausted after a game of football. Every ounce of energy had been spent. We just lay there, and even the Rangers contingent were too knackered to celebrate.

'Shall we go and get blootered?' someone suggested. Everyone leapt from their seats and rushed out the door towards Heraghty's Bar. This meant walking directly past another bar on the way, another place I refuse to grant the oxygen of publicity to, but it's a bar on the south side of a blue persuasion.

There were a bunch of guys standing smoking outside that bar. 'Haw Dominik!' they shouted as we passed. I looked up to be greeted with a volley of Nazi salutes. Well that was just great. A hundred yards from where I lived people were glorifying the premeditated murderers of six million Jews.

'Just keep walking Dominik,' said Irvine. I had no other thought on my mind, being a coward.

When we got to the pub I said to Irvine and Tam, 'How the fuck can you support a club with fans like *that*?'

'Those knuckle draggers are not Rangers supporters,' replied Irvine. 'They are arseholes who happen to support Rangers Football Club. There is a big difference.'

'Every club has a bawjaw element,' added Tam.

Unfortunately Rangers' 'bawjaw element' were on the street where I lived. And for a while I got a little bit paranoid.

Shortly after this David Wells and I had been to some gig or other in town and ended up in The Corinthian, an exceptionally swanky central Glasgow bar with a gigantic brightly lit 'show bar' and a couple of quieter rooms. David and I had opted for one of the quieter rooms so we could continue our post-gig analysis, which normally consisted of David telling me exactly what kind of guitars had been played by the band that night, and a history of said make. Like Noel Gallagher, David Wells plays the guitar. Hadn't you heard?

The room was dimly lit, but I could make out a group of three guys in the corner. Every time the door opened it shed a bit of light across them. Two of them were the biggest, nastiest looking men I'd seen outside of a prison movie. The kind who would be the guys Gene Wilder and Richard Pryor would accidentally fart on if it was a prison comedy. If it was a serious movie they'd just kill a lot of people using home-made shivs. But they weren't the biggest concern for me. The biggest concern was the guy in the middle of them. It was Andy Goram.

If Terry Butcher worried me because he was Rangers through and through, Goram made my sphincter tighten even more. He had links to Belfast. He had switched on the Xmas lights on the Shankhill Road in 1995, there were photos of him at Rangers Supporters Club functions over there with UVF banners in the background and then there had also been the controversy in 1998. During the Ne'erday Old Firm game of that year (by that point moved to 2 January) he had worn a black armband. It was claimed this was a tribute to Loyalist terrorist Billy Wright who had recently been shot in the Maze Prison where he'd been interred for the murder of ten Catholics. Goram claimed it was a tribute to his Aunt Lily.

Goram has since claimed these things were nothing more than innocent coincidences but back then I was drunk, in the same city centre I'd already had a death threat from Combat 18 and the guy was sitting opposite me with two human tanks on either side of him. You can understand why I may have been ever-so-slightly keeching myself.

I said to David that we needed to get out of here. David said not to panic, Goram probably wouldn't recognise me, but we'd finish our pints and leave anyway.

As I was draining my Guinness in something approaching world record pace, the room got darker. I looked up and realised this was because one of the tanks was looming over me, blocking out what little light there was. The tank spoke in what sounded like a Northern Irish accent, although the paranoia was running so thickly through my veins by this point it may have been a Mickey Mouse voice for all I was aware of reality.

'The Goalie wants a word.'

Well I had a word for The Goalie, and that word was shittingmyself.

I got the impression that this wasn't a request, with an option of an RSVP in the negative, so I stood up, keeping my pint glass in my hand just in case I needed to use it as some kind of offensive weapon. David followed me over to where Goram sat. I'd like to say I'd have done the same if the roles had been reversed though to be honest I might have been running down Ingram Street shrieking like a ladyboy on speed by now.

'You're Dominik Diamond,' Goram said, slurring his words slightly.

Again it was a statement, not a question, like I was in some form of court proceedings, which is possibly why I answered with the words, 'Yes m'lud.' Did I ever meet any famous person in my life and NOT say something really dumb?

'The guy off the radio, aye?' he continued. Oh shit, I thought, here it comes. My hand gripped around the pint as I wondered which of the three would kill me the quickest. You know they say that when you're about to die your life flashes before your eyes? Not with me. Not that night. That night I just had an image of Maria, Romano's sister, and how I wished I'd tried to snog her just once in my life.

'Mmm,' I nodded, for I had no time for vowels.

'You're a cheeky wee bastard aren't you?'

I didn't say anything out loud because I didn't know if there was a right or wrong answer to that question and I certainly wasn't going to take the risk. But inside the voice was screaming at me, 'Oh fuck fuck fuck fuck fuck! You're going to die! You're not even forty! You haven't even got a season ticket yet and you never shagged Maria. Still, at least it's in a style bar.'

'But you do some funny stuff.'

What? Did he mean funny 'ha ha' or funny 'rum and peculiar'.

'I heard a thing you did with McCoist the other day.' Well, technically it had been three years before but I did not think it was the time for corrections. 'It was good.'

Finally I plucked up the courage to speak.

'Thank you very much.'

'You boys want a beer?'

It's at this point you might be thinking that we sat with Goram and his mates long into the night, swapping stories and having a great time, becoming firm friends for life.

You must be joking. Don't forget that the press had reported that Goram had been diagnosed as a schizophrenic. I counted myself lucky I was talking to the nicer half but didn't know how long I had with him before the other one popped out. I said we'd love to but my wife was about to give birth and I had to get home. Then we left, another bullet dodged. Metaphorically speaking.

But like Russian roulette, the chances of copping one increased with every year.

Still there was no time to worry about that now, because we were all off to Seville.

# THE HORROR OF SEVILLE

Seville 2003 . . . the greatest moment in Celtic history since the Lisbon Lions . . . 80,000 Celtic fans forming one huge party across Europe . . . laughter, joy, Guinness, adventures.

I had a terrible time. Seriously.

I blame my wife. As well as Rab Douglas, Lubos Michel, Deco, Derlei, Stan Petrov, Shaun Maloney, Spanish cops, the catering manager of the Estadio Olympico, the designer of the City of Seville and Mother Nature. Not necessarily in that order.

Let's start off with my wife. Like many Celtic fans I KNEW I was going to go to Seville. Like many Celtic fans I had no idea how, but I knew I was going to be there. I wasn't going to risk waiting for the ballot and I wasn't going to Do a RodBilly. This is what I called it when a famous Celtic fan used the fact they were famous to try and get a ticket that really should go to a proper fan who pays his hard-earned cash week-in, week-out. As utilised by the likes of Rod Stewart and Billy Connolly.

So I decided to go for the slightly less morally dodgy route of a ticket tout. I had a contact from a friend; a guy in Germany who my friend said ALWAYS had tickets for big games. I emailed him. £200 for each ticket was the answer.

There was only one way I could justify spending this amount

of money plus flights on one match. Spin it to the wife as a holiday. Don't get me wrong, by this time Phoebe had also been baptised in the fire of Celtic Park and loved the Bhoys.

I had taken her to the home leg of the Stuttgart game. She had never been to a football match in her life before; in fact if she'd ever been stuck in a room while I was watching it on TV she would declare the whole affair to be dreadfully dull. She used those exact words. Because she's posh. In fact once we'd gone round to *Caledonia MacBrains* producer Caroline Roberts' house for a meal and Phoebe had shamed me by announcing, right in the middle of an impassioned football discussion, that she couldn't see what all the fuss was about because it was just kicking a ball. Aye, that old chestnut.

But it wasn't just kicking a ball the night I took her to see Celtic play Stuttgart in the UEFA Cup in February 2003. We were blessed with great seats, level with the edge of the penalty box near the top of the North East Lower stand and doubly blessed with the kind of game and atmosphere you'd have to be clinically dead not to get a buzz from.

First of all there was the anger directed at Stuttgart's Marcelo Boron when he got sent off, then the despair when Kuranyi scored for them, then Paul Lambert's storming strike right below us to level it, followed by wee Shaun Maloney's goal on half time, again right in our line of sight. Then there was a second half full of the most beautiful passing from Celtic (admittedly against ten men) finished by a goal from the narrowest of angles by Stan Petrov. In terms of rollercoaster rides of emotions it was up there with any Bruce Willis movie we'd seen together. And she was converted.

Unfortunately she was spoilt by that occasion. It was a bit different in years to come when we had our season tickets and were watching Strachan's team grind out 1-1 draws in howling wind and snow against St Mirren. But for now she was in that first stage of the love affair, when even farts smell like pepper-mint.

I didn't want to push things by taking her to league games, but I knew I could keep her bubbling along with the atmosphere of European nights and though I couldn't get tickets for the Liverpool match, we did get a pair for the semi final against Boavista. Same height as the Stuttgart tickets, but this time back in the 'casual corner' of the Lisbon Lions stand it was a perfect place for Phoebe to see the wave upon wave of Celtic attacks in the first half that night – and the litany of handballs from the Boavistans in their own penalty area (though she would soon learn that being a fan means never having to say you've seen the handball, you just instinctively know it's happened and you should have had a penalty). Once again it was up and down the tracks of that rollercoaster with the green and white waves sparkling under the black night sky, Henrik scoring a goal *and* missing a penalty.

If I say so myself the way I got my wife addicted to Celtic was a long-term game plan the envy of any street-level drug dealer. That said, she would have gone a bit spare at spending £800 to see a game. You can buy a lot of shoes for £800.

So we weren't flying to Seville to see a football match, oh no. We were going to the beautiful cultural bastion of Madrid for five nights, one of which would involve us taking a wee drive in the car to see the Celtic play down the road. I just didn't tell her it was 538km down the road.

Possibly because my wife is posh and English she does not share my love of drinking tons of Guinness and singing rebs and telling grown men that you love them even though you only met them during the first verse. I know, I know, some women are just plain weird. But the only way I was going to get to Seville was by wife-ifying the whole trip. The *Sun* newspaper had already asked me if I wanted to travel in a car with them all the way down, stopping off in various places across Europe on the way, like Didier Agathe's home town. I figured my wife would like this even less than my Editor at *The Star* so I declined. Instead we were going to fly from Glasgow to Luton, Luton to Madrid and stay in some ridiculously trendy overpriced hotel with a sign in lowercase letters that you only hear about through looking in those ridiculously trendy hotel guides you find in the rooms at other ridiculously trendy over-priced hotels with signs in lowercase letters.

My wife loved those hotels and had gleaned an encyclopaedic knowledge of them so it took her about a nanosecond to agree to taking a small fortune from our bank account and giving it to the Urban Hotel in Madrid. That's Urban, Spanish for 'wanker with more money than sense'. The hotel blurb on the website gives the game away perfectly:

*A 21st-century boutique hotel in Madrid: urban, designer and made for pleasure seekers who love luxury and shy away from convention-ality. Five-star, ultra-luxurious personalised service. In the heart of the city there is a new cosmopolitan and heterogeneous meeting place where the established rules do not exist*

'Conventionality' in this context meaning spending the conven-tional amount of money on a hotel room and 'established rules' meaning paying no more than £3 a pint. But I had no choice. The trip was to be wife-ified, the wife was a cosmopolitan trav-eller and the hotel website did claim that 'the hotel is the referent for cosmopolitan travellers.'

Before we set foot on the plane however, we had to get the tickets in our hands. I made contact with the tout in Germany. I wired the money to him. And waited. In the summer of 2009 I had a medical for my Canadian residency. They found a shadow on one of my lungs. I had to get a secondary set of X-rays and wait four weeks to discover whether that shadow was lung cancer or just a shadow. That was the second longest wait of my life.

Waiting for those tickets remains the longest. Then the envelope arrived from Germany. I sat looking at it for a minute or two, like Charlie looking at that precious Willy Wonka chocolate bar, too scared to unwrap it lest it did not contain the golden ticket he so desperately wanted inside.

I ever-so-gently tore open the top so there was no danger of harming the contents, and there the tickets were. And just like Charlie's ticket for the Chocolate Factory they were golden.

Oh alright not golden so much as yellow. And red on the bottom. And with a white border. But golden to my eyes. I read the words 'Estadio Olimpico 21 Mayo 20:45' Hurrah! 'Preferencia Grada Alta.' That sounded cool! Not just an Alta, but a *Grada* Alta. And one that was Preferencia'd as well. Worth every penny of the £200 each ticket had cost. Puerta P! Sector 202 B! Fila 0019 and Asiento 0068. That last bit meant seat. I knew that much.

And the footballer on the ticket, swinging a shot goalwards was left-footed. I was left-footed too! Talk about good omens. There was a list of warnings on the back of the ticket, the like of which I'd never read, mostly because I'd never actually read the small print on any ticket, but this was The Golden Ticket, and I wanted to drink in everything.

There were to be no banners, symbols, emblem or texts that could encourage violence. Not a problem. No weapons or any type of missiles either. Again, I could comply. No booze, OK. No firecrackers, smoke or noise bombs or fireworks of any nature. What? No 'noise bombs'? Had they not seen me at a game? I was one big fat hairy bloody noise bomb.

But it was rule number five that worried me. It read: 'Any person under the influence of alcohol, narcotics, drugs, stimulants or any other similar substance will be denied access to the stadium.'

What? How could they say that? I was with the wife so I wasn't going to be touching the Charlie but I intended on having a skinful. What were they going to do, carry out some test on the outskirts of the stadium to check sobriety? Breathalyse you? Say they'd shagged your mother and wait to see if you punched them? Offer you a kebab and see if you wolfed it down without gagging?

But then I spotted something. It didn't say 'substance' in the above sentence, it said 'susbtance'. It was a misprint. I knew there was a lawyer who was getting famous footballers off the hook with speeding tickets if the policeman in question hadn't joined up letters properly and other such technicalities. If push came to shove and they didn't let me in then I'd just get that lawyer involved and in conjunction with the European Court of Human Rights I'd sue UEFA for millions on a no win no fee basis.

Just to be on the safe side I studied the Portuguese translation on the ticket as well, so I could quite calmly say to a steward, if necessary, that I had 'no bebidas alcoholicas, estupefacientes, psicotropicos, estimulantes o substancias analogas.' It also meant I knew how to ask for them in a bar if the need overcame me.

I put the tickets in my desk drawer in my office and checked two or three times every day to make sure they were still there. I didn't even look after my own children that carefully when they were babies.

One part of the trip that I couldn't wife-ify was the airport. I knew that whether she liked it or not, we would bump into fellow Celtic fans, who might not be quite the cosmopolitan traveller my wife was.

'At least we're flying at 10am in the morning,' she said to

me the night before. 'There's no danger of being mobbed by a load of Celtic fans wanting to get drunk with you.'

The poor woman really had no clue. I had been introduced to the 'aeroplane drinking schedule' with regards to football fans some years before on a jaunt to see Arsenal play AC Milan in the European Super Cup 8 February 1995 with The Woj. The Woj was a legend in the video games industry because he could kill you with one night on the razz. Woj was also a hardcore Gooner and had persuaded the software company he worked for at the time to buy a load of tickets, hire a plane and get Charlie George onboard as MC for the day.

I arrived at Gatwick at 7am for the flight. 'Just got time for breakfast before we board lads,' announced The Woj. I piled my plate high with bacon and eggs and the world's biggest glass of orange juice and headed for the table.

'What the fook do you call that?' asked Woj.

'Breakfast?' I suggested.

'That's not yer fooking breakfast, THIS is your fooking breakfast!' and he handed me a pint of Stella.

The only thing I remember from the rest of that trip is getting my head battered with the butt of an Italian policeman's rifle because I wandered 10cms to the left of where I should have been walking when we exited the stadium. That is all.

I never learned my lesson, though, and continued to drink with The Woj throughout the 90s, nearly dying one night in Manchester when I was out with him because I got so hammered I walked out of the bar saying I was off to Cheetham Hill to hang out with the notorious Cheetham Hill Gang then woke up at dawn face down by the side of the Manchester Ship Canal.

So I knew the score when it came to football fans travelling to Europe for away games. Like the casinos in Las Vegas, time meant nothing. Which is why my wife and I boarded that plane to Madrid absolutely shitfaced.

A bunch of Tims in customs insisted we join them for a drink and then refused to let me put my hand in my pocket for the next ninety minutes. With our new friends we totally cleaned out Easyjet of the booze on the plane, at one point we would have drunk the engine fuel if it had been available with a splash of coke.

My wife was unaware of a lot of this because as soon as we took off from Luton she headed for the toilet and did not emerge until the captain insisted she take her seat for the descent into Madrid.

We made loose arrangements to meet the guys from the airport later that day in Madrid, in that way that you do when you've got drunk and laughed and sung with total strangers. The fact that I am still referring to them as 'the guys from the airport' has probably made you realise that we did not meet up with them, as after a three hour snooze in the most expensive hotel bed in Madrid we had no idea where we were supposed to be. If those guys are reading this then thank you again for the beers and for introducing my wife to early-morning drinking.

This was still a few days before the final, and even though Madrid was one of the more popular entry points for Celtic fans it still only had a light dusting of green and white. I knew there was an Irish bar called The James Joyce that I really wanted to visit. I tried to tempt Phoebe towards it by telling her that Salvador Dali used to drink in there (which was actually true, as did Lorca) but she refused to believe me, thinking this was but a ruse to fall into the company of Guinness-swilling, rebs-singing compatriots. Perish the thought.

So instead we spent the next couple of days in Madrid going to poncy restaurants and hanging out in the Urban's rooftop pool. I know. It's almost as much a betrayal of being a Celtic fan as my being a Rangers fan as a kid. I'm sorry.

The absolute height of my betrayal of what you should be

doing on a football trip was our evening at *La Viridiana*, which Sad Andy informed us was one of the best restaurants in all of Spain. He said it was a nice mix of traditional Spanish cooking and that new molecular gastronomy that Heston Blumenthal would later make popular: where you take a squid and squeeze it through a tractor at -20 degrees so it becomes foam, then you reform it into a squid again, just for a laugh. Remembering that Sad Andy knows everything about everything we booked a table.

I had a fried egg for starter. At least it looked like a fried egg. It was actually a free range egg served with a porcini mousse and black truffles that had been molecularly gastronomised into looking like a fried egg. I had no idea that was what I'd ordered because the menu was in Spanish and I was too embarrassed to ask for an English translation. So I just picked stuff at random and read them out in my best Spanish accent, honed as it had been through watching Manuel on *Fawlty Towers* and Manolito on *The High Chaparal*.

My next course was even crazier. It was cold strawberry soup with pickled herring and garlic slivers in it. On first taste it was the most disgusting thing that had ever entered my mouth. On the second taste I kind of liked it and by the third I was hooked. It was the culinary equivalent of starting smoking.

My main course turned out to be squid in curry sauce, which at least bore some kind of relevance, sounding almost like that Glasgow delicacy of chips in curry sauce. And dessert was foamy stuff that tasted like everything wonderful you'd ever tasted with sugar on the top.

It was the most amazing meal I'd ever eaten in my life. Sod this football malarkey, I thought. Now I know why Gordon Ramsay jacked it all in to go into the restaurant trade – you got to make this stuff *and* swear all day long without getting into trouble. This was how we passed the days and as a result we didn't speak to a Celtic fan from the time we got off the plane to the time we pulled into Seville in the car a few days later.

Actually that's not strictly true. We did meet one Celtic fan, one very important Celtic fan. We were walking past the main Atocha train station on our way to another poncy restaurant and a bunch of Tims had stopped me. I was trying to rush my way through the handshakes as quickly as I could so as not to upset my wife. It's not that she's an unfriendly sort, it's just that she has had to stand there hundreds of times in our relationship while people have come up to say hello. All these people have got a memory of something I've said on the radio or on the telly or in print which is very flattering to me but really boring for her.

When I was doing Xfm Scotland she used to dread going to King Tuts after a while because, even though I always went up the stairs and stood in the darkest shadows of the upper back corner, actually getting from the front door to this spot could take up to half an hour after people came up to say hello.

While talking to these Tims in Madrid I felt a tap on my shoulder. I turned round and, at the risk of sounding gay, there was this guy smiling at me I can only describe as . . . beautiful. Seriously. He was slim with dark hair, skin smooth as alabaster and a really cool leather jacket underneath his Celtic scarf. He looked vaguely familiar almost like a really cool, skinny version of someone I knew a long time ago.

Then the penny dropped. It was Kenny McLeod, the Celtic-supporting, *Subutteo*-rules-bending brother of my childhood best pal Stephen. What were the chances I would ever bump into him again, especially amongst the 80,000 throng heading to Seville of all times?

'I see you finally saw the light, Dominik!' Kenny said. I gave him a hug. I said to Phoebe, 'This is Kenny McLeod; his family lived on the same estate as us in Arbroath. His brother Stephen was my best pal. Hey Kenny, how is Stephen?'

'He's at home watching The Bill,' he replied, in a reference to that wonderful rhyming couplet that came at the end of the umpteenth version of 'Tell All The Huns You Know':

*They'll be watching the Bill*
  *When we're in Seville*

Which the Rangers fans later turned on us with,

*We were watching the Bill*
  *What was the score in Seville?*

Kenny had changed physically since 1980 as much as I had changed mentally. It was amazing to see him, but again there was that recurring shaft of guilt that I really hadn't been a worthy Celtic fan, that no matter how much I tried to bury it, I had once been a Hun and I could never, ever turn back time. It was frustrating. I finally realised what Cher had meant when she was straddling that big gun and singing her heart out surrounding by seamen in that video, 'If I could turn back time, I'd give it all to you.'

I would. But I couldn't. I was attracting more and more attention standing around in the open and Phoebe was getting that antsy look on her face so I told Kenny to say hello to Stephen for me and went off to have another small portion of ridiculously expensive food on a plate in a restaurant with a name that was written in lowercase. By then I'd persuaded Phoebe that in return for the three days we'd spent living like Beckham I'd be allowed one day to be a football fan.

We went to Flaherty's Irish Bar which was the epicentre of Timdom in Seville that day. It was so busy it made the Pope's

Easter Vatican address look like a romantic dinner for two. I drank and sang with the fans and Phoebe did her best to put a brave face on things. But it didn't feel right. It didn't feel how I hoped it'd feel, and again it came down to this guilt I kept feeling about not being worthy of taking my part in this support. I hadn't enjoyed the same build up as these fans had. I hadn't been part of that green and white odyssey where the start, middle and end were all about the game that was happening tonight. I hadn't painted a minibus green and white and driven for a week across Europe with only a faint glimmer of hope of a ticket. For me it had all been ticket touts, rooftop swimming pools and black truffle shavings on everything.

A few of the fans didn't help things. Funnily enough this was the only day as a Celtic fan where some of them made me feel like I didn't belong. One or two would sidle up to me in the bar, 'Awright, Dominik, got a spare ticket, Big Man?' they would ask hopefully. 'Sorry mate, just got the two for me and the wife,' I'd reply. 'D'you pay for your ticket, aye?' they'd ask accusingly.

One or two were a bit more angry and bitter, 'Aye, and I bet you didnae huv tae pay for yir ticket, eh?'

This really annoyed me, especially thinking of all the games I *could* have played the Famous Fan card to get tickets but didn't because I was so desperate to be one of the rank and file supporters of this club. I would never betray them by jumping the queue. OK, I'd bought a ticket from a tout, but it was for the 'neutral' section so I wasn't taking a ticket away from a Celtic fan and I never would.

I never even played the Famous Fan card when it came to Old Firm games. I was lucky that between 2003 and 2007 I took every single away ticket I was offered, so my chances of getting balloted were always pretty high. There were only two occasions when I didn't get balloted and both those times Archie and I dug deep for the £120 corporate packages on offer, so desperate were we to go to Castle Grayskull and cheer on the Bhoys in a polite, restrained and mature manner.

In all my life as a Celtic supporter I have had maybe five negative encounters with Celtic fans and four of them came that day. The other one came in a kebab shop on the south side of Glasgow in that same year when a guy flipped on me because I'd apparently said on the radio back in 1995 that Brian Laudrup deserved to win the Scottish Player of the Year Award ahead of Paul McStay.

The last case I put down to madness. The first four I just put down to how desperate real fans were to get a ticket and how much they rightfully resented the fact that famous people might have got a freebie.

It was one of those drinking sessions you have now and again as what I call a Career Pisshead where you drink and drink and can't seem to get drunk. Christmas Day is always like that for me, no idea why. Sometimes it just happens, like those random bronze medals Britain always gets in the Olympics in things like 1000 Yard Smallbore Live Hairy Target shooting where you see it on the news and wonder 'how the hell did that happen?'

Perhaps I just felt too on edge, too nervous about what was going to happen at the Stadio Olympico in a few hours when all the praying would have to stop and thousands of others would have to just put their faith in God and share the same thought: 'I hope to hell my ticket is genuine!'

This is always my worry whenever I had a ticket for a big event. Whether I'd bought it from an official outlet or a tout, there is still that nagging doubt that until you are actually in your seat you never really know – and in Seville the stakes were high.

We set off deliberately early, much earlier than I normally

would for a game, because I wanted to build in time for Plan B and Plan C which I would use in the event that the tickets were fake. Plan B involved me selling Phoebe in return for a ticket. Plan C involved me turning up to the players' entrance and arguing that even though I'd never played in goals in my life I was still better than Rab Douglas.

To say we walked to the stadium is unfair. It's like saying that Edmund Hillary walked to the top of Mount Everest. It was an epic journey of 5km from Flaherty's to the Stadio Olimpico and there did not seem to be any public transport other than random buses that would pass us occasionally, all of them choc full. So we walked. And this meant Rule Number One of Walking with My Wife. She got a blister.

Now I am a walker. I walk fast. Walking to me is like running without looking like you're desperate. But it's still a way of getting me from A to B in the shortest time possible, especially if I'm paranoid about having a dodgy ticket for the biggest game in my lifetime supporting a football club.

My wife does not walk fast. No wives do. With her blister slowing her down even further it was like we were in two entirely different time zones. It was the most stressful, painful, unpleasant walk of my life – and I once carried a cross for five miles through a Philipinno village in 100 degree heat as part of an Easter Ritual knowing that at the end of it I was going to turn round in front of the world's media and tell a bunch of guys with knives and guns that I *wasn't* going to get crucified after all. This was worse.

I kept consoling myself and my wife with the thought that once we got up to the stadium we'd get some lovely cool juice of some sort. But first we had to get in.

As I remember it there was some bizarre triple entry system. They only took a ticket stub on one of the three so to this day I wonder if the other two were part of that 'no entry if you're inebriated' rule they had on the ticket and the cops were looking out to see if you were indeed showing the 'effectos' of too many 'bebidas' or 'psicotropicos'.

The effectos of our bebidas were obviously not effectos enough to prevent entry and when the steward scanned the ticket it did not produce a red flashing light, an ear-shredding alarm and trap door.

We. Were. In. Into the UEFA Cup Final. Now, where was that cool, refreshing drink?

Nowhere. The Stadio Olimpico had run out of juice. Our Preferencia Grada Alta was as dry as an Oscar Wilde one-liner. I spent the remaining forty five minutes before kick-off queuing for the last remaining bottle of orange. I was hot, tired and thirsty and though the all day drinking had not succeeded in getting me drunk, it had been kind enough to go straight to the hangover. Still, I told myself, it's the UEFA Cup Final! Pull yourself together, big man!

Though we were in what was officially deemed a neutral section, the Celtic fans outnumbered the Porto by a ratio of about three to one, but it was the least recognition I ever had at a game. Who cared if some bloke who talked guff on the radio was here, this was a European final and all eyes were on the pitch.

There have been a million accounts of this game written and there's not a load I can add apart from the fact that Porto were the biggest bunch of shitebags I have ever witnessed in a game of football.

I have never hated a player as much as I hated Deco and Derlei that night (no, not even Nacho Novo). The slightest brush from a Celtic player and they were down as if simultaneously shot by the guy who did JFK rolling around like the possessed girl in *The Exorcist*. It was sickening. There was a Porto fan beside us who kept shaking his head every time it happened. Thank God. It saved me shaking it for him.

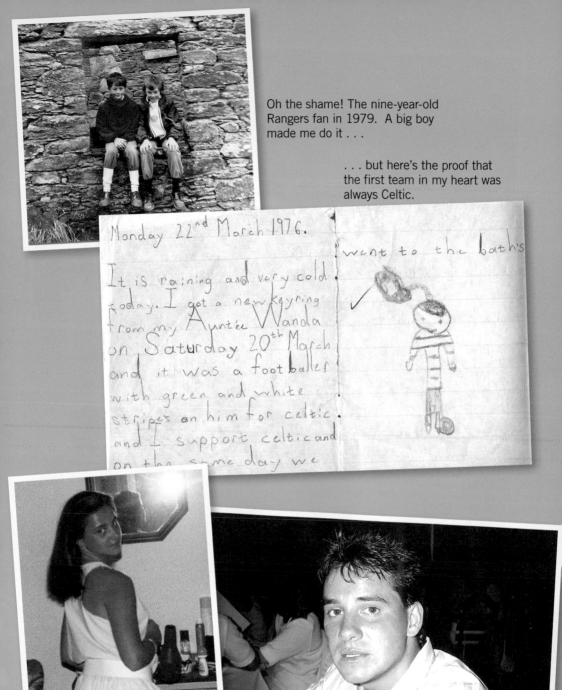

Oh the shame! The nine-year-old Rangers fan in 1979. A big boy made me do it . . .

. . . but here's the proof that the first team in my heart was always Celtic.

Monday 22nd March 1976.

It is raining and very cold today. I got a new keyring from my Auntie Wanda on Saturday 20th March and it was a footballer with green and white stripes on him for celtic. and I support celtic and on the same day we

went to the bath's

Maria Petrucci, the girl who changed my life at seventeen. It helped that she was beautiful.

Romano Petrucci, the boy who changed my life. It helped that he was scary.

On holiday in Greece in 1988 with a bunch of Irish guys after the Republic had beaten England. Having borrowed Morten Harket from Aha's hair.

R-L. Three of Bristol University Drama Department's finest prospects in 1990. David Walliams, future comedy star; Simon Pegg, future moviestar; and a bloke who got free videogames for a while.

## THE BUZZ

**Every THURSDAY at 8.30 p.m., upstairs at the SOUTHERN, Nell Lane, CHORLTON, Manchester** ☎ 061-881 7048.

All concerts £3.50, pay on door, 50p discount for students and unwaged.

| Steaming World Dance Music | plus | Top Quality Comedy |
|---|---|---|
| | | **STEVE COOGAN** |
| 21 Feb **THE BUTTERMOUNTAIN BOYS** + Exciting cajun rockers | | Spitting image's master of voices |
| | | **JOHN THOMSON** |
| 28 Feb **K-PASSA** + Foot-stomping cajun/reggae blend | | Superb Spitting image impressionist |
| | | **SISTER MARY IMMACULATE** |
| 7 Mar **THE BRASSHOPPERS** + Sensational busking brass band | | Revered award-winning nun |
| | | **OTIZ CANNELLONI** |
| 14 Mar **GOD'S LITTLE MONKEYS** + Rootsy Cooking Vinyl heroes | | Spool magician, amazing laughs |
| | | **DOMINIC DIAMOND** |
| 21 Mar **TABOOLA RASA** + Percussive jazz-rock fusion | | Likeable Scotsman tipped for stardom |
| | | **BETTY SPITAL** |
| 28 Mar **WOLLY & THE NEW CRANES** + Slav-rock popsters | | Fully liberated pensioner! |
| | | **KEVIN SEISAY** |
| 4 Apr **JULIAN DAWSON** – Awesome talent + + EDDIE BASKERVILLE – wild reputation | | Inspired performer, 'Buzz' favourite |
| | | **KEVIN McALEER** |
| 11 Apr **CITIZEN SWING** + Crisp Rock 'n' Irish | | Brilliant, off-beat Irishman |
| | | **HATTIE HAYRIDGE** |
| 18 Apr **THE BARELY WORKS** + Indescribable genius | | Deadpan humour 'Red Dwarf' star |
| | | **HENRY NORMAL** |
| 25 Apr **THE GEORGE BOROWSKI BAND** + Dynamic rock guitar legend | | Popular people's performance poet |
| | | **RICHARD MORTON** |
| 2 May **ACCORDIONS GO CRAZY** + Fabulous musical adventurers | | Charismatic and hilarious songs |

| BUZZ SPECIALS | | | |
|---|---|---|---|
| Fri 1 Mar | BLUE JOHN MINES +THE BICH KICKS | £2.50 |
| Wed 6 Mar | TOSS THE FEATHERS – back by request | £3.00 |
| Fri 22 Mar | MIKE ELLIOT – One-Man Comedy Genius | £3.00 |
| Sun 24 Mar | CHERVONA KALYNA (Ukraine) + THE RAGIN' CAJUNS | £3.00 |

presented by AGRAMAN the human anagram
☎ 061-449 7482 with thanks to ...

**THE BODDINGTON**
**PUB · COMPANY**

Flyer from my standup comedian days, alongside Steve Coogan, John Thomson and Sister Mary Immaculate (Caroline Aherne). Whatever happened to those losers, eh? Did they ever get to shake Paul McStay's hand?

Robbie Williams beating the rest of Take That on *Gamesmaster* in 1992. Mr Diamond's wardrobe by Stevie Wonder.

This young man is smiling because he hasn't been banned from using the word Hun yet.

With Mum on my twenty-fifth birthday. She always makes sure I get one piece of ridiculous Celtic merchandise on every birthday. This time it was Celtic change-strip eyeliner.

Assorted members of Diss Utd, stars of FHM and including the wee French genius Berna (in orange), who never understood the Scottish approach to healthy living.

DOMINIK DIAMOND

C.R.SMITH

BLOOD, SWEAT & BEERS

FHM column masthead from the mid 90s. Guess what team I support?

On the pitch in Paris after PSG had given Celtic a footballing lesson in 1995.

With Phil Babb and Graeme le Saux on *Gamesmaster*. Babbsy was a legend, and my ticket to a few mental nights with the Spice Boys in Liverpool.

after all.

**Dominik:** Mellor again. Sorry, David, but I'm sure you'll agree that's a very interesting point.

**Team of the Year other than your own?**
**Nick:** British Ladies Synchronised Swimming Team.
**Dominik:** Richard & Judy. They

and then Phil Babb replying "I should think so, I scored the fifth goal".

**Hand on heart, the worst display by your team and why?**
**Nick:** Barnsley away – I was sober.
**Dominik:** Rushie's testimonial. My Sunday league

*90 Minutes* column picture from the mid 90s. Yes. Not content with having the Celtic top and ball those are rosary beads in shot as well, just to make it clear where I stood.

The deal was I wore a Celtic top in my *90 Minutes* column pictures . . .

# DIAMOND GEEZER

**The beginning of a new year just wouldn't be the same without some random Scottish bloke dishing out awards for a host of fictitious and farcical categories. So, without further ado, let us hand you over to your host for the evening, Mr Dominik Diamond**

It's that time of year again, boys and girls, when an exhausted Santa Dominik concludes his deliveries by rummaging around in his big red sack

wearing a dress. Prat

**Most Charitable Man In Football**
Frank Clark for helping out the poor and needy by buying them for millions and playing them up front. And then resigning

**Team Of The Year**
Oxford United. Only just promoted and they're banging on the door of the Premiership already. Sad Andy is already thinking of changing his name to 'Andy'

**Anchorman Of The Year**
Richard Keys for his wit, intelligence and 'Lego man' style haircut

**Broadcaster Of The Year**
Gary Lineker

# DIAMOND GEEZER

**Bored to death during those long 'off on international duty' weekends? Dominik Diamond has come up with a few alternatives ideas to keep both the fans and players amused when matches are few and far between**

I have just had one of the dullest sporting weekends ever, thank you very much for asking. From dawn on Saturday 5 to sunset on Sunday 6 October, a footballing vacuum sucked any possible entertainment out of the weekend. There wasn't even so much as a Grand Prix or a cricket match to stave the hunger of quality sport. The reason – this ridiculous system whereby the Premierships in England and Scotland get the weekend off because of internationals. Whoever decided that should be shot, or

**3) PAIN**
Business enhance business to work of forest building country would artistic against the pain of Wimb

**4) IT'S**
Same back ma me y

"Aaaagh! Get this thing offa me!" Yep, Rangers beat Celtic, so Dominik has to don the dreaded blue shirt

. . . unless Rangers beat Celtic, then I had to wear their shirt. Which always made me . . . er . . . smile.

games: North v South, etc. Why not have the equivalent

Skinheads v Perms, Wedges

This was not the disguise Kirk and I used while sitting with the Rangers, sorry Airdrie fans in 1995. But it was considered. This was from *Gamesmaster*. We got paid to dress like this.

One of these guys is a legend called Andy. The other is a fine sports commentator. Andy Gray, Sad Andy and myself, mortalled at the World Cup in Paris 1998.

The beautiful, amazing, perfect wee baby daughter God blessed me with in 1998 and whose birth sent me spiralling towards drink, drugs and depression. Kids, eh? What are they like?

Back in Scotland with Karen Dunbar and Fred MacAuley on the set of *Caledonia MacBrains*. If I had known the show would start the insomnia that wrecked my life I wouldn't have been smiling.

The finest Hun who ever walked the earth. My *Star* colleague and friend Irvine Hunter. I am blessing him here and he is giving me the finger. Just so you know.

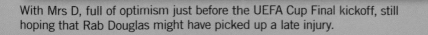

With Mrs D, full of optimism just before the UEFA Cup Final kickoff, still hoping that Rab Douglas might have picked up a late injury.

L-R. Claire Pattenden (boss), Marisa de Andrade (news/drums), Dominik Diamond (vocals/verbals), Scott Shaw (bass/producer). The Xfm Scotland team and the best job I ever had in my life.

The new life in 2010. Onstage at The Al Whittle Theatre in Wolfville, Nova Scotia. A world away from Celtic Park but still with the shamrock on my cap.

I queued up with all the other punters outside Celtic Park to get my photo taken with Craig Bellamy. It was worth every second, in spite of my hair malfunction. What a player!

It's one of the things that stupifies me about football: you never see bad players cheat. It always seems to be the good ones, the Decos, the Eduardos, the Ronaldos and the Henrys, the players who have been granted such a naturally gifted advantage that they should not need to try and steal another one through sleight of hand and dishonesty. This is why I have always respected David Beckham. In spite of the run ins I had with him and his fragrant wife during my time at *The Star* (and you have NEVER heard a human being swear so much as the day he phoned me on my mobile to tear a strip off me for saying his kids always looked miserable. And he was right too, I had stepped over the line) I have never seen David Beckham cheat on a football pitch.

I would love to say that the game was all about Henrik's two goals epitomising that he was a genuine attacking legend who could pull it off at the highest level under the highest pressure, but it wasn't. I would love to say that the game was all about the rebirth of Celtic as a football dynasty on the European stage again, the rehabilitation started off the pitch by Fergus McCann completed on the pitch by Martin O'Neill, but it wasn't. I would love to say that the game was all about the Celtic fans showing they could arrive en masse to a European city that was too small and poorly equipped to handle them and conduct them-selves in a manner in and around the stadium that would do the team and the country proud. But it wasn't.

For me it was all about those wee bastards Deco and Derlei proving that on the football pitch goodness and fairness do not triumph. And then, adding insult to injury, Rab Douglas spilled the ball for the reprehensible Derlei to score the winner in extra time. I was so angry. It just felt so unfair. And it capped a miser-able trip for me. I know thousands of Celtic fans look back on the occasion with joy and pride, but I can't.

We lost the game. Worse than that, we lost the game through

a mixture of refereeing incompetence and cheating. And Rab Douglas. The worst thing the game of football has to offer is losing games you should have won. Actually the worst thing the game of football has to offer is losing games you should have won in a cauldron hotter than Satan's bawsack with no available water and a two hour walk back into town with a blistered wife having spent a small fortune getting there in the first place to find there are no pubs open.

Maybe they expected that having lost the game, this Green and White Army would lay siege to their town in the manner of other clubs' supporters, so they stopped the flow of booze. But that's not the Celtic way. That's not to say our fans don't drink, indeed the centre of Seville was awash with fans lying on park benches and in doorways sleeping that deep sleep that is only possible using that soporific cocktail of Guinness and sadness.

We found one little place that was open and I attempted to get drunk again from a standing start, but it wasn't to be. We got back to the hotel room and Phoebe and her blister went to sleep. I sat up drinking the most revolting red wine and trying to convince myself that we may have lost the game but this heralded a new dawn of Celtic as a genuine European footballing superpower. The board would realise that it was the serious money invested in players like Sutton and Hartson that had got us to this level and it was obvious that we needed to take the huge amounts of money the board was raking in from seasons like this and get more players of this ilk.

Jeez. Even my fingers are laughing as I type that. I didn't realise that this was the peak for the club and from the next day it would start to crumble as a result of poor investment, short-term business decisions and misguided loyalty. Nor did I realise that, once again, the path of the club would mirror the path of my own life's descent over the next five years too.

We flew back the next day, after the return leg of that 538 km journey that was made even more frustrating by a Spanish police car that sat in front of us all the way back to Madrid doing the exact speed limit, taunting me to try and overtake them in the way that men who should know better do. But I didn't. I had left all my testosterone back in Seville. There was that sick feeling you get when something really bad has happened and you can't quite believe it so you feel that there really must, in a good and just world, be some kind of reset switch you can hit to rerun said event with a fairer result.

But you can't. Not in football. Not in life either. And like every true horror film, there was the bit at the end when you think the horror is over but something even more horrible happens. And that was the final day of the SPL season, four days later.

Celtic playing Kilmarnock at Rugby Park, Rangers taking on Dunfermline at Ibrox, Dominik Diamond watching with Archie and Riff in McPhabbs, a terrific bar at Glasgow's Charing Cross.

It was always a great place to watch the football and had become our 'good luck pub' for Celtic's UEFA Cup away games that season. What was incredible about this pub on the season ending day was that they had tellies showing both games, with the result that there was a 50/50 split among the viewing public. On the last day of the season. With free-flowing alcohol.

It should have been a bloodbath. But it wasn't. It was kind of . . . cool. I know the result went Rangers' way with them getting 6-1 against our 4-0 in the Battle of the Goals, and please understand that it was totally and utterly heart shredding, but it was a great atmosphere, among the best I've ever experienced in a pub watching football. It showed that it is possible to have both sets of fans together without anyone getting their heads kicked in.

Mind you, that's looking back at it now. On the day it was worse than being dumped by Rachel Smith all those years ago.

It was as bad as when my dad walked out on us. Seriously. I was in so much pain I hoped I'd never have to go through that depth of despair on the last day of a season again. Of course I would a couple of years later, and this time I would be sitting with the away fans at Motherwell on that particular Black Sunday.

But in 2003 there was only one way to deal with the pain, blot it out with whatever came to hand. Riff, Archie and I got absolutely tonto'd after that game. McPhabbs, then a few other places, then Bairds Bar to sing songs of defiance and revolution, then a few other places and then Paisley.

You know when you live in Glasgow and you *finish* your night in Paisley that it's been particularly brutal. It was one of those nights where you know you're literally killing yourself with the amount you're imbibing; it gets to the stage where every ingestion is actually painful because your body is screaming at you to stop. You can almost see future days you might have lived, packing their things and heading out of your body and you take a perverse pleasure in it because you simply cannot be bothered facing up to the sober reality of the situation.

I have always said that music was my biggest passion in my life, but music has never left me feeling as mentally obliterated as being a Celtic fan. And I've never been to a gig and felt so let down afterwards that I almost killed myself with drink. And I've seen the Black Eyed Peas live.

We should have been UEFA Cup and SPL trophy holders, but that glittering team, the best since The Lisbon Lions, ended up with nothing.

# 13

## A DREAM FULFILLED

'Dear Mr Diamond,' the letter began, 'we would like to offer you a season ticket for the 2003/2004 season at Celtic Park in spite of the fact that you are a drunk and a mental case and occasional cokehead and you used to support the Huns. Yours sincerely, The Celtic Ticket Office.'

Well that was how *my* brain translated the letter. But there it was. In black and white.

I ran through the house like a wee boy on Christmas day who got the Scalextric set. 'Phoebe, Phoebe, Phoebe! We got the season tickets! We got the season tickets!' I was so excited. I couldn't wait for this season to begin after the disappointment of Seville then the final day of the season.

'Very good dear,' she replied. 'Do we get those nice seats we had for the Stuttgart game?'

I checked the letter. Not quite. It was the Lisbon Lions Upper, section 419 which I knew was in a corner, and the fact that it said Row EE meant it was probably quite high up.

'Yes my love. Just as good. In fact actually an even better view.'

Boy! Did I catch it when we turned up for that opening game against Dundee United. First of all we had to walk all the way up the stairs to the Upper Deck level. My wife had never had to do this before. The games she'd come to with me after Stuttgart had continued to be in that corner section of the Lisbon Lions Lower. We'd also gone to the pre season friendly against Arsenal a couple of weeks before where we'd been in the second row section 119 just behind the goalpost. She'd found that 'terribly exciting' but I hated being that low down, it was so confusing. It did give an insight into just how chaotic a goalmouth can seem from the player's angle, though, which almost makes me understand why Rab Douglas struggled. Almost.

Luckily, by the end of the year Phoebe was pregnant so we would point her swelling belly out to the nearest steward and get a ride up in the lifts. That's not the only reason I got her pregnant. I did get a lovely son into the bargain. In fact I got all six numbers and the bonus ball because I got a lovely son who took after his mother.

Even after we got into the seating part, Phoebe looked up into the seats that stretched almost into the heavens. 'Bloody hell! They're not right up at the top of that are they?'

'No my dear, course not!' I replied. They weren't *right* up at the top. They were third row from the back. That was always a hell of a trek up to those seats. When I used to go to Celtic Park on my own I'd run up and down with my head bowed, so I wasn't recognised, but my wife is no Zola Budd so we would get up the stairs at the same kind of pace Hannibal's elephants got up The Alps.

I'd like to apologise to all the people who ever said hello to me as I was ascending the North face of the Lisbon Lions Upper, because I never said more in reply than 'alright mate, how're you doing?' It wasn't that I didn't want to chat, it was just that the wife and I were always late, we'd had to run all the way from the car (having negotiated a knockdown rate of £1 with the young men who kindly offered to watch it for us) and I simply did not have the breath to speak any more than a few words.

By the time we got to the top of section 419 each time I'd be sweating like John Leslie's defence lawyer. That first time was amazing though. We edged our way in the nine seats until we reached ours. And we sat down. Phoebe turned to me and started to speak.

'Shh!' I cut her off, 'Don't say anything. Just give me a second.'

And I sat. And I just looked out over Celtic Park. From my seat. My season seat. For the first time. Lisbon Lions Upper 419 EE9. This was my little bit of Celtic Park at last. My seat at the family dinner table. My backside as part of this whole collection. Who gave a damn if I was a Hun at fifteen? Who cares that I was too busy sprinting down the TV treadmill of the 90s to get to a game? Now I was here, now I was just a fan, just one of the thousands. It was all I ever wanted to be with regards to this club. I never wanted to be the 'famous Celtic diehard' or have a seat for life given to me by the board in recognition for sticking the name of Celtic in a song. I just wanted to fit in, anonymously, and feel I belonged to something.

But that was only part of what I was thinking. As the teams trooped onto the pitch, most of my brain was repeating two words. Sensible. Soccer.

That's what it looked like. We were so damned high up the players looked like they did in *Sensible Soccer* all those years ago when I sat in my Notting Hill flat with Sad Andy making Brian O'Neil curl in another sensational ball for Simon Donnelly to poke home.

From where we were you could hardly read out the numbers on the back of players' shirts, let alone any distinguishing physical characteristics. You could tell Bobo because he was big and black and in defence, and you could tell Stan Varga because he was big and not black and in defence and you could tell Henrik Larsson because of the runs he was making. I also knew that

Magnus Hedman was in goal because my Rab Douglas Muppetometer was not flashing.

Five guys scored goals for us that day: four guys and Henrik Larsson. Actually I had a hunch that Shaun Maloney scored the first because he was so small that from where we were sitting it looked like the ball changed direction in mid air, so I can only assume wee Shaun was that invisible speck.

First game as a season ticket holder and five nil! Ha! That laid to rest the Dundee Utd game we'd drawn because of my getting those free tickets from Danny McGrain. I walked down the steps at the end of the game, hypnotised by the sight of the pitch and all the fans walking out.

They were rubbish seats, though. It wasn't just that the players were tiny specks but the PA system did not reach to the heavens where we sat. You would hear frustrating snatches of announcements as if it was being remixed by a really bad rapper.

There were some interesting characters around us. There was a guy sat directly to my right who spoke to me about the team each week. That may sound boring but by that I mean that he didn't talk to me about telly or radio or Dominik Diamond or any of that guff. He and I were just two guys moaning about Bobby Petta's infuriating inconsistency and how Liam Miller was going to be a Celtic legend. Hey! I didn't say we were experts.

We sat in those seats for a whole season and I never once got the guy's name. So if you were that bloke who sat next to me in 2003/04, the guy who would always make his voice twice as loud when it got to the Free Derry part of This Land Is Your Land then thank you for whiling away the hours on the top deck with me and making me feel like a normal fan.

There was a guy who sat a few rows down who was part of what to this day is the finest hip hop act ever to emerge from . . . er . . . the south side of Glasgow, The Sentinalez, who are also the only hip hop act ever to use Jackie MacNamara as one half of a rhyming couplet. Unless there's a line in a remix of NWA's *Fuck Tha Police* I'm unfamiliar with.

There was another guy called Danny who used to call me up on the radio and he sat two rows in front of us with his wife, there were a bunch of Nigerian guys in the back row who never said a thing all match but just sat there with the biggest smiles on their faces and then there was Shouty Man.

It was Phoebe who named him, pretty early on in the season. Every part of every football ground has someone like him. Slightly unkempt appearance, always goes to games on his own and talks from first to last whistle. Loudly. Always on foot-balling matters and always using only the surnames of players, like the commentator who never was.

Shouty Man was also English, which made his voice stand out even more. The Cockney Catweazel would sit there and utter things like,

'Thompson, up the left, look Larsson's making a run.'

'MacNamara that's your ball. Yes. That's the way to tidy it up.'

'This referee is having a shocker, but you must not let it get you Lennon.'

Now and again he would look round for a small sign of support from his fellow fans to his latest testimony and people would look down at their Bovril.

I'm not decrying the guy. Hell, I'd rather have a thousand people like him than a lot of the latter day customers at Celtic Park who sit there and say nothing. In fact within a few years Phoebe had christened me Shouty Man 2 as I morphed into the same kind of unkempt vocalist who seemed to be describing the game loudly to no-one in particular.

Talking of noise, there really wasn't any in section 419. I used to gaze over at the Jock Stein Stand and the west side of the

North Stand Upper because that's where all the songs seemed to come from. That was the next part of the plan. To get over to that side. Not only would I be part of the fans who sung, but it also meant I would get to see the Rangers games as well. I sat in what was their allocated section for Old Firm games and it was heartbreaking to watch those games on telly for those two seasons and look up and see my seats covered in red white and blue.

Those were lucky seats that season in terms of results. Phoebe and I never saw Celtic lose there until 21 May when what were more or less an Aberdeen youth team brought what was then a seventy one game unbeaten home run to an end in the last minute of the game. In the team's defence they had been crowned Champions three days before with a 1-0 win at Rugby Park which in turn had followed the agony of the UEFA Cup exit in Spain at the hands of Villareal four days before that. So you could forgive them for not having that final bit of puff.

What we did see from those lofty positions that season was the way that whole team moved together like a symphony. Not a showy one by Mozart, full of trills and grace notes and flights of fancy pushing the limits of exponential musical development to blindside the listener, more like something JS Bach would offer. A nice enough tune, with the odd bit of counterpoint but a fairly rigid bass line holding things together and notes going pretty much the way you know they're going to.

You knew that when Alan Thompson got the ball Henrik Larrson would run from the centre down towards the left corner at which point Thommo would hit a long pass that curled outside his opposite man but just stay on the pitch. You knew that as soon as the opposition had the ball Neil Lennon would close them down and nudge it to Stan Petrov. You knew that Didier Agathe would beat a man, run to the by-line and cross. You knew once that cross was fired in it was either going near post for Henrik to glance it in or to the top of the penalty box for Chris Sutton. You knew that if that ball happened to dally for a second in that penalty box somehow John Hartson would be there in a flash that belied his physical attributes to knock it home.

It was utterly conventional, predictable 4-4-2 football, but to see it in operation with that efficiency from on high was like gazing on the workings of a Swiss watch.

The problems would come for Martin the following season, when the parts of this watch were getting older and rusty and he didn't replace them, or rather the board in its infinite wisdom decided the watch would work forever and didn't need money spent on replacement parts.

It wasn't just my wife whom I was dragging into the Celtic family; I was using the club to build bridges with other members too. I had applied for everything at the start of that season: Champions League Home Ticket Package, Champions League Away Tickets, SPL Away Support Registration, Scottish Cup, League Cup, everything I possibly could. All I wanted to do was go and watch Celtic play. Unfortunately I hadn't got enough credits in the supporters' bank to get balloted for many away games, so I got in touch with my old tout pal in Germany when Celtic drew Bayern Munich in the Champions League. I was going to go to the football with my dad.

As I've written earlier, my dad had walked out on my mum when I was at university – money problems, in a nutshell. I was so angry with him about this that I refused to have anything to do with him for the next ten years. In fact it was only after I had sacked my mum from my production company that he got in touch and effectively said, 'Look, you need to sort things out with your mum, and while you're at it, we should sort things out between us too.'

It was a slow process. He had missed out on all those years

of me being on the telly and had never seen his granddaughter. But by 2003 I thought we were close enough to have the kind of trip away to the football that a boy and his dad should always have, even if they are thirty four and fifty four by this stage.

I said at the beginning of this book that my dad was never a football fan, in fact as a kid my mum went to more matches than he did. Football was a game for 'nobbys' and 'poofs' as far as he was concerned. If this was a work of fiction my dad and I would have gone off to Munich and bonded like no two men have ever bonded before. Perhaps there would have been a fight and he'd have saved my life, perhaps I'd have saved his, or maybe watching Celtic together would have forged a different relationship between us: one that saw him too become a season ticket holder and we'd walk down London Road together into the sunset.

It wasn't quite like that but, just like my wife, he was another person who was captivated by the Celtic experience. First and foremost he was stunned that there *was* no fighting or trouble of any kind. As a non-football fan, especially a non-football fan right-wing tabloid reader living in England, he just assumed that every foreign football trip would involve the fans of that British team laying waste to city centres. I'm proud the Celtic fans proved him wrong.

Like the trip to Seville, I didn't just head for the biggest Irish bar and get bladdered, I was with my dad so I wanted it to be a big cultural trip as well. We went to the famous Hofbrauhaus and ate sausages to the strain of an oompah band, we went to the fantastic toy museum they have there and we went to Dachau concentration camp.

We bonded more over our trip to Dachau than any other part of the trip. Like Auschwitz, which I'd visited with my mum and Phoebe while we were in Poland in 1996, the place was silent. No birds sing there. Unlike Auschwitz, this place was full of Celtic fans. That's a surreal sight, let me tell you. To be poring over the worst excesses of horror the human race has been capable of and the place be full of guys in green and white hooped shirts.

I felt proud of the number of Celtic fans who took the time to visit Dachau on that trip. It wasn't just about the football, it wasn't just about the beer and it wasn't just about getting away from their work for a day or two. It was about taking the time to pay tribute to innocent people who had been murdered in the name of fascism. I wonder if fans from the other side went to places like that, would they then return to their club and stand there while the guy in the seat next to them gave a Nazi salute? Put simply, if you go to Dachau or Auschwitz you don't laugh at a racist joke again.

A sobering place to visit and the experience allied to fact that this was the longest time I had spent in my father's company since I had gone off to university at eighteen, brought us closer together as father and son. My dad didn't quite see it solely in terms of the evils of fascism. 'This is why we should never allow Britain to be ruled by Europe,' he said. Have I mentioned he's a *Daily Mail* reader?

It was also one of only two times in my life where I've wanted to be recognised, where I've been desperate for that which others in my profession seem to be willing to sell their soul for: fame. Once was when I took my daughter Molly to T in the Park in 2008, the other time was that night in Munich. Both times were for the same reason. I wanted my dad and my daughter to see that I was somebody. I wanted them to be proud and impressed by me. It may be pathetic and shallow but it's what every man wants from his dad and his children. So I lingered at road crossings, I gazed around myself nonchalantly in bars instead of keeping a hat pressed down over my eyes; I met people's gaze and tried to burrow into their mind.

'Yes. I *am* who you think I am. It is me. Dominik Diamond. Please, roll up, roll up! Don't be shy. Come see the desperately insecure man and tell him how much you like him in front of his dad!'

When we walked into our seats in the beautiful Olympic Stadium that night it hit my dad like a bolt. He saw what Phoebe saw that night against Stuttgart and what I saw that day in 1986 with Romano: that sea of green and white. And what's more you could buy beer in the stadium! And drink it in your seat! It was almost as if they treated football fans like mature adults instead of errant children.

It was another brilliant Celtic performance in all but one position. Agathe and Thommo ran the show down the flanks, Henrik and Hartson ran their backsides off, Lennon marked Ballack out of the game and Balde was imperious at the back. I'm sure Roy Makaay bought a huge house with his cut of the £18 million Bayern had just spent on him but for seventy minutes he was living in Bobo's pocket.

It's just a pity that Bobo missed a chance to follow up Thommo's opener because moments after that Makaay gave eighteen million reasons why you needed to spend that kind of money to compete in Europe. He had half a chance to shoot from a poor Varga clearance. Bang! 1-1. Then there was *that* free kick.

You will notice again that I fail to give plaudits to the man in the Celtic goalkeeping shirt, but that night it wasn't Rab Douglas, it was Magnus Hedman who fell asleep on duty and let a free kick from Makaay literally float past him with all the pace and venom of a soap bubble.

I will never forget the taunting sound of the stadium announcer that night, one of those guys who stretches the name of the goal scorer into infinity and beyond. 'Maaaaaaaaaaaakkkkkkkkkkkaaaaaaayyyyyyyyyy!' he screamed.

The final syllable was still reverberating around the Munich night when the final whistle went.

Yet another big European night Celtic should have won but didn't. I was almost as deflated as I had been in Seville. My dad and I got the train back into town and nipped into this lovely wee Italian café where we consoled ourselves with something called Grappa that we'd never tasted before and after the amount we had that night never wanted to taste again.

'So what was that like then dad?' I asked as we boarded the plane back to the UK. What would he mention? His new love of the Hoops? The sobering experience of Dachau? The fact that we'd finally gone on that father-son trip after all these years?

'What a remarkably tidy city, Dominik,' he said. 'You never saw any rubbish lying around, no graffiti, nothing. From the station to the ground to the airport – absolutely spotless.'

Dads eh? Can't live with them, can't stop them being *Daily Mail* readers.

# INVESTING IN THE FUTURE

The rest of the season was a peach. Celtic steamrollered everyone domestically, as you would expect looking at the final table: ninety-eight points in total with a goal difference of eighty, seventeen points ahead of Rangers who only had a goal difference of forty-three.

It was goals, goals, goals. At one point the team scored twenty-two of them in the five SPL games between the Anderlecht and Bayern Champions League games. I could not have wished for a better first session as a season ticket holder.

Even though Celtic didn't progress past the Champions League group stage, the wins against Lyon and Anderlecht were great nights to be at Celtic Park and at that point it did look as if Liam Miller was going to be the next hooped hero. But sadly he was to become another in a long line of those who seek their fame and fortune away from Celtic only to never reach the heights they scaled in Glasgow's East End.

The exit from the Champions League that year was especially annoying for me because I had a ticket for the away game in Lyon. I'd finally been balloted a ticket for an away European game. The bad news is that it was just a single. What the hell? I thought. I'll go on my own. I was filming in London the day of the match so I'd just hop on a plane to France, watch the game, find myself an Irish bar afterwards then fall asleep in whatever place was linked to my BMI rewards card. And then the storm hit.

My original flight got cancelled and then the next one was delayed meaning it wouldn't land in Lyon till half an hour after the game had kicked off. I decided to cut my losses and fly back to Glasgow, figuring I'd just go and watch it in Sammy Dow's on the south side with my neighbour Archie. So I paid full whack for a ticket and headed through to the BMI Lounge.

'Good evening Mr Diamond. How are you today?' asked the friendly flight attendant on the reception. With all the filming in London that lounge and its bar had become my second home.

'Fine thank you, I have an appointment with Mr Guinness, can you show me to the fridge please?'

That flight was then delayed. Still, by the time we boarded the plane I calculated that by the time I got to Sammy's I'd have missed the first quarter hour of the game. And then we sat there. On the runway. For over an hour while the storm closed in. By the time we landed in Glasgow it was actually nine o clock. I sprinted through the airport and into a taxi. 'Awright big man?' Asked the cabbie. 'Surprised you're not watching the game.'

Sometimes there are no words to express yourself.

Got to Sammy Dow's, saw Archie, grabbed the pint he'd got in for me like the good friend he was, drank heavily from it, looked up. Just in time to see the ball brush Bobo Balde's arm. Penalty to Lyon. Goal to Lyon. Goodbye Champions League Second Stage. It could have been worse. I could have been in Lyon.

We could have won the UEFA Cup that season as well, but the writing was on the wall in that Champions League game against Bayern. They could spend £18 million on a striker, we didn't. I say didn't, not couldn't, because of course we could have. But no. When some clubs would get the UEFA Cup final, their board sees it was a sign of encouragement and strengthen the squad to go one better, Celtic didn't. Even when the greatest striker in the club's history left at the end of that season, did we go out and spend £18 million on someone similarly world class? No. We spent a million and a half on a one-year loan deal for Henri Camara. Why? Because of that seventeen point margin over Rangers. Because all the board has ever done since the turn of the millennium is look towards Govan and base Celtic's spending on what's happening over there. It's like Irn Bru worrying about lemonade from Bon Accord instead of trying to take on Pepsi.

Sure we managed to beat Barcelona at home in the second greatest Celtic Park European night I ever witnessed then knocked them out of the UEFA Cup with that incredible draw at the Nou Camp, but only because Rab Douglas got himself sent off in the tunnel at Celtic Park and we had a decent goal-keeper in David Marshall for the majority of the rubber.

But the two games against Villareal showed that as good as that Celtic team were domestically, we simply were not good enough to win a European trophy unless everything went our way on the night. We would need stunning saves, Larsson to take all his chances, no defensive slip ups and the lion's share of the refereeing decisions to go through. It worked against Barca. The luck ran out against Villareal.

Dominating the league by that margin in 2003/2004 was the worst thing that could have happened to Celtic. Investment should have been made to make us a modern European giant. It wasn't, which is why the club is still a bargain basement team as soon as it gets outside of Scotland. All because the board looks towards Ibrox instead of Europe.

Talking of our friends south of the river . . .

Towards the end of that season I was speaking to a guy on a flight up to Glasgow from London bemoaning the fact that by only having a season ticket for the Lisbon Lions Upper I couldn't get a ticket for the Rangers games. He said that wasn't necessarily the case. He said he had mates who always managed to get tickets just by phoning up the ticket office the week before and seeing if there were any on general sale. Sometimes the players and staff and whoever wouldn't take up their full allocation and they'd stick them on general sale at the last minute.

So first thing that Monday morning I went to the ticket office when it opened and asked if they had any tickets left. They did. Literally just the one. So I took it. North Stand Upper Area 402 Row Z Seat 1. The last seat in the house. I like to think it was one of those occasions when Rod Stewart or Billy Connolly were too busy to take their freebies.

Not that I cared. This was my first Rangers game at Celtic Park since that day Romano took me there. It would be amazing to see if it matched the level of intensity I witnessed back then. It would be amazing to see if we could make it a clean sweep of wins over Rangers that season. It would be amazing just to find somewhere to park.

I couldn't get down the road to my normal parking spot on the grass fields to the south of the stadium. No one told me that's where the Rangers fans were allowed to park. So I had to double back and head right down almost all the way back to the Shawfield Dog Track before I could find a space to park. And driving there I realised that a legion of blue and white shirts stood between me and Celtic Park. It was like going to the Scottish Cup Final against Airdrie all over again.

Shirt tucked right into the jeans, scarf tied around chest, jacket zipped right up over my chin, baseball cap pulled right down, sunglasses on and sprinting like a bastard for over a mile through the Hun hordes, heart racing, blood pumping, paranoia working overtime.

'Hey pal?' one of them shouted. 'Got the time!'

'Sorry maaaayyyyyte!' I gasped out of breath, with the return of the World's Worst Cockney Accent.

I got to the front of the stadium on the wrong side of the divide and tried to run through to the Celtic section, at which point my ribcage was nearly broken by one of Strathclyde's finest who had clotheslined me thinking I was a Rangers casual attempting a run on enemy territory.

'Fuck sake man!' I cried. 'I'm a Celtic fan.'

I pulled the jacket down and took the cap off to reveal that well known multiple chin and baldy napper combo.

'Jesus Christ! Dominik Diamond! Are you a total fucking madman?' The policeman replied, and ushered me through towards the Jock Stein end of London Road.

I bombed it up to Turnstyle 14, jogged up the stairs, entered section 402 and just stopped. And looked. Taking in the sea of green and white divided in the South East corner by that slash of red, white and blue. The contrast was, and always is, dizzying. It was like those adverts where they show a screen from a normal TV next to one that's HD. There are football matches and then there are Old Firm matches which even to the eye seem to be in almost unnatural superfocus: it's the hyper-reality of Celtic v Rangers.

The game was about to kick-off so I dragged my fat, sweating carcass up to Row Z and settled down for the game.

Aye, right! Settled down? For an Old Firm game? For the next two hours 'lull' is nothing but a four letter word.

People are often asked – what would you do if you were told you had cancer and could do one thing before you died? Well I'm sure it's a giggle doing a bungee jump, parachuting out of a plane, seeing the ruins at Machu Pichu or shaking the Dalai

Lama's hand but you can keep them. For me it would be an Old Firm game. Every. Single. Time. It is the most intense experience life has to offer.

It's why if you're a fan you really don't care that the standard of football is almost always poor. This one was end to end stuff though.

I thought we'd won the game after three minutes, with Stan Varga touching in from a Thommo free kick, but Mr Hugh Dallas in his always impeccable judgement decided that famously dirty player Henrik Larrson had assaulted that delicate flower Frank de Boer, so it was chalked off.

There could have been half a dozen goals in that first half: Henrik, Sutton, Ricksen, Mols, Stephen Hughes all on different days could have scored for their respective sides of the Glasgow divide.

Each time someone went close it was like a balloon being blown closer to bursting. People talk about tension being a palpable thing, but in an Old Firm game it's not just touchable, it infects your body like one of those aliens from the Ridley Scott movie then grows with each passing incident as the excitement threatens to burst out of your chest and assume its own independent life. I have almost thrown up during Celtic-Rangers games, it's felt so uncomfortable.

The second half was more Celtic, with attack after attack tearing the Bears to shreds, but Stefan Klos, like Goram before him, seemed to have the Superman cape on in the Rangers goal. Luckily in the last minute Chris Sutton pulled out one of the best Celtic goals I ever saw, heading on a long ball to Henrik, who in turn touched on the most inch perfect pass for Chris to run on to. He holds off, or pushes over, the Rangers defender before curling a shot past Klos into the top right hand corner.

And that's why we called him The Hunskelper.

To say the place went ballistic for the Celtic fans in there is like saying the moon landings were a holiday for Neil Armstrong. The cheer almost sucked the air out of the stadium and only then, in spite of the seated nature of Celtic Park, did it become a seething throng of arms and heads and bodies like it did that time in The Jungle with Romano. The throng was still a-seething when the referee blew, and for about twenty minutes afterwards. Nobody wanted to leave, nobody wanted to go home, especially not me, because my car was still parked right in the middle of where the Rangers fans were driving and as fast as the Subway Loyal were leaving I thought it best I left it as long as possible before putting on the cap, zipping up the jacket, hiding the shirt and scarf and assuming my secret identity as Anonoman again.

League wrapped up, whitewash against *them*, just one thing left now: the Scottish Cup Final against Dunfermline at Hampden. Something of a grudge match after their capitulation against Rangers on the last day of the previous season. But more importantly, Henrik's last competitive match for us.

Phoebe was eight months pregnant at the time so it was one of those rare occasions where we couldn't turn up with a minute until kick-off and sprint from the car, we had to be there in plenty time. So we turned up two minutes before kick-off instead, and were smack bang in the middle of Row L in the South Lower, so it required something of a military operation to get everyone to stand up and let us past.

Poor Phoebe, she couldn't jump up and down that game at all, so not only could she not go daft and celebrate Larsson's final brace for the Bhoys, she pretty much missed seeing them thanks to the guys in front being a bit premature with their risings, which was pretty much how we'd conceived Charlie in the first place. Catholics and contraception, eh? What are they like?

All that left was to get through Henrik's farewell testimonial against Seville a few days later. Epic fail. My eyes were bawled out and it felt great. I finally felt like I belonged to the Celtic family and if you can't cry in front of your own family who can you cry in front of?

A few weeks later my own family was added to with the traumatic birth of my son. Not just the birth itself, which involved an all lights-flashing sprint down the corridors to an emergency Caesarean for Phoebe, but the fact he was born in the Southern General in Govan right in the middle of Marching Season. Phoebe had to stay in the hospital for a while after the birth, and my daily trips up there involved a backdrop of The Sash and numerous diversions around bowler-hatted gentlemen in aprons and their followers. This is what my son was born into, spilled from the serenity of the womb into the cauldron of Scottish religious conflict. Charming.

A few weeks later we took him the civic offices to register the birth.

'Surname?' asked the lady filling out the form.

'Diamond,' I replied.

'First name?'

'Charlie.'

'Middle name?'

'Henrik.'

'Christ! No anither wan!' she exclaimed.

What else could I do? By giving him the middle name of Celtic's greatest ever striker I gave my son a part of Celtic. It's in his blood, it's in his name. He would never have to take that long twisting journey full of self-doubt and feelings of guilt and unworthiness. He is Celtic from birth.

Not sure I should have named my third child Neil Lennon GIRUY Ya Hun Bassas Diamond though. Not with her being a girl and all.

# PASSING IT ON

I would not be a Celtic fan if it hadn't been for Romano Petrucci 'adopting' me into the Celtic family when I was seventeen. So I was pleased to be able to do the same thing for someone else many years later, even though the man in question was nearly old enough to be my dad. OK, he'd technically have been an eleven-year-old dad but stranger things have happened. I'm from Arbroath.

Archie was my neighbour across the road from us when we moved to Glasgow in late 2001. With a wife called Theresa and five kids with names like Gabriel and Francesca it was pretty obvious what side of the religious and footballing divide he was on.

His wife kept him on a very short leash. He never got out and it was obvious that their relationship was not a happy one. She was a terrifyingly controlling woman who once, in the middle of a rainstorm, refused to let her husband help my eight month pregnant wife get into our house when she'd locked herself out because they were having their tea at the time.

This was a shame, because Archie loved life. The first Halloween we spent in Glasgow he was up and down the street dressed as Freddie Mercury with all his kids and even though he was in his mid 40s I could tell that there was so much untapped energy in him as a person, so much of life that had not been lived. His kids were lovely too. I did a live Halloween broadcast for the *Richard & Judy* show from my front garden the next year with his kids doing the famous witches scene from *Macbeth*. It was as cultured as my life had been since I sat my A levels.

Like my own experience with Romano, Archie was to be baptised into the Celtic way in the cauldron of The Old Firm, but only by accident. He was always a jammy bastard that way.

After that first season in the Lisbon Lions Upper I'd got a transfer to the North Stand Upper, finally getting automatic tickets for the Rangers games. Phoebe was not happy.

Everything I loved about the Old Firm encounters, she hated. My wife was the complete opposite of me. She was born posh, I was born poor. She grew up with horses in stables. I grew up on a council estate. She was an angel. I was a wanker. She saw the good in everyone. I kept looking for the bad. She was very friendly in new company, thinking that strangers are simply friends you haven't met yet. I was quiet and withdrawn (until I'd had a drink), thinking that strangers were simply friends you haven't been fucked over by yet. The biggest difference between us and the reason why she disliked Old Firm games was that she really did not like anger. By contrast I thought that line in the PiL song – 'anger is an energy' – was one of the best lines ever written.

I was always angry at something. Angry at posh people at school, angry at political correctness at university, angry at media types in London, but what I didn't realise throughout most of my life is that anger is actually a mental illness and depression is anger directed at yourself. But it took me years of therapy and a religious rebirth to grasp that.

Back on 29 August 2004 I still just simply hated the Huns. And my wife really does not like hate. She won't even let the kids use the word in the house. Seriously. If they use the word she shouts and screams at them and calls them all the names under the sun.

Oh alright, the last sentence was made up, but the Old Firm atmosphere was not for her. She loved the European nights, because there was something altogether more positive and wholesome about the energy. Every time she looked over at me during ninety minutes against Barcelona or Anderlecht I was smiling. When she looked over at me during ninety minutes against Rangers it was quite different. I was up and down and out of my seat and banging my hands on my head like a really bad actor playing the role of someone in a lunatic asylum. Draw any number of parallels from that if you will.

Phoebe said she didn't even recognise me as the person she knew and loved. She wasn't a big fan of some of the comments flying around either – 'Fuck the Queen!', 'Ya fucking Brit bastards!' and 'Fucking burn that English flag ya cunts' – being three of them. Like I have said, my wife is English and rather posh. She's probably related to the Queen in some way.

The new seats were fantastic: Section 445 Row D Seats 5 and 6 were perfectly in line with the West goal-line and near enough the front of the upper tier to give you a perfect view no matter where the ball was in play. No more *Sensible Soccer*, this was like FIFA 10. This meant that we had a great view of the Celtic board's ambition that season, specifically our new superstar signings: an aging Brazilian fud and an unknown Senegalese striker. To be fair Juninho and Camara had good games against Rangers that day, but neither of them lasted more than seven months at the club.

They still featured in more Old Firm games than my wife. After that one she said she never wanted to be surrounded by such a hostile atmosphere again. Posh, nice people are funny like that. So Archie got the golden ticket – he got all of Phoebe's

Old Firm tickets from that day on. And that was the start of our amazing Celtic adventures together. Our first Old Firm match together was actually at Ibrox, the first time I had ever been there for a game too – 10 November 2004, Scottish League Cup. I took Archie right up the Broomloan Rear, right up to row EE seat 137.

This was an evening kick-off so Archie and I were spared the hairiness of future drives from Strathbungo to Ibrox which took us through a number of streets used by Rangers fans. Archie and I soon learned that the combination of my face; green and white scarves and rebel songs on the car CD player were not the most inauspicious combination.

There is nothing like watching Celtic at Ibrox; it's better than watching them in the Nou Camp, the San Siro or even Celtic Park on a European night; it's a raid on the enemy camp against vastly superior forces and taps into that whole underdog feeling of being a Celtic fan.

The underdog feeling at Ibrox is exacerbated by the fact that they absolutely deafen you with their songs beforehand. 'Rule Britannia', 'Follow Follow', 'The Dambusters' theme get absolutely blasted. I'm sure they're using noise-terrorism techniques developed by the East German Stasi in the Cold War because it's psychologically really intimidating as an away fan, which is the way it should be. By comparison Celtic's sound system is like a few wasps being rattled in a jar.

The other great thing about seeing Celtic at Ibrox is that it's a hundred times sweeter if you win and yet not nearly as traumatic if you lose, which we did that night. For the first time in a year and a half. Just as well I'm not the kind of egocentric, superstitious, neurotic mess that reads too much into events and would blame himself for things like that if that first loss coincided with his first trip to Ibrox, eh?

This was another Old Firm match with a ridiculously high

tempo matched by a ridiculously low level of skill. There were only a handful of meaningful passes from either team. But it was still the most ridiculously exciting 120 minutes (including extra time) of football on atmosphere alone. Every mistimed tackle, every poor shot on goal, every woeful pass was refracted through the Oldfirmometer and emerged as something beautiful in a way that is and always will remain a mystery to non-Old Firm fans.

The bare facts of that night were that Stan Varga hit the bar, Big Bad John scored but he could have, should have, had two, Craig Beattie had a shot cleared virtually off the line and Henri Camara expelled wide with a few minutes of extra time to go. Life without Larsson . . .

In the blue corner, some of their guys nearly scored. Two of them did; a head-bandaged Prso and a relentlessly impudent Arveladze.

You could just see instantly what it meant to Archie. The excitement in his voice, the light in his eyes, that way he just connected with the Celtic family in the same way I had all those years ago during the Billy Stark Old Firm game with Romano. As we went to more and more matches home and away together it seemed that it was only as a part of this crowd of supporters that he finally discovered who he was as an individual. He'd lived all his life in Glasgow, but only now was he at home.

Neither of us were too bothered by the result that night. It was just The Diddy Cup, and we were just buzzing so much from cheering on the Bhoys at Ibrox. And getting back home safe for a few pints in Heraghty's after.

Within a year Archie had got Season Books for himself and Gabriel and he became my constant companion for away games, but the relationship with me and Celtic also helped end his marriage. Archie was making up for lost time; he was getting a bit of independence and a lot of new pals that were nothing to do with his wife. Eventually they separated. Normally it's sad when anyone splits up with their wife. Not in this case. I thought she was a nightmare.

Archie is now the happiest guy I know, in an amazing relationship with a girl who also went through a horrible divorce; who also has a hundred kids who get on great with his hundred kids and who just happened to be a pal of mine from school.

As I keep saying throughout this book, all these things come to pass for a reason and it's just another example of the incredible destiny my life as a Celtic fan took on. My pal Archie is finally happy, all because of a journey I was started on by my pal Romano nearly a quarter of a century before.

If there are any Celtic fans reading this who are scratching their heads wondering if they ever saw Archie with me at a game, then there are two words that might jog the memory.

The second word is 'vest'. The first word is 'gay'.

Don't ask me why, but for some reason Archie would always wear a tight black vest under his Celtic top, which he would remove at the earliest opportunity whenever we were in any pub that was warmer than freezing. I suspect that, because he has always been a thin guy who wanted to make up for lost time when it came to women, Archie figured that this svelte, vested figure would stand up well when contrasted with the larger baggy hoop shirted figures around him.

But he forgot the most basic of facts. People don't go to the likes of the Brazen Head or The Spirit Bar in Glasgow to watch Shebeen or Gary Og because they're trying to meet women. So most of the people we came across just assumed Archie was my 'wee gay mate'.

What made this even more bizarre was that later that season we gained another mate, Big Mick, who's name was the biggest understatement since Helen of Troy was described as 'not bad looking'. Mick was the biggest, scariest-looking guy in the world. You know in the movies, when someone comes across a biker gang just when they don't want to and they end up pinned against the wall by the one that's ten foot tall with the shaved head and the goatee?

That was Big Mick. More about him later . . .

For now the dream was complete. Season ticket holder, now with the Rangers games included and credits in the bank with the away registration scheme and a pal to go to the games with. It doesn't get any better as a Celtic fan.

Professionally I fulfilled another dream that season; I *finally* got the move into music radio I had dreamed of my whole career. Unfortunately I took the job without listening to the station first, or even realising what being a music radio DJ entailed. Specifically, a music radio DJ on Real Radio.

I thought, in my infinite naivety, I would just turn up and pick a load of records and play them. Honestly. I had been working in the media for over a decade and I was that dumb.

Part of the problem was that I didn't actually listen to music radio. I was a Radio 5 live man through and through. If I happened to catch a music radio station in the car the dumb Smashy'n'Niceyness of it had me retching in seconds. The only exception was Jim Gellatly, my old schoolmate who had edited the *Socialist* magazine at school and who now, I was chuffed to discover by complete accident, had a new music show on a station called Beat 106.

All I knew about Real was what my agent told me – they were the biggest radio station in Scotland and their boss Jay Crawford thought that they could put me up against Jonathan Ross in Scotland and do well. That was good enough for me. First of all I had to do a couple of overnight slots to get used to the equipment, then a week filling in for Robin Galloway on the Breakfast Show.

I didn't pay too much attention to the music I was playing at first. I was so nervous about pushing the wrong button and having the faders at the correct level. Well that and the odd abusive phone call. Don't ever do late night radio if you're a sensitive soul. Especially if you're a sensitive soul who's a well-known Celtic fan in the city of Glasgow. Many people up at that time of night are drunk, mental or both. I know. I'm up at those times.

I'd only been in the overnight chair at Real for about fifteen minutes when the phone lit up. Wonderful! I thought. It's the first well-wisher of my music radio career! I picked up the receiver.

'Hello Real Radio, Dominik here.'

'Ya fucking Fenian Bastard!'

Ah! *Now* I understood why you had to pre-record all calls with listeners!

By the third abusive call I gave up answering, but I was so unnerved by this I wasn't listening to the music, I was watching the door monitors to make sure I wasn't getting a welcoming committee.

When I was doing the *Real Breakfast* I wasn't even listening to the music going out either. By then I was too busy having a laugh with co-host Cat Harvey and producer Michael Wilson, who was also given the onerous task of keeping an eye on me in general, poor sod.

It was only when I started the Saturday show and was sitting there on my own that I realised I was playing Westlife. And Dido. And George Michael. Pish. Pish. Pish. 'Right,' I thought to myself. 'We need to do something about that.' So I started changing all the songs I didn't like. Nobody told me these things were decided by committees based on listener research and scheduled by a supercomputer bigger than NASA to give people exactly what they wanted. I just thought the computer programmed the songs in case you didn't have time to do so yourself.

So Jay called me into his office to tell me in the nicest way possible that the playlist was the playlist and if it was possible could I try and stick to it because that's the way it works, bozo. So I went back and played Westlife and Dido and George Michael as I was told. Only this time I was technically proficient enough to find a sound effects CD and play vomiting noises over the top of them. So Jay called me into his office again. And again he was nice. So I stopped playing the vomiting sound effects over the top and instead I would just play Dido then apologise for doing so afterwards.

There was also a small incident whereby I said the weather was worse than testicular cancer, which didn't go down well either. Actually it's a testament to Jay that throughout this short, but intense period, when I quickly turned from his great white hope to his biggest nightmare, he was always so nice to me, and to this day we get on great.

But it was obvious I was a round peg in a Real square hole and it was only a matter of time before someone above Jay in the pecking order said. 'Enough!' Ironically enough I sent an email to Jay asking if I could take Saturday, 20 November off because I had finally been awarded a pair of tickets for the Ibrox game in the away registration ballot.

The title of the email was 'Assuming I haven't been sacked by then . . .' By the time the game came around I had been.

Real were doing this thing whereby a load of their DJs were in some Big Brother-style house at the SECC during some exhibition or other and I had to do a live link-up with them from my Saturday show. I can't remember how it came about but for some reason I'd mentioned the words 'Radio' and 'Clyde' in the same sentence. Quick as a flash Robin Galloway said that

I shouldn't mention other radio stations on the air. I then said. 'Who cares, everyone knows that Clyde is pish and only listened to by morons.' Even quicker than the previous flash Robin said. 'I can't believe you said that. If any of the rest of us said something like that we'd be sacked.'

As if by magic, the following week I was called into Bossman Jay's office for the final roasting. Michael Wilson was in there too, so I knew it was bad news. Poor Jay was almost in tears as he said he really had no choice this time. I had caused some major headaches at board level because Clyde could take Real to OFCOM and start an investigation which could get Real fined or shut down, so they had to let me go.

I argued that surely if it went to OFCOM we could claim 'fair comment' and Radio Clyde would have to prove that they were not 'pish', something I felt they would struggle to do in any form of court.

Michael shook his big ginger head and Jay gave me that look for the umpteenth time that meant even he was still staggered by how clueless I was about these things. I felt bad I had let Jay and Michael down. I was contrite, I was humble and I fought like a tiger for my job in that meeting and managed to talk my way from a sacking down to a suspension instead.

Then I walked out of Real and phoned my agent and told him to write them a letter saying I was quitting. Technically it meant that I had held onto my 100% record of walking away from every job and never getting sacked, though I don't think there was a more relieved man in the world than Jay Crawford when he read that resignation letter.

He and I knew it was only a matter of time before I misbehaved again and I couldn't keep doing that to Jay, not when there were lots of other potential bosses I could be doing it to. That would be selfish.

Anyway, this all coincided with that first trip to Ibrox with

Archie, then another one on 20 November almost immediately after which I was flying to Barcelona with Phoebe for the Champions League tie. It was the most intense Celtic fortnight of my life to date, so you can see why walking out on the biggest radio station in the country was not at the forefront of my mind. Career? Give a damn?

For some reason Archie couldn't make the Ibrox game, for some other reason I managed to persuade Phoebe to go instead. I think I told her that as a posh English lady almost certainly related to the Queen she'd feel right at home amidst all those Union Jacks and Rule Britannia tunes. I promised her it would be different than it was at Celtic Park.

It certainly was. We were pretty much on the south edge of the lower Broomloan Stand in full view of the Main Stand West Enclosure. And didn't they let me know. 'Dominik Diamond is a wanker' alternated with 'who ate all the pies?' throughout half-time. Phoebe was shocked. I had never felt so proud. I turned round and conducted them, possibly because there always seemed to be far less Nazi salutes from that side than there was from the West corner of the Govan Stand.

I actually got an email from one of the Rangers fans after that game. It read thus.

*Mr Diamond,*

*Just a quick email to apologise for any rude gestures and/or expletives that me and my two mates may have aimed in you direction at half time on Saturday. While all around were losing their heads both on and off the park I fully accept that simulating 'Playstation thumb' and chanting 'Gamesmaster Gamesmaster What's the Score?' was both inflammatory and provocative. Singling out someone on the basis of race, religion or career choice is not acceptable in today's society and I hope you accept my sincerest apologies.*

# PASSING IT ON

*I hope you find future success within your career and look forward to a barren year or ten following the Tic.*

I won't put the guy's name, just in case he works somewhere supporting Rangers might be frowned upon, like Glasgow City Council.

Some people reading this book may at times fear that I'm delusional when I constantly hint at the destiny I had mapped out as a Celtic fan. But when I look back at the events that happened it is impossible for me to think that there wasn't some higher power with a hand on the tiller. Take Barcelona that season, for example.

# FRIENDS OLD AND NEW

Once again I cleverly pitched a Celtic European away game as a chance for Phoebe and I to have a few nights away from the kids. Like the trip to Seville my wife made me pay by lodging us in another ridiculously overpriced trendy hotel but this time we did have a rather big session in Flaherty's off the Ramblas in Barcelona before the game and my wife may have even joined in the odd song as well. That's the beauty of Guinness.

We were a bit worse for wear by the time we got to a tiny bar on one of the roads in sight of the Nou Camp and I decided to check where our seats were so I could ask a local the best direction to head in, what with my internal compass having been drowned by this stage.

I took my wallet out of my pocket to get the tickets. The tickets were not there. We had got so hammered in Flaherty's we hadn't gone back to the hotel to pick them up. The hotel was at least half an hour away, and the game started in fifteen minutes.

'I've left the tickets back in the hotel!' I screamed and grabbed Phoebe. Actually being a typical man I probably screamed, 'YOU'VE left the tickets back in the hotel!'

We ran out in the general direction of the train station. Even though this was one of the few months during the noughties when my wife wasn't pregnant, it was pretty slow going. Booze and jogging go together like *Grand Theft Auto* and the Dalai Lama and we stopped within a few minutes.

'This is crazy,' my panting wife said, face the colour of an Aberdeen kit. 'We'll never get back in time.'

'We might make the second half though,' I pleaded and was about to throw her over my shoulder and run back to the Ramblas if necessary when a calm voice cut through the panic.

'Do you need tickets?'

I looked around us to see where the voice had come from. I couldn't see any Celtic fans around, all I could see was a priest.

'Do you need tickets? I've got two spare. Two of my brothers couldn't make it.'

The words were being spoken by the priest.

Now do you understand why I think there has been a higher power guiding me through my Celtic life? But wait, it gets even stranger.

I bought the two tickets from the priest (for face value I hasten to add) and we headed back into section 531 row 27 seats 12 and 13. We just made it in just after kick-off and I was nearly weeping with relief. Then I felt a tap on my shoulder and heard a West of Scotland accent that made my heart leap out of my chest.

'All those years a Celtic fan and you still can't make it on time to a game. I thought I'd taught you better than that.'

It was Romano Petrucci! I had not seen the guy for nearly fifteen years and here he is, in the seat directly behind me. A seat I would not have been close to if I hadn't left our original tickets back in the hotel and hadn't bumped into that priest on that street at that time.

'Phoebe,' I said. 'This is Romano.'

'THE Romano?' asked Phoebe.

'The very one, the reason we're here supporting this team.'

Unbelievable, or not, if you believe in a higher power which, ironically, I didn't back then. I had lost my faith after the insanity of my insomnia and it took a journey to Jerusalem and the Philippines some fifteen months later to get it back. But whether I still believed in God or not at this point, I certainly believed in miracles.

There was a miracle on the pitch that night as well. Barcelona could have scored some half dozen goals but Magnus Hedman actually had a great game and in spite of going 1-0 down after twenty-five minutes, the team fought doggedly against far superior opponents in the shape of Eto'o, Puyol, Xavi, Ronaldinho and that wee bastard Deco from Seville.

The battle on the pitch however was nothing compared to the battle my bladder was fighting against the umpteen pints of the black stuff still shipping around inside me. I was trying to hold on till half-time, but with a few minutes to go I could keep it in no longer and headed for the toilet.

I sighed with relief as I let the floodgates open, then the sigh became the biggest roar I had heard in my life. But it wasn't coming from me; it was coming from the Celtic fans who had more control over their bladder. John Hartson had scored.

Celtic's first away point in the Champions League and I missed the goal. Still, I think that over the course of the evening my luck was in.

We returned to Glasgow and I carried on passing the legacy Romano gave me on to Archie. We had such a laugh going to away games that season. Most of the time they were a catalogue of errors as we tried to find places like Almondvale and Fir Park for the first time. We were almost always late, which resulted in constant sprints from car to ground. What's annoying is that Archie is a jogger so he'd sprint off like a wee boy leaving me like the big fat dad puffing behind, even though I was the younger man by over a decade.

Part of the fun was to be had from mixing with other away fans, who were of a slightly more intense variety than the home support. The finest of these were the kids we met at the cup tie against Clyde, 27 February 2005. This match was significant because it was the most dazzling I ever saw a Martin O'Neill team play. With Henrik Larsson gone and the likes of Thompson, Sutton and Hartson slowing down, the by-line style of play was foundering on the rocks of predictability while exciting teenage geniuses like Aiden McGeady languished on the bench.

But in this game Martin picked his tactics straight out of the Harlem Globetrotters rule book. For over twenty minutes we had recent loan signing Craig Bellamy, Shaun Maloney and McGeady on the same pitch, three magicians with pace in their feet and in their heads who combined for the last goal in a 5-0 victory. Added to this the combination of Stan Petrov and Juninho in one of the few games when he looked like the player who had dazzled Middlesborough and it was my favourite ever Celtic away performance.

Come on, you say, it was only against Clyde! Yes, the same Clyde that knocked us out of the same competition less than a year later in that less than auspicious Roy Keane debut. There are still fans like me who were at that earlier game and swear blind they saw a big Chinese international called Du Wei play, but I think that was just more Sheidt.

The football was mesmerising that day, scintillating one touch pass-and-move stuff. However the best bit of play in the Hoops that day came from Alan Thompson, not from his boot but from his mouth.

Celtic were 4-0 up and one of the Clyde players was getting a bit antsy with him. Archie and I were sitting about ten feet away from Thommo at this time and clearly heard him say to this lad in his thick Geordie brogue, 'Listen ya fooking twat, you're 4-0 down, there's no point in being a bellend, aye?'

But even this patter was outshone by the young lads in front of us who had decided to make the diminutive, overweight linesmen the target of their humorous abuse. Every time he came anywhere near us they would start singing the Oompah Loompah song from *Willie Wonka and The Chocolate Factory*.

*Oompah loompah, loompadee do*
*I'm going to wave my wee flag for you*

There was a young policeman patrolling our section who happened to be standing beside the linesman during one of these verses when, before he could stop himself, he let out a snigger. Quick as a flash one of the lads put on a mock serious voice, the one people use when they're trying to convey someone who is tight of ass and Masonic. 'Excuse me officer, is there something amusing you?'

Of course this only made the policeman laugh even more, which egged on the Buckfast boys and so on. Don't ever think being a policeman at a football match is easy.

They were also giving dog's abuse to one of the Clyde players whenever he touched the ball. I can't remember what his name was but it had Archie and me scratching our heads trying to work out why. Normally this kind of abuse was reserved for those whose career paths had intersected with the Red, White and Blue Sons of Govan.

'What's up with that guy?' Archie asked. 'Did he used to play for Rangers?'

'Naw,' one of the lads replied. 'He lives in oor street an he's a pure fud!'

I loved the away games. I'd take one of them over ten home games any time. At away games we didn't have the Celtic Park customers sitting there all nice and quiet, we weren't answerable to a plc who seemed ashamed of the club's Irish roots. We didn't have stewards patrolling and throwing you out for singing 'the wrong songs'. You had fans that cared – and you had much better food.

The food at Celtic Park from 2001-2008 was a disgrace. The steak pies just about pass muster, but pale into insignificance next to the offerings from Rugby Park or Tannadice. The burgers were a slice of cardboard with a few cold dry chips and the pizza is so arid that if swallowed without a pint of the flat urine they call Coca Cola there's a danger it can dry your mouth out so much it turns itself inside out, creating a wormhole in the universe.

That's the other good thing about Archie. He was a physics teacher. I took him to Celtic games, in return he taught me about wormholes. It was a good deal.

It was good to have friends in the Celtic family, because very soon the club itself would stab me in the heart.

## 17

# THE HEARTBROKEN HUDDLER

Though I was having the time of my life whizzing all over Scotland with Archie, it was obvious that the club itself was not having such a good time of it in 2004/2005.

The 3-0 defeat away to Shaktar Donetsk in the Champions League had been bad enough but the 3-2 loss at home to Aberdeen was worse because it was the first sign that the giants of Seville were on the wane domestically. Aberdeen went 2-0 up within minutes, and then produced a winner where the virtually unknown John Stewart skipped through a defence that had rendered the Barcelona attack impotent the season before.

Even when we won, it was more and more just by a single goal, and away draws with Dundee would have been unthinkable a year previously.

The style of play was now so predictable teams seemed to know exactly what the likes of Thompson, Sutton, Big Bad John and Petrov were going to do with the ball and they themselves were doing it slower than before. We needed a new Larsson, a new genius to confound the opposition. Frustratingly, there were youngsters who could do this: Ross Wallace was one, Aiden McGeady was the other. But Martin was sticking by his old favourites.

The season was one of those where we were always neck and neck with Rangers. Then we played them at Celtic Park on 20 February. Although Martin gave the on-loan Craig Bellamy his debut, we still had Wallace, Maloney and McGeady languishing on the bench. And Juninho who, although not consistently good, at least provided something a bit unpredictable.

And we lost 2-0. At home. The first time they'd beaten us there for eleven games and a crucial psychological advantage to them in the race for the title. What made it worse was that this was the third time in a row I'd been in the stands to watch them beat us. Need I also mention that one of their goals was the result of a Gregory Vignal shot slipping right through Rab Douglas's fingers?

The next game was the Clyde game I mentioned in the previous chapter, with all the fancy dans playing and it was the best football I ever saw in my time as a season ticket holder. It was just so obvious to anyone in the stands that this was the way to win the league that season.

This was only compounded by the ensuing 6-0 win over Dunfermline. Aiden started that game and was magnificent; scoring a peach as he cut in from the right after Bellamy had made the most fantastic dummy run. But it wasn't obvious to Martin. Almost certainly because he was distracted by his wife's illness that would eventually make him leave the club and take time off from management. But as a fan I did not know this. So by the time I was asked to go on Celtic TV I was a frustrated wee boy.

The appearance came about because I had just recorded *Extreme Celebrity Detox* for Channel 4, a show that involved me doing Tai Chi and climbing Slovenian rock faces with Jack Osbourne and Jilly Goolden in an attempt to cure my fear of heights. Another epic fail, though the show was a great lesson in why you should never base your opinions on people from how they come across on the TV.

Based on the spoilt child who had appeared on *The Osbournes* I had thought Jack O would an absolute arse of the first degree. I couldn't have been further from the truth. He had been clean and sober for a while by this point and what I found instead was a really clever, thoughtful guy who could at the same time match me when it came to dodgy jokes. Jilly Goolden on the other hand was someone I'd admired for years on the box. And we fought like cat and dog.

Celtic TV had contacted my agent to ask if I wanted to come on Ally Begg's chat show to plug the show and talk about all things Celtic with him and Jim Craig on 15 March. It turned out to be one of the worst, and best, decisions I ever made.

It was the worst because I didn't have a subscription to Celtic TV and naively didn't realise its sole purpose was to massage the egos of all at the club and give an unrelentingly positive spin to everything that was happening, even getting whipped three times in a row by Rangers. I thought they'd got me on to be Dominik Diamond.

So when Ally Begg asked me how I felt about Rab Douglas being selected for the next Scotland squad, I naturally replied

'I don't care if Douglas plays for Scotland, as long as he doesn't play for us again. In fact I hope he gets injured on international duty just so he can't play for us again.'

I heard a crash to my left. It was Jim Craig's jaw hitting the floor. The remainder of the interview was another masterclass from my career on how to lose friends and alienate people wearing suits. Here's a selection of other choice comments.

'I love Lennon because he winds *them* up.'

'We need a youth system in place because let's face it we aren't going to buy anyone.'

'If you played football with your mouth Alan Thompson would be Maradona.'

'Thompson in ahead of Wallace is bad enough, but ahead of McGeady!?!? McGeady must look around that squad and think – hang on a minute, I'm the most talented player here by a country mile!'

'Martin O'Neill should have a clause in his contract that says if Aiden McGeady isn't in the first eleven then he should be sacked.'

'Stephen Hawkins couldn't even calculate how much cash Dermot Desmond has. He needs to stick his hand in his big fat pockets and buy Bellamy NOW!'

'If we don't win the league this season Martin needs to go.'

'Celtic Park sounds like a morgue on a Saturday.'

Each time I was speaking I could see Ally Begg's eyes widening, but I was on a roll. And I was not on there as Dominik Diamond the TV guy, I was on there as Dominik Diamond the Celtic fan, the season ticket holder, home and away and this was my chance to express what I was feeling that season. Of course I loved Martin to bits and realised the good that he (and Alan Thompson and the other players) had done for the club, but the fact was that they were all underperforming now. Would you let Linford Christie run the 100m for you aged forty-five just because he was fast when he was in his twenties?

Jim Craig literally couldn't speak to me after the cameras stopped. It was like my chat was a disease he was worried about catching if he got too close. In fact nobody really met my gaze after the show, except for Ally Begg. He at least had the balls to say to me. 'Dominik, I have wanted to meet you for a long time and you did not disappoint, but I'm not sure we'll meet in this studio again.'

And sure enough my agent called the next day.

'How did you enjoy your Celtic TV appearance?'

'Good, I think I said everything I wanted to say.'

'Good, because it won't be happening again. They've banned you.'

'What?'

'You're not allowed back on again.'

'Under whose orders?'

'They won't say.'

Apparently the next show that went out they crucified me with a load of emails from Celtic fans complaining about my comments. I do not know who instigated the ban. Martin? Brian Quinn? Dermot Desmond?

I was really upset. I don't know why. It seems obvious looking back that there was no way you could go on the club's own TV channel and systematically undermine the board, the manager and the players. But the way I saw it was that the club I loved had cut me off.

Then I bumped into some random guy on Buchanan Street in Glasgow.

'Haw Dominik – ya legend!' he said. 'Saw those bastards banned you fae Celtic TV? Fucking shitebags so they are.'

'Well thanks for your support mate, I appreciate it.'

'It's not just me, pal. You should see what they're saying on the Huddleboard. They're pure raging about it.'

I had heard about the Huddleboard from a guy called Francis Donnelly I'd bumped into a few weeks before in The Spirit Bar in Glasgow. It was one of many Celtic fan forums out there. I'd never gone onto a forum because I just assume that world would be an intimidating club full of anoraks who just poured out statistics and ruthlessly ripped apart anyone who couldn't say who was the assistant Celtic kit bag man in 1973. So I went home and logged on and my heart was repaired.

There was post after post after post about my Celtic TV appearances. A guy on the Huddleboard called Chuck seemed to have started it. Others were piling in with exotic internames like SeanCeltic 1916, Hoopyboy, Kenny 79, 1967-revivalist, Pat Mustard, davedbhoygreen, Guv, Bilbaobohy, Martin O'Neill (presumably not the Celtic manager) and my personal favourite, Tiochfaidh Armani, fellow fans, up in arms about my ban, saying how I was only reflecting the views of supporters on the terraces. It wasn't just on the Huddleboard either. Kerrydale Street, another forum, was showing waves of support.

I'm not someone who trawls the internet looking for people to kiss their backside. As I think I've made quite clear, apart from the two times I mentioned (Munich with my dad, T in the Park with my daughter) I never enjoyed the recognition factor of broadcasting. But it made me feel incredible that day. All I had ever wanted was to be a normal Celtic fan and here were hundreds of normal Celtic fans posting that I had just represented what they were all feeling. It meant the world to me. If you were one of them, I thank you.

Though I was grateful for all the backing on the assorted forums, there was something about the Huddleboard in partic- ular that drew me in. I think it was because there were as many people talking about cheese toasties and meercats as there were about football. It reminded me of the golden days of Popbitch around the turn of the millennium, when it was the funniest place on the World Wide Web.

I posted a few times under my own name to say how much I appreciated the support and I got another login so I could just become an anonymous contributor. Many people twigged it was me, though. The first to do so was Big Mick.

He had got in touch shortly after the Celtic TV fiasco and we hit it off immediately. He mentioned there was a Shebeen gig that weekend in the Spirit and did I fancy meeting up. Fine, I wrote back. How will I know it's you? You'll just know, he said. Sure enough when I went into The Spirit Bar that Saturday this giant came up to me with a big smile on his face. He was so intimidating looking that I didn't care whether he was Big Mick or not, he was going to be my friend. And he was.

Actually he was more than that. Big Mick had my back, not just from opposing fans, but from some of our own. There was once in the Brazen Heid he gave a guy a telling who had got slightly psychotic with me.

This didn't happen often, and in this case it was just a guy who was a bit drunk who'd been talking to me for a while and then hit me with the old. 'Sorry Dominik, you probably just think I'm kissing your arse cos you're on the telly.'

'Not at all mate,' I replied. 'No worries.'

'Because I'm not you understand.'

'No, I'm sure you're not.'

'You being sarcastic?' the guy said, with an edge to his voice now.

'What?'

'You're *sure* I'm not, eh? Well what *are* you sure I am then? Huh?'

'Look mate I'm not looking for trouble . . .'

'Go on; tell me, what am I then, huh?' His eyes were now a bit mad and starey, a bit Terry Butcher.

Mick stepped in and gently pushed him away for a chat. 'I'll tell you what you are; you're in fucking trouble now,' I thought.

The guy later came up and apologised.

Mick was ever-vigilant when we were out, as people who have done the odd bit of security-orientated work tend to be. So many times guys would run up to me with mobile phones already filming, miming the IRA rifles and chanting 'alright Dominik, Up the Ra! Dominik's a Provo!' Mick would just step in between their camera and me and tell them to beat it. I would always be going up to the guys afterwards and saying things like. 'I'm sorry lads. Don't get me wrong, I believe what happened to the Irish Catholics in Ireland is a disgrace and people who have been subjected to that kind of invasion have every right to fight for freedom against that invading army but I really can't be wandering around saying I'm a Provo or any of that nonsense, what with Enniskillen being the indefensible atrocity it was. Even if those who carried out that act are not actually anything to do with the Republican Movement we sing about in rebel songs, you know The *Daily Record* is always desperate for an anti-Celtic story.'

Mick would just stand there and shake his head and laugh, 'You know you don't actually have to go up and justify everything to every single Celtic fan all the time. If guys bug you or are being eejits you can just tell them to fuck off like anyone else would.'

But it was the guilt at work again, the guilt at being held in such esteem by these people when I felt I never deserved it because no matter the support I gave to the club on air during the dark times I never stopped my media career long enough to actually go up to the games or lend what could have been a useful voice to things like Celts For Change. And if I'm boring the reader with my incessant repetition of this I hope the reader can only imagine how boring it is when you've got that voice in your head constantly making you feel guilty day in day out, match after match. In many ways it was like being adopted by a family and being surrounded by the most immense amount of love but feeling guilty because the adoption papers had been forged.

Anyway, I spent a couple of fantastic years kicking about with Mick, but he had a bit of a temper as well and we fell out in Milan when he mistakenly thought another pal of mine messed him around over tickets and I haven't heard from him since, though I still see his posts on the Huddleboard. Anyway, if you're reading this Mick, thanks again for all those times you had my back, mo chara. And thanks for introducing me to Kopparberg Pear Cider and letting me know it was perfectly acceptable for a man to drink a bottle of fruity pop in public as long as it was teeming with booze.

It was always the most bizarre sight though, myself, Big Mick and Archie yomping our way through whatever part of Scotland Celtic were frequenting that weekend. Mick was genuinely twice the size of Archie and wherever we went people stared agog at the scary looking giant, the wee gay guy in the tight black vest and the bloke off the telly.

Moments still blaze through my mind and always will: Mick lobbing 10p coins at Archie's back while he was in a world of his own jigging around topless to Shebeen in The Spirit and encouraging me to do the same to see who could get the most of them to stick to the sweat that clung to him.

We also had mad moments with other Huddleboard characters. Pre match meetings with Sellic and Tall Paul in The Spirit, afternoons holding court in the Portman in Kilmarnock with Irvinebhoy, evenings of madness in the Ruggie Vogue with Henke and Rod C, singing rebs at the Brazen with Toi Tim and the Burnside Sniper, drinks in Milan with Martin D and Edinburgh with Keefybhoy and many more bars with many more Huddlers. But Mick was always at the centre.

What became clear in 2005 was that while I had probably burned my bridges with Celtic FC plc, I was part of the family of fans. And that meant more. I still stand by everything I said on Celtic TV that day about the team and the direction in which it was heading. The chickens came home to roost that season in Fir Park, on the day forevermore known as Black Sunday.

I had finally managed to get a music radio show at a station where I not only had checked out the music beforehand but actually loved it: Beat 106. My old pal Jim Gellatly had put in a word for me with the boss Richard Wilkinson who, after what seemed like an interminably long series of auditions, had finally given me the same weekend slot I had on Real Radio. It had meant turning down a few shows on Talksport but with two kids now I didn't want to spend all my time working in London (the irony was that Richard was only an interim boss because Claire Pattenden was on maternity leave and Claire had already knocked me back for a job there a year before, on the grounds that she thought I was a bit of a dick. This is why the most successful organisations in the UK media are run by women; they are *much* better judges of character).

The fact that these were weekend shows meant getting to the football could sometimes be problematic, especially if the kick-off was two o'clock. I had asked for the day off but Richard had refused. Even though it was the deciding match of the season, as it was on 22 May 2005. So Archie was sitting in the studio with me when the show ended at 13:50 and was sprinted straight out into my car (there was no way I was letting Archie plod along at 5mph on this occasion) and absolutely flew down to Fir Park.

To be honest we could have run the car off our own hearts as a battery, we were so excited. The only way we could lose the league was if Rangers won and we didn't. And we had Bellamy. Archie and I had been at Tannadice with Mick a few weeks before to see him single-handedly break Dundee Utd hearts with a hat-trick and an attacking display as good as anything Henrik ever produced.

We had also been at Ibrox to see him score the winner a month later and laughed as fans above us unfurled a banner which read 'Welcome to the Craig Bellamy Show'.

In fact the only recent slip up, the 3-1 defeat at home to Hibs, had come when the wee Welsh genius was injured. Now he was back in the starting line up there was no doubt. We would win this. Easy.

With the match already started there were no parking spaces anywhere near the ground, so we had an even longer sprint to the ground. And we were right up near the top of the South Stand Upper Tier. So by the time we got in half an hour had gone and I had to run the gamut of all the comedians.

'Nice of you tae turn up Dominik, ya part-timing bastard!'

'Fuck sake Dominik, did ye no set yer alarm this morning?'

'State of you, big man, yer as well just running tae the St John's Ambulance people.'

And then a familiar voice.

'This is even worse than in Barcelona, Diamond!'

It was Romano. Once again. This time about twenty rows or so down from us. I said I'd catch him at half time and then all bedlam broke loose as Chris Sutton scored. I didn't even see the goal because I was still running up the stairs. But I didn't care. We were one nil up against Motherwell. We were going to win the title – and Terry Butcher was their manager. Ha! Try and out me as a teenage Hun now you slightly sinister starey-eyed bawbag! As long as we won it didn't matter what Rangers did in their game against Hibs and we couldn't lose now, not after scoring first, not with Craig Bellamy in the team.

At half-time we went down to Romano and I proudly intro-duced Archie to him. The man I had introduced to the Celtic Family was now meeting the man who had introduced me. It was a perfect moment. After the game we'd all go off and cele-brate together.

'Mind you,' Romano said as Archie and I left him to return to our seats. 'If we lose then fuck yez I'm going straight home.'

We laughed. We laughed less when John Hartson and Craig Bellamy missed chances to put the game beyond Motherwell in the second half. We stopped laughing when we heard that

Rangers had gone one up against Hibs. Of course it was Nacho Novo, the most unpopular of theirs among the Celtic support. We were tight-lipped when Scott McDonald took it on his chest in the eighty fifth minute, turned and shot past Rab Douglas to make it 1-1. We were shaking our heads in disbelief when his deflected shot sailed over Douglas a few minutes later. We were empty when the final whistle blew. We'd lost the league.

We said nothing, Archie and I. We just walked down the stairs. There is always talk about how players try so hard in some games they leave it all out on the pitch. Well the fans are the same. That day we left it all in the South Stand at Fir Park.

We walked down the steps.

Romano had gone.

And so had The Craig Bellamy Show.

And so had St Martin.

And a few weeks before this fateful Sunday I was nearly gone too.

# DEATH BY KEBAB

I love kebabs, kebabs of every kind. From the pseudo-healthy chunks of lamb that are cooked to a crisp on an open grill then sliced in front of you right down the food chain to the elephant's foot of a doner that contains Lord-only-knows what, there is something about them that connects with my taste buds the way Henrik Larsson used to connect with a ball from Alan Thompson.

'Those kebabs will be the death of you!' friends would warn as I tore into another pile of greasy grey slivers. What is interesting is that one night my love of kebabs *did* nearly cost me my life, and then saved it, though not in the way any of my friends could have envisaged.

Archie and I were off on another away adventure, this time to the mystical land of Almondvale. There were seven games to go in the 2004/2005 season and a victory over Livingston would take us back to the top of the league over our Orc friends. Archie and I were both feeling optimistic. After all, we'd driven to Almondvale before and this time knew how close it was to the motorway. This time we would not get lost and miss the first ten minutes.

Plans started to go awry when I woke up that morning with one of those horrific back pains where every step you take feels like a little man is jabbing your internal organs with a stick. No doctor in the world would recommend I moved a muscle that day, so I prescribed my own cure of eight Nurofen and four pints of Guinness in Kelly's before we hopped on the supporters' bus.

Ah yes, the supporters' bus! Normally I drove us to the away games but the midget back-jabber prevented that and there was no way I was going to let Archie drive because he is one of those men who has difficulty finding the accelerator pedal in a car. In some cultures they call those men 'ladies'. A quick online trip to the Huddleboard revealed a supporters' bus was leaving from Kelly's round the corner on Pollokshaws Road. Archie and I had never been on a supporters' bus before and we were as excited as two wee boys the night before Xmas when you've picked your toy out of the catalogue months before and have actually seen it lying under your parents' bed.

This was the Kelly's Supporters' Bus after all. Kelly's was the pub just down from Heraghty's, both were Tim pubs but I always viewed Kelly's as Heraghty's badly-behaved little brother. Heraghty's was classy, sophisticated and bohemian; Kelly's was like a war zone. Go in there towards the end of any day when Celtic were playing and it was like the opening scene from Saving Private Ryan. Instead of half-dead US Marines wading through a sea of blood to get to Omaha Beach as German bullets flew all round, Kelly's would see half-cut Tims wading through a sea of spilt drink to get to the toilet while sweary words and songs flew about their ears.

It was a crazy place. It also had by far the most beautiful barmaid I had ever seen in Glasgow. I wish there was more to this aspect of the story but whenever Archie and I were in there we just stared at her, too entranced to speak. And now we were about to get on that pub's supporters' bus. We envisaged a raucous affair of rebel songs, carry outs and crack-a-plenty, with arses hanging out the back window every time we passed a car with a Rangers sticker on the M8 and maybe that barmaid dishing out cans of Guinness using her breasts instead of her hands.

The reality was something different. Quiet? This bus made a library sound like a concert by The Who. The average age was such that it made even Archie look urchinesque in comparison and there were more sensible cardigans than Celtic tops. I can only imagine that the hardcore amongst Kelly's customers had a separate mode of transport to away games. Possibly a tank. With nothing to distract us the journey was spent focussing on our bodies' respective frailties. In my case my back, in Archie's a bladder that was not used to having four pints of Guinness forcibly inserted in it before teatime.

If this bus had been what I imagined the Kelly's Supporters' Bus to be like, then Archie's bladder would not have been a problem. He could simply have peed in a bottle held by some guy twenty feet down the bus as part of some form of gambling entertainment. But this being Val Doonican's Green and White Army there was no choice for Archie but to try and hold it in. I did what any friend would do in that position.

'Aw Archie, imagine how great it would be to have a pee right now, eh? It would be magic! Imagine that relief as the pish flowed gently out . . . and your bladder, think for a second how this bladder currently stretched to breaking point as painful as any mediaeval torture, would quickly return to deflated bliss.'

'Shut up!'

'You know I think in a lot of ways a good piss is nicer than a good shag. Seriously. The feeling of just letting go is so good.'

'Please, I'll pay you,' Archie begged.

'Did I ever tell you of that time we went to Niagara Falls?'

By the time we drew into the shopping centre in Livingston

that plays host to the Almondvale Ground, Archie had had enough. He begged the driver to stop and he actually fell out of the door, unzipping his flies and was peeing as he rolled away to find some kind of car for cover.

Unfortunately it would not be the most pain Archie found himself in that fateful night.

Almondvale is my favourite Scottish away ground, because it has not just a bar for away fans, but an actual discotheque. I always felt the club should have been given an extra half a dozen points a season for this fact alone, it's just so damned civilised. We popped in there and had ample time to refill Archie's bladder before kick-off and throw my stick-wielding back midget a couple of codeine to keep him happy.

It was one of those times I wished for a standard 1-0 away win for Celtic, just so I wouldn't have to keep jerking my back by standing up but no, they had to go and make it hard on me by winning 4-0. I was up and down like a groom on his honeymoon. Not a bad analogy to use because Aiden McGeady actually got on for a few minutes at the end which obviously gave me a semi.

I felt sorry for the Celtic fans who came up to chat to me that night. The talk of the steamie was still about my ban from Celtic TV. Guys were coming up and giving me their support in the most passionate and eloquent of terms and I was so bombed all I could say was 'Fankshhhhvewwymushpal!' I'd like to take this opportunity to apologise to all of them now for my chat, which verily was pish.

Back to the game, and even in my stoned state it was obvious that Craig Bellamy was once again running the show, his pace causing Livingston, and my slow vision, problem after problem. John Hartson showed once again that night why he was one of the greatest forwards I'd ever seen. He had been suffering one of his classic fallow periods, where he hadn't scored for

207

something approaching twenty seven years. When that happened with Big Bad John he seemed to grow bigger, fatter and slower with every match he failed to score. But that night he got a hat-trick: a penalty and two classic pieces of Hartson: a header and shot, neither from more than a handful of yards out. That to me was his magnificence as a player. In spite of the fact he looked less athletic than your average Celtic supporter, he always got in positions to poke the ball home in a flash from close in. How the hell did someone who was so immobile achieve that? I suspect that he used some form of invisible Tardis to get around the pitch. It's the only explanation that could possibly make sense, especially in the zonked out condition I was in that night.

Dr Diamond prescribed a hip flask full of Glenfiddich and another half dozen Nurofen for the bus trip back. Knowing full well that professional sportsmen are encouraged to consume slow-burning carbohydrates last thing at night to help their bodies recover from injuries while they slept, I was forced for medical reasons to tan another few pints of Guinness on our return to Heraghty's after which a kebab from Shahed's across the road was the only sensible option.

After my initial bout of kebab shop aggro I was ridiculously careful when it came to venturing into places where drunken people congregate in an enclosed space with the scent of meat in their nostrils, that heady combination would lead to a fight between the Dalai Lama and Dylan from *The Magic Roundabout*. I soon learned only to enter if they were empty and even then I'd order, pay then go out and wait round the corner in the dark till it was ready.

Tonight was different; tonight I was so spaced out on booze and painkillers I had floated through the doors of Shahed's without thinking. It wasn't empty. There was a bald guy getting served at the counter who, if he didn't have a dotted line tattooed on his neck with the words CUT HERE underneath, it was surely only a matter of time. He was the kind of fellow I used to refer to in my younger days as a skinhead, until I realised that sometimes God curses you with such a lack of fringe that shaving your head is a necessity rather than a deliberate lifestyle choice.

I tried to focus on Baldy's face to look for the tell-tale snarl and steam coming from his ears. But my vision was swimming like David Wilkie and it was all I could do to focus on the all-important menu. The guy walked past me out the door. I decided to go old school with a large doner and chilli sauce and turned to Archie while what passed for a meal was undergoing what passed as cooking.

'I think that guy was looking at me funny. Do you think there's going to be any trouble?'

'Don't be daft. You're too paranoid about these things,' he replied.

I felt relieved by this. Archie, after all, was a teacher. Unfortunately, he was a teacher who'd been battering Guinness for the best part of twelve hours so I probably should not have relied on his assessment of a potential urban-warfare situation.

We waited for our kebabs while wondering again who would ever order the omelette from an establishment such as this, then walked out into the night. As I raised the dripping meat offering to my hungry lips a cry rang out in the night.

'Haw! Ya cheeky Fenian bastard!' Four guys were running towards us, including the Baldy Kebab Fan.

Oh shit.

I had learned by now that when people include the words 'Fenian' and 'Bastard' in the first sentence they're not about to ask for an autograph, especially at 11.10pm at night. I knew that something was going to kick off here. To make matters worse, they were running from the direction of the very same pub Nazi salutes had been thrown towards me previously, but I'm sure that was just a coincidence.

Now I have been blessed by God with a few talents. I can carry a tune, make the odd joke and have a freakish ability to read words backwards. But I would trade them all in for the ability to think clearly in a fight situation. That's the difference between guys who win fights and guys who lose. It's not actually about having the strength of a lion and a nice array of Vulcan neck grips, it's about having the calmness to let your brain work out what you're going to do next instead of the terror paralysing it. In my case, I don't get scared as such, I just get really confused. It's like this brain that can work so quickly on a live radio show when every machine blows up and I have to fill ten minutes with talk about something, just stops in a fight situation and all I can do is mumble like a stroke victim (this actually saved my life once in Notting Hill when a bloke attempted to mug me at knifepoint and I kept saying 'What?' until a combination of passers-by and his own boredom caused him to run off).

So faced with four guys coming at me like this all my brain could process in reply was to smile in a doped-up manner and say 'Good evening!'

Good evening! GOOD EVENING! What the fuck? These guys were intent on battering us, we were outnumbered two to one and for some reason I thought speaking as if I was in an Oscar Wilde play was the answer, it was like the tsunami of Guinness and Nurofen had taken the normal brain fuzziness I get in these situations and twisted it into some surreal brain version of a balloon animal.

This did not exactly stop them in their tracks. They advanced towards me. Their leader, a man Archie later referred to the police as 'looking like Chief O'Brien from *Star Trek Deep Space Nine*', shouted. 'Think you're fucking funny on the fucking radio don't ya, ya Fenian Bastard, not so fucking funny now, are you?'

'Good evening,' I repeated, for absolutely no reason.

He lifted his knuckles off the ground and swung at me with a fist. And then something magical happened. The confusion I normally feel in those situations melted away, and a primal protective voice took over the inside of my head and guided me. It felt like Ben Kenobi guiding Luke Skywalker from beyond the grave while he flies down the Death Star trench. Except this voice wasn't saying 'Feel the Force.'

It was saying, 'Protect the kebab.'

The kebab was in my mouth. So, with all the dexterity of a prize fighter I moved my head back to protect the kebab. As a result the punch harmlessly grazed my cheek. If it had connected I would have been on the ground and it would have been all over. But my love of the kebab had saved my life.

Having protected the kebab from the first attack my thoughts now obviously focussed on keeping it safe. I ran round the side of Bloke from *Deep Space Nine*'s back into the kebab shop, possibly thinking that a return to its womb was the safest place for it.

I ran in and slammed the door shut just as three of them crashed into it. I say three because in my attempts to protect the kebab I had forgotten all about Archie. He was still stuck outside on his own and while three of the guys were coming after me, Baldy was dealing with him.

What happened next reminded my why Archie is one of the greatest friends I'd ever had. This wee man, approaching fifty, five-foot-two inches tall, father of five, skinny as a rake and to my knowledge never having been in a fight in his life, took a run at this thug and launched into an almost perfect flying dropkick (Archie had no martial arts training so I can only imagine this technique was the result of years of watching

Bruce Lee and *The Matrix* movies). Anyway, it was an *almost* perfect flying dropkick because although the take-off and shape were technically superb, he didn't actually get within three feet of the knuckledragger and crashed flat on his back in the street.

I would have hosed myself laughing if I wasn't also trying to hold the door closed on three of my own assailants, which through a combination of my own seventeen stone and inner kebab protection strength I was just about managing to do.

'Get your fucking arse out here ya Fenian Bastard. We'll fucking cut ye!' One of the trio screamed. I cannot recall which character from a Sci-Fi television show *he* resembled most and I apologise for this oversight.

But he was stupid, obviously. Did he really think an invite like that would get me out there? Surely if he was smart he'd have said. 'Get your fucking arse out here ya Fenian Bastard and we WON'T fucking cut ye!' In my stoned state I probably would have fallen for that, in return for a guarantee of kebab amnesty of course.

It was surreal, there was I being threatened with a stabbing, a hundred yards away from my own house where my children slept and for some reason all I could still think about was losing my kebab. I looked round hoping to see the Shahed's staff running to my aid with those big knives of theirs, but they were nowhere to be seen. I made a mental note to start patronising Danny Singh's up in Shawlands Cross instead.

Things were getting a bit serious. Every time the three thugs pushed against the door the lumps of doner meat got closer to the edge of the pitta bread. Any minute now they were going to fall off. And I knew I'd bend over to pick the bits off the floor which would probably mean the thugs would get in, as well as being generally against basic food hygiene practice.

Then Archie came to the rescue. He picked himself up off the road and shouted at the guys. 'Ah'm phonin' the polis!' He even took his mobile phone out of his pocket for good measure. For some reason this appealed to their better judgement and they ran off, with the obligatory hand-slitting-the-throat-gesture.

Now the kebab was safe the reality sunk in. I had nearly been stabbed. This was not funny. Not any more. But I was a strange mix of emotions. Part of me (the terrified and paranoid part) just wanted to turn back the clock to whenever it was I'd first slagged off the Huns on air and keep my big stupid mouth shut. The other part (the angry part) felt that if those were the kind of people I'd upset over the years then it was a war worth fighting because they were scum. Unfortunately, they were scum who could have killed me.

Archie had called the police and the fact that a high profile Catholic was being attacked in the street at knifepoint meant Strathclyde's finest broke all records and got there in thirty minutes. Thanks, guys!

So I did what any sensible person would have done. I had a word with a friend who had a word with another friend of ours who was the kind of person you did not mess about with on the south side and he put the word out in a certain south side pub that this was not to happen again. But that didn't make me feel any safer. I looked over my shoulder twice as much as I did before and started to wonder what kind of madness I'd ended up in the middle of, a madness that was spilling over into violence a stone's throw from my young sleeping children.

I bought some pepper spray on the internet and carried it around for a while whenever I went out at night. Then I realised that if this ever happened again I would have to drop the kebab to set off the pepper spray so I left it in a drawer at home instead.

# THE BEST YEARS OF OUR LIVES

With the exception of the odd knife attack in the street round the corner from my house and heartbreaking end-of-season letdowns, 2005 was a good year. We were now enmeshed in the most wonderful community on the south side of Glasgow. We had made friends with a load of families who had kids the same age as Molly and I now had a fantastic circle of pals dubbed The Tuesday Night Gang, a bunch of senior figures from the Scottish tabloids and Rikki Brown, who would meet in The Ivory Bar every week and put the world to rights while Martel Maxwell asked advice on how to further her media career, so it wasn't only the Celtic family I now felt a part of, but our own little part of Glasgow really was home – apart from the odd knife attack.

I didn't even mind that Martin had gone. Because of the understandable distraction of his wife's illness he was not focussed on the job. He also had not got the backing of the board after Seville. It was right that he took a break.

I was more upset about Craig Bellamy leaving to be honest; here was a player who could have been the new Larsson. I managed to meet Craig before he went back down south, one of those complete fanboy situations where I was in getting tickets from the club shop and joined the fans waiting outside the club doors to see what players were emerging. One of them was Bellamy and I queued up to get my photo taken with him.

It is the worst photo I have ever had taken in my life. You know when a guy's hair recedes to that point that long hair is simply not an option? This was that day. My head looks like it belongs to one of those Playpeople toys, the ones where you can pull the hair off in a block? It looks like mine has been pulled off then put back on again, but not in the correct place – a bit too high up and a hell of a lot too far back.

I was excited about Gordon Strachan becoming manager, though, unlike others. There was roughly a 50/50 split on the Huddleboard between those who thought he would bring an exciting dimension to Celtic and others concerned that his reputation as a 'relegation escaper' down in England and an 'antsy ginger smartarse who used to wind up Celtic fans' would not be suitable. After interviewing him at Coventry I felt confident that he'd do great. He had the big personality for the job and he was ginger. I was telling everyone who would listen that Gordon Strachan would be a fantastic Celtic manager.

And then we got pumped by Artmedia Bratislava and drew 4-4 with Motherwell in his first two games. But sometimes even horrible things happen for a reason and the nine goals conceded in two games meant Strachan changed goalkeepers, putting in some random Polish guy called Artur Boruc for the home leg against Artmedia. We scored four that night, in what was an ultimately disappointing but hugely exciting night at Celtic Park. Artur went on to become a folk hero and Strachan's team would only lose one more game before becoming champions that season.

Strachan's style of football was infinitely superior to the last season of O'Neill. Shaun Maloney was in the form of his life, Aiden McGeady started getting more regular games, Craig

Beattie was full of pace up front and we now had Shunsuke Nakamura, whose every touch was so cultured his left foot was almost Shakespearian. Like David Beckham and Paul McStay, he was one of those players who seemed to watch the game from fifty feet up in the sky, so he could see the space that other players could run into in a way that defied logic from ground level. His passes, both the long ones and the deft dinks, followed a mathematical precision Pythagoras would have been proud of. Imagine if he'd played in the same team as Larsson!

Strachan had managed to graft this blend of young and imported creativity and pace onto Martin's mainstays like Petrov and Hartson. I know it seems criminally insane to write these words knowing what we know today, but Stephen McManus actually looked like a future Celtic great when lining up with Bobo Balde in the centre of defence.

The only weakness Naka had was a tendency to disappear against Rangers, but he wasn't the first cultured player to get lost in the melee of an Old Firm match, especially when he had assorted blueshirts trying to kick lumps out of him.

This happened in the first Rangers game that season, which again saw Archie and I take our place in the Broomloan Lower. Celtic were bossed out of the game and any attempts to respond to the physical nature of Rangers with like challenges of their own were met with cards yellow and red. Thompson, who by this stage had completely crossed the divide from being one of my favourite players to one of the names I groaned at upon discovering on the team sheet, got sent off for a shocking lunge on an opposition player. The fact that it was Nacho Novo didn't even make it forgivable. At least Neil Lennon had the intelligence to wait until the final whistle to pick up his marching orders, having let referee Stuart McDougal know exactly what he thought of the way he'd handled the match.

That was another one of those games at Ibrox I didn't mind

losing. The fact that we had been reduced to ten men and had been kicked off the park just added to that underdog feeling that drew me to Celtic, and railing at the injustices kept Archie and I going well into a dozen beers afterwards at Kelly's.

Though Lennon, like Thompson, was half the player he was under O'Neill, I still wanted him to be the first name on the team sheet for his passion alone. I almost met him once. He was in Bar Blue, an exceptional pizza place in the West End of Glasgow, when I was in there. I sat there for about an hour, trying to pluck up the courage to go over and introduce myself but I was too nervous. He was my hero and I was so desperate for the guy to like me that I wasn't prepared to risk another one of my cack-handed chats with celebrities a la Noel Gallagher years before so I just ate my Capricciosa quickly and left.

After the initial disappointment of Motherwell, Artmedia and Rangers, I loved that season. I'd got to know some of the guys sitting around our seats: a group I called The Militant Posties. As far as I was aware they all worked for the Post Office and they would sit around discussing socialism in between cheering the team on. It was fantastic listening to them because they'd slip from one to the other without missing a beat.

'The problem with attempting to instigate unilateral change in Cuba from outside is, fucksake Gravesen move your arse you are taking a consumerist attitude and attempting to, come on Hartson that was a sitter, graft it onto a socialist mindset.' It was brilliant.

There were a mother and daughter who we initially, unfairly dubbed The Sours because they always turned up late with that wee tight Glasgow mouth thing going on which makes you look really grumpy. My mate Kirk's wife is the greatest practitioner of it in the world. Seriously. Her mouth can get so tight and puckered up when she's cross it creates a black hole somewhere in the universe. As it turned out, The Sours were lovely once you started chatting to them.

Less lovely was The Phantom Farter. Through conversations with others over time I have come to realise that this occurs in every football stadium wherever you sit. Someone, at some point, lets one drop that is the worst fart of all time. The kind that makes you physically retch. The kind that can kill wasps. These olfactory weapons of mass destruction would tend to leak out shortly after half-time, which can only lead me to believe they were the result of some form of offering from Celtic's pitiful version of catering. I have mentioned this before but it's worth saying again how poor it was, with the exception of a Cornish Pasty that seemed to appear on the menu for about three months in 2006 before disappearing forever. Perhaps like Stan Petrov and Shaun Maloney it got taken to Aston Villa by Martin O'Neill.

When faced with the phantom fart, I would just sit there and man it out bravely, gagging away in stoic silence. My wife is made of more vocal stuff, however, and the stand would ring to the sounds of a posh English accent exclaiming 'oh my God that is *disgusting*.' This did not result in the culprit guiltily identifying him or herself, though it did make a sizable portion of the North Stand Upper look around to see where Camilla Parker Bowles was sitting.

The season was good, the team was playing great football, and my life was about to be the best it had ever been. Claire Pattenden had returned from maternity leave to resume her job as boss of Beat 106. Far from dumping me, as I thought she would, she called me into the meeting room one day to tell me that the station was getting rebranded as Xfm Scotland and asked if I would I like to do the breakfast show.

It was a dream come true. Xfm had been the only music station I listened to when I lived in London. It had a dangerous, off-centre attitude and vigorously championed new music. By this stage in Glasgow I was spending as much time in King Tuts as I was at Celtic Park and I knew there were a ton of Scottish guitar bands out there who could really benefit from a station like this. It was a chance not just to have my dream job but also play a part in a new Scottish musical movement.

But there was one small problem, two small problems actually – Paul Harper and Fraser Thompson. They hosted the breakfast show on Beat 106 and had become good pals.

'I'm not taking a job that takes a job away from friends of mine,' I said.

It was then I noticed that there were also a few men in the room, men wearing suits. One of them spoke.

'Listen Dominik, it's horrible but it's a reality of radio. If a station rebrands it has to change its breakfast team. Whether you take the job or not, Paul and Fraser will lose that show.'

Well that was clear. I said I'd take the job on the condition that Paul and Fraser were to be told as soon as possible. I did not want to be going for beers with these guys and keeping secrets from them. As it turned out, it wasn't the worst thing in the world that happened to them. Fraser ended up getting his own show on Xfm and Paul got to travel the world before getting mid-mornings at Real Radio.

And it was the best thing that ever happened to me. The other condition I asked for was that I got to have Scott Shaw as producer and Marisa de Andrade as newscaster. Not only did we have more fun than I ever thought it was possible to have while working, the three of us ended up forming a band, The AMs, through which I finally got my dream of playing on the King Tuts stage.

I was also able to make amends for being a tit in front of Noel Gallagher at the first T in the Park all those years ago. The station set up an interview with him as one of the launch events, so I turned up to the SECC on an afternoon in December 2005 to meet him backstage and try and come up with a better opening line than 'here's my mate David, he plays guitar too.'

As it happened I didn't have to worry about opening lines, because Noel started talking as soon as he opened the door.

'Here he fookin is, world's smartest fookin' man: Dominik Diamond. Is that really your name?' Noel didn't wait for me to answer. 'You know I sit in the 'ouse and watch you on all those Top 40 fookin War Film shows and I shout through to my wife 'here's this fookin Dominik Diamond again, do you really think he fookin knows everything about this shite all the time?' And she says 'No, he's a smart-arsed twat.' Anyway, 'ow are you?'

I was left with no choice but to reply.

'You can tell your wife, Mr Gallagher, she can fuck off. I do know all that stuff I say, because I get a list from the producers of all the movies and I pretty much watch them all again just so I can be that smart arsed.'

He laughed. I laughed. We did a storming interview and afterwards spent a good ten minutes talking about the Hoops. Noel loves the Hoops. Legend. Total legend.

It was also through the Xfm show that I also came in contact with another band that were to write its own chapter in Celtic's history, The Fratellis.

I saw them for the first time at the end of December 2005 at King Tuts where I think they were supporting The Hussys. I went along with Jim Gellatly who was raving about both bands. There must have been only about forty people in Tuts when The Fratellis took the stage but within a few lines of the first song it was clear these guys were like nothing else that had come along in years. They had the tunes, they had the swagger and they had the ability to sing 'la la la' or 'ba da ba' in the middle of a song and make it sound like it was the best lyric you'd ever heard. It was a perfect mix of retro and modern and was obvious they would be destined for greatness if they got the radio play.

I raved about them on the very first Xfm show and pushed at every opportunity for the chance to play them, as I went on to do with other Scottish bands like Biffy Clyro, The View, The Dykeenies and Glasvegas, with differing degrees of success. They wouldn't let me play Biffy, for example, until they coincidentally signed to a major label that year and I remember being told by the then deputy boss of Xfm Stuart Barrie that I couldn't play Glasvegas on the breakfast show because 'they're just a novelty band'. So I just talked about them every single day instead.

However, the station did get behind The Fratellis in a major way, and rightly so. They were great guys as well, real men of principle. I remember bumping into Barry when watching Radiohead at Meadowbank Stadium that summer and he refused to let me buy a drink that evening, just to show he appreciated the support. That's the kind of principles I like. The best example of this was when the guys won the Best Breakthrough Act at the NME Awards in February 2007. Jon publicly thanked Jim Gellatly and myself for playing their songs before anybody else would, in spite of the fact that interview was on the BBC and it was Radio 1 who had sponsored the award. That is class.

And they were all Celtic fans, which made it amazing when they started playing Chelsea Dagger at Celtic Park whenever the Bhoys scored a goal. I texted Barry the first time it happened. He was sitting with Mince in (I think) the Jock Stein. 'OMFG! They're playing your fucking song!' I typed. 'Greatest moment of my life!' Barry replied.

I would continue to get random texts from Barry in the middle of games, often when Celtic scored, often when he was in places like New Orleans on tour and he'd managed to find some random bar in the early hours to watch the game, often when he was somewhere really exotic and hot and I was freezing my nuts off in the cold and wet of the North Stand Upper.

# THE FINAL PIECE OF THE JIGSAW

The only thing that was missing from my life at the start of 2006 was God. And that was also the only thing missing from my checklist of being a Celtic fan. I'm not saying you have to be religious to support Celtic, and I'm certainly not saying you have to be Catholic, but if I wanted to be an Uber Tim there was one part of the checklist I wasn't fulfilling.

Irish connections? CHECK

Ireland for the Irish? CHECK

Living in Glasgow? CHECK

Supporter of the underdog in most political situations in the world? CHECK

Paranoid? CHECK

Believe all referees are in the payment of Rangers FC? CHECK

Catholic? Mmmmmm . . .

I had lost my faith in God when I fell victim to insomnia. I prayed so often to be delivered from that illness and nothing had happened. It made my life so tortuous and painful that I simply stopped believing a benevolent, omniscient and omnipotent God could let that happen. I felt I was a good guy, with evil things happening to him. Then one day I had asked Molly to go and tidy her room or something and when she asked why, I replied, 'Because I say so. And I'm the boss.'

'You're not the boss. God is the boss.'

'Not in this house he's not. Now go and tidy your room.'

A bizarre conversation to have with your seven-year-old daughter, but one that got me thinking. Molly was having religious assembly at school and I hadn't joined the dots enough to realise that sooner or later she'd mention God to me. I couldn't tell her I believed in God, because I didn't, and I was still in that wonderfully naïve stage of parenthood where I thought you should never lie to your kids.

At the same time I felt it would be wrong of me to tell her something like 'there is no God, or Heaven. After you die it's just blackness'. I imagine that would freak a small child out somewhat. So I decided I should have another look for God myself.

In another example of things seemingly being made-to-order in my bizarre life, later that month Ginger Productions got in touch. They had made the *Extreme Celebrity Detox* programme I'd done with Jack Osbourne and their boss Ed Stobart had been struck by something I'd said in that show about having a gap in the centre of my being where God used to be, but one that was now empty and always looking for something to fill it.

He told me about the Kalbaryo, a ritual in the Philipinnes where Catholics got crucified so they could better understand what Christ went through. He thought it would be fascinating to make a documentary where someone who had lapsed would go on a religious journey with this at the end, 'Just to see what happened on the way.'

When I later met Ed face to face he uttered what became legendary words, 'I'm not saying you actually have to get crucified.' This came as a relief to me, because I told him that would not happen. So we came up with this journey, which would start in the Cathedral in Glasgow, then go back to the Parish Church of St Vigeans in Arbroath, then Jerusalem where I would walk the Stations of the Cross in Christ's footsteps, then go to a Jesuit centre in Manila to study before finally going to Pampanga for Easter Friday. A little bit different from making knob gags about Super Mario.

Jerusalem changed me forever. My guide for the Jerusalem part of the trip was the Reverend Clarence Musgrave, head of the Church of Scotland. The experience was too great to cram into this book and a million miracles happened along the way. One day I'll write a proper book about how I found God again, but for now two parts in particular were crucial to my reconversion.

Firstly, I was allowed into the Garden of Gethsemane, where Christ spent his final evening with the disciples before being arrested. Tourists can walk around the outside, I was allowed to go in and sit among the trees. At one point I reached out and touched one of them and my life changed in that moment. There was just something living and breathing in that ancient, gnarled tree which Jesus himself had quite possibly rested his head against. It was like seeing your life flash before your eyes, but now it was a life full of God.

I then walked the Via Dolorosa, then entered the Church of the Holy Sepulchre wherein lies the tomb in which Jesus was buried. There is space under the altar where you can reach in and touch the rock. Again, the moment I touched it something reverberated deep inside.

I would say that God entered my life that day, but the true realisation was that he had never left. We all have a choice when it comes to interpreting events in our life. I had always viewed the insomnia as a curse, something that pretty much wrecked my TV career, but that's not the whole truth. As a result of insomnia I started seeing a therapist. As a result of seeing a therapist I gave up cocaine and stopped being an arsehole, or at least stopped being as much an arsehole as I was before. I became a better husband, a better father and a better friend, which was probably more important than spending the rest of my life doing cooking quiz shows for STV.

By the time I went to the Philippines a week or so later I felt that the work of the documentary had been done. I had undergone my Damascene conversion. I made it quite clear to the production company once again that I was not going to get crucified, there was no need. My mum begged me not to do it, Phoebe said she would leave me if I did and my therapist said that if I got up on that cross it would really render all our work to that point meaningless.

I left the production company to sort out any problems this would cause with Channel 5 while I entered the Sacred Heart Novitiate to study with Father Ramon Bautista, the most senior Jesuit Priest in the Philipinnes. What this entailed was five days where I took a vow of silence, breaking it only for daily lessons with him and occasional discussions with the TV crew.

Again I do the experience a disservice to attempt to cram it into a few paragraphs but suffice to say I went through my whole life, reanalysing it in terms of God and where he'd been for me. He had been everywhere. I had to undergo a General Confession, where I confessed every sin I had ever carried out. Then I was atoned by Father Ramon in what was another incredible moment.

Then Father Ramon got down on his knees in front of me and started to speak. I can't reveal the exact nature of what was said because it's bound by the laws of confession but by the time I left his room there was no way, even if I wanted to do it, that I could have gone through with the crucifixion. I couldn't do that to my priest.

There then followed the most surreal situation whereby it

was explained to me that Channel 5 would be extremely unlikely to broadcast the documentary if I did not go through with the crucifixion ritual.

'But I'm not going to get crucified at the end of it,' I explained.

It was suggested that I still had to be seen to go through with it right up to the end. The transmission of the film would depend on it.

So that was the deal. I travelled up to this poor village of Pampanga, the most poverty-stricken place I had ever seen. As they saw it I had been afforded the ultimate honour of being the first Westerner to take part in their ritual in front of the world's media which would in turn grant it and them enormous credibility in return.

I had to go up there, stay in the house of the Chief of Police, meet with them, talk with them, pray with them, break bread with them and get pigs slaughtered in my honour – and lie to them. And then shit all over them by refusing to go through with the crucifixion itself. Humiliating them in front of the world's media – and humiliating myself in the process.

I'd like to say that last part didn't bother me, but I'd be lying. It made me furious. I was being accused of taking part in 'a stunt', when surely if it had been a stunt I would have gone through with it.

I was accused of being a coward, as if this was something I'd chickened out of at the last minute. Let me tell you that surrounded by blokes with machetes, many of whom have spent the morning whipping their own backs into bloody ribbons in the name of religion and you've just effectively told them to shove their most revered religious ritual right up their ying yang, then you kneel down and close your eyes and pray – that is the bravest thing in the world.

Unfortunately, even though I did go through with the ritual, Channel 5 did not get the money shot they were after: namely

227

me writhing in agony on a cross. So they buried the documentary, putting it out in a quiet slot after originally trailblazing it with a huge fanfare of publicity. This was a great shame, but I still got hundreds of letters, many from lapsed Catholics who had been inspired by my journey to rekindle their own faith. Ultimately that's far more important.

The main point is that I was now a Catholic again, as trite as it seems to type that. I don't think I've missed a Sunday Mass since, God is at the centre of my life and it feels amazing.

To hell with what the rest of the world may have thought, I had found God and I had also undergone a radical rethink of my priorities. Much of my General Confession had involved the realisation of the number of times I'd said to Molly that I was 'too busy' to do things with her. In fact I'd been such a slave to my career I'd been too busy to do a lot of family things. That changed from that day on.

I started taking Molly to Celtic matches with me. She was bored to tears.

Ah well, my heart was in the right place.

So by the end of the season Celtic had romped home in the league and cup, I was having the time of my life on air, doing the greatest radio show I'd ever done, hanging out with cool bands, I'd found God and my third child, Honor Belle Diamond had been born, so named because my wife had gone into labour right in the middle of the Belle and Sebastian gig at the ABC in Glasgow. One of my most prized possessions is a photo of myself, Honor Belle and Stevie Jackson from Belle and Sebastian at T in the Back that summer.

That's T in the Back, not T in the Park. T in the Back was put on by my pal Big Tony Gaughan and comprised of a tent in his back garden where a load of pals played. Those pals included Stevie, Norman Blake from Teenage Fanclub, Duglas Stewart from the BMX Bandits and myself, Scott and Marisa

AKA the AMs. In CV terms that translates as 'the day we supported the BMX Bandits, Belle and Sebastian and Teenage Fanclub'.

It was a year in which everything went right. Take the Arctic Monkeys for example. They released their debut album *Whatever People Say I Am That's What I'm Not* a few weeks after Xfm Scotland launched. It was the fastest selling UK debut album of all time; they were a musical phenomenon unlike anything the UK had witnessed since Take That, though I'm sure they'd hate the comparison. They were playing at Glasgow's Carling Academy and every single radio station and newspaper in Scotland were hanging around the gig venue desperate to get a photo or a few words.

I was on their tour bus. Talking about *Gamesmaster*. It turned out it was one of their favourite shows when they were kids. This happened throughout that first year of Xfm: Fratellis, Kaiser Chiefs, Maximo Park, Ash, The Streets and countless others gave Xfm Scotland interviews we wouldn't otherwise have had because years ago they'd watched a speccy gobshite talk about video games in a vaguely amusing manner. That show, which I felt would destroy my career, ended up being responsible for my greatest success.

The only negative note in that whole first half of 2006 was that I missed the away game against Dunfermline and missed the monumental occasion of Neil Lennon scoring during an 8-1 victory.

You can tell it's a good season when God lets you become champions by beating Hearts at Celtic Park. Next to beating Rangers there, this was the best way to win it. Archie and I were like two wee boys, two very silly, stupid wee boys. We got in my car, with his son Gabriel in the back and went on a tour round all the classic Rangers pubs in Glasgow: flags and scarves out of the window, blaring the horn like we were in traffic in New York City. We ended it with another pilgrimage to Ibrox where, while Gabriel guarded the motor, us two daft diddies tied Celtic scarves to the gates and took photos on mobile phones which we then deleted by accident when we got drunk.

# 21

# WEE GORDON'S FINEST HOUR
# AND A HALF

After a glorious summer that for me, as usual, revolved around T in the Park, Strachan's Celtic started the 2006/2007 season in much the same manner they finished the last one. Nakamura was such an expert from a dead ball by this stage it was a disappointment when he *didn't* score from a direct free kick, Zurawski was looking like a decent striker, McGeady was getting better and better with every touch of the ball and Boruc was a rock behind the back four.

But tiny cracks were there. Stan Petrov was still the best box to box midfielder in Scotland but towards the end of the previous season he too often seemed to be carrying a petted lip as well as the ball. Kenny Miller was a curious buy: putting aside the baggage that came with being an ex-Rangers player, his dazzling pace was in inverse proportion to his shooting ability. Now and again capable of screamers when he didn't have time to think about them, he was inconsistent.

It was this more than anything that came to mark Strachan's signings. Jiri Jarosik, Evander Sno and Mo Camara being three prime examples of players that season who, on their day, could look brilliant, at least in the SPL. But more often than not they were just diddymungous. Martin O'Neill's Celtic team were the same level week in week out. Dependable players. You knew exactly how the likes of Valgaeren, Agathe, Lennon, Jackie Mac, Thompson, Sutton and Henrik would all play. They never let you down.

With players like Sno and Jarosik you didn't know what would happen from one touch to the next, added to this was Strachan's habit of buying players then not playing them. No Celtic fan can truly say whether the likes of Derek Riordan or Stephen Pearson were good buys because they simply did not get enough playing time to answer the question. Then there were signings like Steven Pressley that made no sense at all. Take a player who was never good enough to play for Celtic and wait until he was too old. What? You could lock a team of monkeys in a room full of typewriters for infinity and they wouldn't be able to write an explanation to that one.

This remained the case for the remainder of Strachan's reign, bizarre signings that made no sense, players not given their proper chance, maddening inconsistency. Add to this the trait that O'Neill also had: loyalty to players even when they're obviously not up to it, and you can sense disaster looming before you can say Paul Telfer.

But let's not dwell on the negatives yet, because there were still moments of magic to come on the pitch in the second half of 2006: the moment Kenny Miller scored against Rangers in the first Old Firm game of the season when, for a second, I loved him as much as I ever loved anybody in a Celtic top; Nakamura's hat trick against Dundee Utd in October; the 3-0 win against Benfica on one of those nights when Kenny Miller *did* look international class; a crazy game against Hearts where we were one nil down with four minutes to go then Jarosik got a header and Craig Gordon scored the most hilariously inept goalkeeping own goal right in front of my seat . . .

But what am I talking about these other games for? Why

bother? Sure there were fine victories but there was only one game in the first half of the 2006/2007 season. One encounter. One fixture that as soon as it was announced you crossed off the weeks, then the days and finally the hours until it happened.

Manchester United. Champions League. Celtic Park. 21 November.

It was the biggest game since Seville, made bigger by the fact that, as he revealed in my interview with him years before, there is a needle between Strachan and Sir Alex Ferguson as large as that one in Seattle. In addition, there were two previous encounters with Man U that season which had really stung. First there was the pre-season friendly where their reserve team pumped us 3-0 at home. Not so big a deal, but they'd also beaten us 1-0 in Roy Keane's testimonial back in May and it all adds up. But then there was the first Champions league encounter at Manchester. Where do I start with that one?

I don't think I've ever been so terrified as a Celtic supporter in terms of watching the club try and punch above its weight. For the first twenty minutes of that game it just seemed that a Celtic player hardly touched the ball. United were immense. Pass-and-move may be the most fundamental football tactic, but they did it at such a dizzying speed, with laser accuracy it didn't seem fair to let Celtic on the same pitch as them.

Then a ball pumped long from Boruc found Jan Vennegoor of Hesselink who walked through a momentarily invisible Rio Ferdinand then fired home from eighteen yards. It was the very definition of 'against the run of play'. That's why I couldn't feel too aggrieved when United were awarded a soft penalty and Saha equalised.

And then we got the two opposite extremes of that Celtic squad, in fact the two opposite extremes of Gordon Strachan's tenure as manager. You had Nakamura with the technique of a ballerina and the temperament of an East German policeman placing the most exquisite free kick past Van der Sar, as good a free kick as United's own dead ballmeister Beckham had ever scored at Old Trafford, and then you had the bonkers bit – the player who was supposed to be brilliant turning into a combination of Wile E Coyote and The Keystone Cops. That man was Thomas Gravesen.

I still scratch my head when I think of him. He was a brilliant player in his day, and I remember phoning Archie up and screaming with excitement when I heard we'd bought him. But it was like the Gravesen who'd been peerless at Everton and initially so successful at Real Madrid had been kidnapped by aliens and possessed by an evil Mr Bean-type demon.

Of course he had flashes of greatness in a Celtic shirt: scoring against Rangers that season and running the show against St Mirren when he got a hat-trick. But those were rare moments when the real Gravesen managed to break free from the Mr Bean demon. In other games he was genuinely the most incompetent player I'd ever seen in a Celtic shirt – and I saw every single one of Gary Caldwell's games.

That night he was easily dispossessed by Paul Scholes to set up one goal then virtually passed directly to the same player for another. If it wasn't for some heroics by Artur Boruc in the goal, the 3-2 score line could have been a lot, lot worse.

So Celtic Park on 21 November was a big game and to this day it's the best atmosphere I remember from any European game at Celtic Park. It's difficult to describe it without resorting to cliché but the whole point about a cliché is that it's true. The sound *was* deafening. The atmosphere *was* so thick you could cut it with a knife and once again Manchester United were technically so in advance of Celtic it *did* scare the shit out of me.

But enough about the pre-match drinks in the Spirit Bar and

the mobs of English casuals roaming the streets looking for a fight, up at the stadium it was electrifying.

From the whistle, just as at Old Trafford, they were all over us with those perfectly orchestrated Speedy Gonzales passes. However tonight they foundered on two solid walls of defence. Gordon Strachan had got his tactics spot on. This was not about charging into them from the off, backed by the roar of the Celtic Park crowd and grabbing a goal then resolutely defending until the end. Oh no. This was the rope-a-dope, famously used by Muhammad Ali against George Foreman in the Rumble in the Jungle in Zaire, 1974. Ali sat back against the ropes and took everything the superior athlete could throw at him until Foreman started to tire in round five. Then Ali went on the attack and a few rounds later had floored his exhausted opponent in the greatest tactical battle boxing had ever seen.

In that first half the Celtic defence and midfield were Ali on the ropes, soaking up punch after punch from Manchester United. Gravesen, Lennon, Sno and even Naka all sticking to defensive roles and Bobo Balde and Stephen McManus were working like a well-oiled machine with Lee Naylor and Paul Telfer to nullify the threats from Ronaldo and Rooney. Any time Celtic won the ball it was more or less pumped long and high up to Vennegoor of Hesselink and Zurawski. Alright maybe I'm flattering Sno somewhat because he was a bit of a liability that night, but Strachan's theory was sound.

Then after half-time came the switch. Jarosik on for Sno after Strachan realised he was out of his depth and Maloney on for Zurawski. It meant more quality possession in midfield when the United players were tired after all that Speedy Gonzalez passing. The ball was played much more into the feet of Maloney and Nakamura now. And we started to attack. From our seats in the North Stand Upper we were perfectly placed to see this advancing army and perfectly placed to be just as conned as the referee was when Jiri Jarosik did his outrageous twisting fall with ten minutes to go (it was only after watching the highlights I realised Vidic never touched him but so what? In Europe in particular we had more than our fair share of dodgy decisions go against us) and we were then perfectly placed to watch Naka's free kick.

Except I didn't. I could not look. As Naka lined up I said to Phoebe. 'He can't put this the same way he did at Old Trafford, he has to try and stick it in the other corner.'

He didn't. You could tell from the second he struck it that it was going in exactly the same spot: top right-hand corner. As opposed to when he did this at the Stretford End in Manchester, I saw Van der Sar actually move in the right direction this time and my head sunk into my hands. He was going to save it.

Then the roar went up. Then I felt the hands thumping my back. I looked up into the face of one of the militant posties. 'Yaaaaaaasssss!' he was screaming. The rest of them were jumping up and down like popcorn in a bag in a microwave. It was louder than any cheer I'd heard in my life, louder even than that primal cry in the Jungle in 1986.

1-0 up against Manchester United. Four of the most expensive players in the country in that Manchester United wall, all jumping at the right time. Van der Sar, just about the best goalkeeper in world football, diving the right way, but the ball still went in because it was the immaculate strike. Unbelievable.

But it wasn't over yet. We had ten minutes to ride out, ten minutes that felt like every Christmas Eve you ever had as a child rolled into 600 seconds. Then they got their penalty. A soft one, obviously. But in the light of the Jarosik dive it was honours even. 'We're fucked now,' I said to my wife, 'Typical Celtic. They'll not only score this but I bet they'll get a winner before the final whistle.'

I've never been so happy to be so wrong. Under a backdrop of twirling green and white scarves Boruc dived the right direction and saved Saha's spot kick because, well, because he was The Holy Goalie and God had decided his name was going to be etched on the stone tablets of Celtic's history books in one way or another.

When the final whistle went we were so jubilant that we'd not only beaten Manchester United but, over the two legs, had won the Battle of Britain that it wasn't until we were back in the car with Archie on the way home that we heard on the radio we'd actually got through to the last sixteen of the Champions League for the first time in the club's history. Regardless of mistakes Strachan may have made during his reign as manager, that result and those tactics deserve to stand up there with anything any Celtic manager achieved before.

What a night! What a year! What a life I had now!

Ten years before I'd been speaking to the *Gamesmaster* producer Jonny Ffinch about what I really wanted to do with my life. 'I just want a music radio show,' I said. 'One where I can turn up every day, play music I like and get to talk funny pish in-between. I don't care if it's only for 100 people. It's all I want.'

Well I had that now. And God. And three wonderful kids. And a Celtic team on top of their game.

And then it all started to go wrong.

# 22

# SNATCHING DEFEAT FROM
# THE JAWS OF VICTORY

Men in suits, corporate monkeys, idiots in ties – they ruin everything sooner or later – people obsessed with balance sheets and short term views, guys who just want a black tick on a spreadsheet and think nothing of passion, or culture, or community or love or soul for they have none, they ruined my life in Scotland and they ruined Celtic Football Club.

If proper investment had been made in Celtic after Seville it would be one of the top teams in Europe today. If we'd looked to competing with Europe's top tier instead of simply Scotland's we'd have been so far in advance of Rangers the duopoly would have been broken and the Old Firm put to rest, at least until we'd got ten in a row.

Instead we got Camaras and Telfers and Caldwells when we should have got Keanes and Laursens and Vidics, or even Vidices, but as long as we were beating Rangers that didn't matter to the board. Don't get me wrong, I want to beat them too, but if you stand still while the dragon is lying on the ground eventually its wounds will heal. You've got to kill it or it will leap up and fry you. It happened to Rangers towards the end of nine in a row and it happened to Celtic during Strachan. From Seville onwards we should not have lost an SPL league title. Considering that a one goal swing at any point during the Seville season would have won the title that year too, we should have been sitting at the start of the 2009/2010 season going for the record of ten in a row, given the state of Rangers FC during this decade.

But the suits thought differently and they thought incorrectly. It was almost like they wanted to sit atop some kind of economically moral high ground by not getting into that horrible debt that Rangers were in. Maybe they felt the cry from David Murray of 'for every fiver they spend we'll spend ten' was arrogant and unseemly and did not want to be tarred by the same brush. 'Look at our balance sheets!' they seemed to cry. 'Our red numbers are not nearly so big and obscene as theirs! In fact by 2009 some of those red numbers will be black.'

It's one of the perversities of the capitalist system that when it enters a global economic crisis as the direct result of people borrowing too much money, the interest rates get cut so low that it makes it pointless to try and save money. The middle of an economic crisis with miniscule interest rates is *exactly* the time to borrow because debt is far more manageable, so Peter Lawwell's obsession with having zero debt didn't just fail to make any footballing sense, it makes no financial sense either.

It was also unfair to the fans. They were paying more and more money each year on tickets while the board were paying less and less for players, ultimately leading to a worse and worse deal for the supporters. That's not right.

Neither was the suits attitude to Xfm Scotland. With proper investment it could have been a great station. When it launched though, it launched without any billboards advertising any shows. Instead there were a few posters with babies dressed as rock stars.

How creative.

How cool.

How clever.

How pointless.

By comparison I had to walk through the Gallowgate after every Celtic match and see what seemed like the biggest billboard in the world advertising the *Real Breakfast Show*. A big picture of Robin Galloway and Cat Harvey with sausages stuck in front of their mouths making a smile . . . naff, cheesy and brilliant. You didn't need a degree in marketing to realise that these were the two people who did the breakfast show and they liked to have a laugh. I would have tuned into listen to them after seeing that.

After a year on Xfm I was still getting into taxis in Glasgow and having drivers saying 'Awright big man – what are you up to these days?' That should not have been happening. I'd have been far happier if they'd said. 'Awright big man, heard you on that Xfm the other day, you were shite.'

Because then it would have been my fault. I would not have been doing my job properly. But I was. That's why I got the Scottish Radio Presenter of the Year Award at the beginning of 2007. That's why I was nominated as Sony UK Music Radio Personality of the Year at the same time. The other nominees? Chris Evans, Jonathan Ross, Mark Radcliffe and Andy Kershaw. It was the biggest award at the biggest award show in the country. And I was there. Finally. After years of personal and professional struggle, admittedly much of my own making. But this was it. Surely?

Unfortunately, the true nature of commercial radio was about to rear its ugly head. My boss Claire Pattenden had left to go on another maternity leave and was replaced by a guy called Owen Ryan. I am sure Owen performed spectacularly at previous mainstream radio stations (he certainly never stopped telling us he did) and I can't say he will not go on to perform adequately in future jobs. Hell he may have even met financial targets he was asked to meet at Xfm but personally speaking in my dealings with him I found the guy to be a complete arsehole. I would like to go into more details but the libel laws on these things are tediously old-fashioned. I just wish I'd recorded every conversation I ever had with the guy.

The suits had panicked after the first couple of ratings for Xfm had been low. This was entirely to be expected because they had no advertising. It was the equivalent of planting a tree in the middle of the forest and expecting people not only to find it, but like it and tell every person they met that this was the best tree in the world.

So we had a station that wasn't getting great ratings, but was playing the most exciting new guitar music at a time when Scotland was full of brilliant new guitar bands desperate for a chance to play their music to people. We should have stayed firm to this original vision and accepted that Xfm was not competing with Real or Clyde or Forth.

But the suits shat it. They changed the music ethos of the station and started playing the same ten songs with guitars in them that every other station was playing. Every other station that had big billboards and TV adverts and was giving away cars every week as competition prizes.

Our biggest prize? A holiday that took people about ten weeks of listening to win. It was a terrible idea. One of those horribly cynical cheap ideas they use in commercial radio to hook listeners in and con them.

I had been promised a pay rise after my first year at Xfm by Claire Pattenden. It wasn't specified how much and to be honest I didn't care. It was a principle thing. But when it came to new negotiations they actually wanted to *cut* my wages.

My argument was that I made the show a huge critical success. I was starting to win awards. I deserved a token raise. I was told they didn't have any money.

Fair enough. I could have understood that. But then I went down to the Sony Awards.

It was supposed to be the greatest night of my professional life. It turned out to be the worst. It wasn't helped by the fact that I had my leg and arm in plaster, the result of snapping my Achilles playing for Xfm in a five-a-side match against Little Man Tate then discovering once I started using crutches that I had fractured my wrist some weeks before, again playing football.

Some bits of the night were great. Bob Shennan, still the Boss of Radio 5 live came up to speak to me and said how happy he was that all the potential I had shown at the BBC was finally coming to fruition. In return I apologised for saying he could stick his station up his arse all those years ago. I spoke with Danny Baker, another man I'd crossed swords with years ago after I took over the football phone-in 606 when he was sacked. A war of words had developed between us and the hatchet was buried that night too. I was particularly pleased about that because Danny is the greatest exponent of radio since Marconi first flicked a switch. He does things with words that normal broadcasters simply can't. He is one of my all-time broadcasting heroes. But I had never told him that because I was young and a twat.

I just felt that if I could win the award and beat the likes of Chris Evans and Jonathan Ross then the stations owners would *have* to put a bit of money into some billboards to advertise the fact. Then once people knew about the station they'd listen. When they listened they'd like it, the ratings would go up and even the suits would be happy.

But I didn't win. Not only did I not win, but I saw the reality of Xfm's owners that night. Our table was full of various managers. And the drink flowed. And flowed. And flowed. I stopped drinking after I didn't win, I was so fed up but even after the awards do had finished, the drink continued to flow in the hotel bar.

The hotel was The Grosvenor, a five star hotel on London's Park Lane. The beer was about £10 a bottle. 'Come on Dominik!' one of the senior figures of Xfm drawled to me in a drunken stupor, 'Have a drink! It's all on expenses!'

They must have spent thousands and thousands of pounds that night. This was at the same time they were laying off DJs because they said they couldn't afford the budgets. Some of those DJs were only getting paid £80 a show, the price of about half a round those corporate bastards guzzled that night. It disgusted me. This was the reality behind my dream job. I wanted no more part of it. I knew that the station was going to die with idiots like this running it so I left. Then so did the remaining listeners. And it died.

I feel sorry for the DJs who worked their backsides off and, unlike many of their counterparts on other stations, actually lived, ate and breathed the music. People like Jim Gellatly, Fraser Thompson, Martin Bate, Ali Campbell, Al Lorraine, Susan Hay, most of them now not even on air (as a contrast I won't reveal the name of the Real Radio DJ who told me when I worked there to keep my head down and tune out the music and concentrate on the money because it was a great place to cash in. That guy is still on air. There is no justice).

I feel sorrier for an entire generation of Scottish bands who were inspired by hearing the likes of The Fratellis, The View and Biffy Clyro on Xfm Scotland and took up guitars only to find there was no outlet for their music. I remember talking about this on an internet forum some time after I left and an anonymous poster accused me of being bitter. Damn right I am. I always will be.

The Xfm bosses killed an entire generation of DJs and bands in Scotland. The only consolation I had was that Glasvegas, deemed 'a novelty band' by one of Xfm's corporate lackeys, didn't need Xfm to survive, they had the musical ability *and* the brilliant management to ensure the NME and Radio 1 got onboard and they went on to become the biggest new band in Britain the following year.

Scott, Marissa and I were lucky enough to support them at King Tuts as that was all starting and James and Rab sang on stage with me at my Xfm leaving do in June. It was worth going through all the heartache at the end of Xfm just for that.

For Xfm read Celtic Football Club. A generation of fans inspired by the road to Seville, a tantalising glimpse of what could have been, then forced to live off inconsistent scraps.

On paper it was still good. Gordon Strachan won the league again in 2006 and in 2007. But once you take out the Old Firm games and European nights I struggle to remember more than a handful of games in each of those seasons, and I was there for every moment home and away with the exception of Aberdeen, Inverness and Hearts which I was never balloted for, in spite of taking every single away game ticket I was offered over the course of four years.

This constantly frustrated me. I would have loved to have been in Inverness for any of the games, the talk on the Huddleboard before, during and after those weekends always made it seem like the best away trip to go on. Instead I sat in a pub in Glasgow with Archie, in January 2007 as Jan Vennegoor of Hesselink scored the winner in time added on then got booked for celebrating.

That, of course, was the great thing about Strachan's Celtic: their never-say-die attitude. We were simply never out of a game. Partly due to some inspired substitutions by WGS, but mostly because those players, I think, realised they weren't that brilliant in ability alone, so had to try that bit harder, for that bit longer in every game.

For example if Strachan had been in charge of the Seville team in 2003? We may have won the UEFA Cup. We'd probably have equalised then scored a winner in the last sixty seconds. That was just what Strachan teams did.

But take away the last five minutes of games and they were getting really boring, with over-elaborate build-ups and nobody willing to take enough shots on goal. It was almost as if that win over Manchester United at Celtic Park had installed a blueprint for all future tactics. Sit back for the first half, soak up the pressure, try and knock it around a bit then come out fighting in the second half. Now that's necessary against Man Utd but pointless against Hibs. All you do is constrict the time you have left to win the game and it means that if a goalkeeper or defender makes an error (as they became increasingly likely to do under Strachan) it puts you under more pressure. And as for those Strachan signings? They still didn't make sense.

I remember a cracking away day with Archie at St Mirren, 2 September 2007, where we won 5-0 because not only was it my first trip to their ground but Derek Riordan got a rare start, and scored (Strachan had rested many of his first team favourites after their exertions in the win on penalties against Spartak Moscow a few days before). But the most abiding memory was Archie and I hosing ourselves laughing at Scott Brown's showboating that day. We'd just signed him from Hibs for £4.4 million in the kind of transfer move we *should* have been making all the time. But not on Scott Brown, though, who has never lived up to his billing at Celtic and indeed that season it was only because his injury forced Strachan to pair Paul Hartley and Barry Robson in central midfield that we rallied to win the title.

That day, however, Brown was simply unplayable. From our position in the stand we had a perfect view as he humiliated their left back Maranda time and time again. Turning him inside, then out, pulling faces, giving him that blank 100-yard stare then sticking his tongue out.

He never played as well as that day again, unfortunately, and with all respect to the Buddies, Celtic needed players who could do that against a higher calibre of opposition, but instead that 2007/2008 season started with a 0-0 draw at home against Kilmarnock, with Killen starting instead of Riordan. What? Was no-one creative allowed to work in Scotland any more?

There were great wins at the start of that season, two 5-0 pumpings of Hearts and Inverness Caley Thistle where Massimo Donati scored a cracker in each and the 2-1 win against Milan in the Champions League stand out. The best bit about that last game was sitting beside Susan Hay while we were all singing 'they gave us Johnstone, Tully, Murdoch, Auld and Hay' then us both realising that was her Uncle Davie they were singing about and beaming from ear to ear!

But the team, like Brown and Donati, were so inconsistent. Two months after that destruction of Hearts they knocked us out of the League Cup – at Parkhead. Two months after we beat Milan at Parkhead, Phoebe and I once again sat in the San Siro and watched us be the very definition of mediocrity as they beat us 1-0. Yes we still got through to the last sixteen but without scoring a single goal away from home, and only because Shaktar Donetsk fell apart over the course of the autumn.

But there was one thing working in Strachan's favour. If his Celtic team was often frustratingly inconsistent, this era coincided happily with a time when our friends across the town were consistent – consistently pish. Rangers' ineptitude during Strachan's time at Celtic is every bit as responsible for the Hoops' success as anything Wee Gordon managed to do.

But then they beat us 3-0 in October. McGeady was left out of the team in the first signs that Strachan and he were not seeing eye to eye. In another perfect example of our inconsistency at the time Evander Sno, who made a goal-saving tackle at the end of the game in the San Siro two months later, had an awful game here and gave away a penalty from which Novo scored one of his two goals that day. Two things were telling that day. Firstly, we had no bite in midfield at all and Barry Ferguson controlled the whole game. Secondly, Rangers *had* bite, and you could tell with Walter Smith and Ally McCoist back they had a renewed spirit, in spite of their lack of footballing talent.

That really got to me. The sectarianism was really getting to me as well. Certain Rangers forums were posting pubs where I drunk in, with recommendations that assorted members wait outside them with an assortment of implements. At one stage some nice people even posted where Molly was attending school.

I had gone onstage to host Xfm's Winter Wonderland concert at the end of 2006, the climax of that first wonderful year, and there had been a few boos from Rangers fans. 'How do you know they were from Rangers fans?' You might ask. See the guys who boo while standing there with their right hand raised in that funny salute? It's a dead giveaway. To coin a line from a popular song 'that's why I'm paranoid.'

I realised pretty quickly that night the best way to handle this was to announce the name of the band that had just played, so the cheers would drown out the odd negative comment. And it was a stunning line-up that night: Biffy Clyro, The View, Idlewild and Ocean Colour Scene; so there were a lot of cheers to go round. It got a bit hairy after the Fratellis played, because I was onstage on my own trying to get them to come back on for an encore. Their manager had said 'give us a minute' so I was onstage on my own. With a capacity crowd at the Carling Academy, with a sizeable portion who were disposed to dislike me.

So I launched into the 'do do do' bit of Chelsea Dagger. With my arms flapping above my head in that 'easy, easy' fashion. Of course that was exactly the same refrain and the same movement 57,000 Celtic fans had performed when Kenny Miller scored our second against Rangers that season, which was obviously too much for one Son of Orange in the crowd who threw a pint right at me. His aim was true and it caught me right on the left shoulder.

I just made an ornate bow. What I really wanted to do was to make the sign of the cross in the direction the pint had come from, but luckily that night I hadn't been drinking, so common sense prevailed.

Anyway, I'd seen no less musical emissaries than Morrissey, Alex Turner from the Arctic Monkeys and Brandon Flowers from the Killers get hit in that exact same spot with the exact same weapon, so I was in good company.

Luckily the Fratellis were ready to go so I just screamed. 'Here are the Fratellis!' and left the stage. Again if I had been drunk there was a very real chance I would have screamed. 'Here are the Fratellis, and they're all Tims! And we're top of the league and in the last sixteen of the Champions League so youse can all fuck yourselves!'

I can look back on it with some degree of humour now, but it was because of events like this I started leaving it to the last minute before going into gigs. King Tuts wasn't so bad; it was a relatively short walk up the stairs to the shadows of the back corner. But Barrowlands could be a nightmare. The queue for the security, where the allegiance of the bouncer could sometimes mean a five-minute search of every pocket and every section of my wallet while the guy smirked at me, loving his tiny moment of power. Then there would be the three flights of brightly-lit stairs, then the walk right across the width of the ballroom to get to the raised platform in the back left corner, where it was darkest and quietest. As always 99% of the time the cries were 'alright big man!' but there was always that 1% still saying 'ya Fenian bastard.' When you've been told you're on a Neo Nazi death list and been attacked in the street by guys with knives it's those 1% that you take more notice of. Which is a real shame, Scotland's Shame, in fact.

I used to get a lot of shout-outs from the stage by bands, or 'menshies' as Susan Hay used to call them. I would dread them. The minute a band would say 'we just want to thank Dominik Diamond for the support he's given us on the radio' I started to shrink knowing that for every cheer there would be a boo.

I remember going to see Manic Street Preachers at the Barrowlands in May 2007 when they were promoting *Send Away The Tigers*. After following them around like a lovesick puppy during the *Smash Hits* days it had been great to catch up with them again as a proper music DJ. Towards the end of the set Nicky Wire said. 'I just want to say thank you on behalf of the band to someone who has been the biggest supporter of ours since *Generation Terrorists*. Dominik Diamond.'

Some cheers, some boos. It seemed more boos than cheers this time. Nicky continued, 'I know some people up here don't like him for silly reasons, but we have always loved him. This is for him!'

And they launched into 'You Love Us'. One of the proudest moments of my life? In some ways, but a horrible one too. I was too embarrassed to go to the after show party.

Leaving Xfm in June put me into another depression, I had just had my dream job shattered and I was still in plaster because of the snapped Achilles. The two things combined to send my weight ballooning, over seventeen stone to be precise. I started drinking heavily again and it was only through a chance blood test before an ear operation that I discovered my liver was paying the price for the years of booze and sleeping tablets and was starting to resemble the rock of Gibraltar.

Things had to change. I had to get out of Glasgow. Too many bad memories now, too many people potentially waiting outside pubs and schools when I picked up my kids. The tiny seeds of hate I had planted years ago as an indestructible gobshite on the radio in London had now grown into fields of hate. Hate directed at me, but hate that would ultimately affect my wife and kids. I couldn't put the genie back in the bottle and to be honest with the abuse I was getting did I really want to? Did I want to apologise for calling these people scum when certain sections of them were behaving just like that to me?

Why not just leave it all behind? The dream job was gone, the dream Celtic team was gone and the pressure of living in the goldfish bowl of Glasgow was not worth it any more. So why not leave Glasgow and all the troubles behind?

# 23

# SCOTLAND'S SHAME
# AND THE END OF THE ROAD

Edinburgh held great memories for me. It was the city I had frequented as an underage-drinking schoolboy with assorted posh pals, selling our Five Nations tickets then buying a carryout and getting hammered under some bridge before returning to the school bus.

It was where my first girlfriend Kari had got a job and a flat after she left that school and we briefly played at being grown-ups in Stockbridge. It was where I had stayed many times with Phoebe on stolen weekends while Granny watched the kids, revelling in the romance that dripped from its ancient buildings.

Now we had a huge apartment in a mansion block on North Bridge, with two balconies overlooking Princes Street and the Castle. In the summer the sun streamed in so you could actually sunbathe in the living room, in the winter when the snow fell it was like looking out on a film set. I could walk about with less of the constant recognition I got in Glasgow because, well, because people in Edinburgh are a bit more aloof and unfriendly. It was the best place I ever lived in Scotland.

It was a bloody long way from Celtic Park though.

The M8, the damned M8, that pitiful excuse for a road that

grudgingly links the east and west of Scotland. It's supposed to be a healthy tributary but in reality it's a blocked artery of slow-moving metal boxes of anger spewing out poison, though I do like the sculptures of horses and heads along the way. That's a nice touch.

There is nothing more stressful than using it to get to a Celtic game in the evening, especially if you're doing a *Drivetime* show on the radio and you can't leave until 7pm.

I can honestly say the drive through to see Celtic take on Barcelona in the Champions League 20 February 2008 was the most stressful hour of my life. As soon as the last words had been uttered by Diamond and de Andrade I flew into the car and screeched away down South Gyle Broadway. I reckon I was at the Glasgow Road roundabout before I even closed the door.

I slammed it down the bypass to the Hermiston Gait round-about overtaking on the inside and outside lanes like it was *The Wacky Races* then onto the M8, cursing anybody who dared to drive below 'the regulation speed limit' (the previous phrase may have been rewritten by my lawyers). As always with the M8 from Edinburgh to Glasgow there was that deceptively smooth flowing bit at the start, with towns appearing as nothing but signs passing in a blur: Broxburn, Bathgate, Whitburn, Shotts. Then you'd hit that wall of traffic just after the Dakota Hotel when the motorway would turn into something resembling the fall of Saigon, but with people trying to get *into* Glasgow rather than out.

It's not the most original observation to say that being stuck in traffic is a nightmare, but being stuck in traffic when you're trying to see Celtic play in the last sixteen of the Champions League is like one you wake from to find that Freddy Krueger is under the bed and Nazi werewolves are behind the hospital curtains.

Once again I got into a big Celtic game late, this time just as Jan Vennegoor of Hesselink opened the scoring after fifteen minutes. Given the seventeen stone I was carrying at the time I was sweating even more than my usual twenty buckets.

An administrative error (i.e. I hadn't paid attention to a letter) meant I had lost my fantastic seats in front of the Militant Posties but luckily managed to get another pair only about twenty feet away. This meant I was sitting behind Mick and Anne. Mick had been a long-time texter to my Xfm show and was a guy who like me loved his music as much as he loved Celtic. He was a postie too. What IS it with that section at Celtic Park?

We were all in agony that night as we took the lead twice only to get pegged back then defeated by a team who were on such a different level of playing ability it was terrifying. They had Henry and Messi up front; we had Caldwell and McManus in defence. If that doesn't perfectly illustrate the gulf in class I don't know what does.

It was the first time I ever hated Thierry Henry. After he scored his goal he 'shooshed' the crowd. I know that's his standard goal celebration but when you're the recipient it makes you fizz. And I fizzed all the way back to Edinburgh. Eventually. The traffic getting out of the East End of Glasgow was such a nightmare I pulled over in some random street and went to sleep for an hour. This was definitely not so much fun anymore.

Neither was my career. I was initially excited by the prospect of working for Edinburgh's Talk 107 when I met its boss Mike Graham shortly after leaving Xfm. We'd arranged to meet in Harthill Service Station and I liked the clandestine nature of this, it was like we were organising a football transfer.

Mike Graham had been a fan of my newspaper columns when he was Editor of the *Daily Mirror* in Scotland and he was the kind of straight-talking boss I liked. You can say what you like about the tabloids but I wrote for the *Daily Star* for a decade and know many, many people who write for other tabloids and you will not meet more honest, decent and honourable people in your life. Seriously. They are a world away from the duplicitous, backstabbing, two-faced inhabitants of TV and radio. Another bonus was that Michael Wilson, who looked after me during my brief period at Real Radio, was now a producer at Talk 107, so I had the chance to make his life miserable again.

As far as joining Talk 107 went I had one condition, but it was non-negotiable. I wanted to work with Marisa de Andrade. We'd had a connection at Xfm unlike anything I'd experienced and I knew she hated being stuck there after I left. Mike agreed.

Marisa and I started on weekends then moved to do the daily *Drivetime* show. Once again I was having the time of my life. Once again suits came in and spoiled it. This time it was a bit more understandable than the Xfm experience. A talk radio station in Edinburgh was always going to struggle, especially after its initial launch, when a less than stellar line up of presenters and ridiculous adherence to only talking about things in Edinburgh had damned it from birth. It never recovered from that and was losing money hand over fist.

As a result, shortly after Marisa and I started doing *Drivetime* they got rid of all the producers and phone ops as a cost-cutting measure and we were in the situation of having to devise, research, set up and produce twenty hours of speech radio a week, including answering the phones while we were live on air.

This meant that Marisa and I would ask people to phone up to talk about something like troop withdrawal from Iraq. Without callers we wouldn't be able to do the next portion of the show. The board would light up with a call coming through and we couldn't actually answer the call because we were talking live on air at the time! So we had to cross our fingers and hope the caller would keep ringing until we went to a break so we could answer the phone.

By contrast at BBC Scotland someone like Fred MacAuley would have a small army of producers, researchers, engineers and phone ops so all he had to do was turn up fifteen minutes before the show started, read a script someone's written for him, facts and figures someone else has researched for him and guests a producer has lined up.

It made me rue the day I'd quit Radio 5 live. Anybody who asks me about going into radio I offer them the same advice. Go for the BBC or don't bother. I never worked so hard in my life, though, and as a result we still ended up with a line up of programmes and guests I'd have put up against any speech show at the time: Alex Salmond, Cherie Blair, Kenny Richey, Irvine Welsh and my own personal favourite – the marketing manager of the biggest bubble wrap manufacturer in the UK.

But the stress was killing me. I remember one day in particular when I was supposed to take Molly out for sushi. It was something I'd made a point of doing every week since I'd got back from the Philipinnes. Just Molly and I having a couple of hours of father and daughter time in an attempt to make up for the early years when I'd been too wrapped up in work or depression to spend enough time with her.

I'd had four books to read over a weekend tied in with the next week's guests on Talk 107. So I told her we couldn't go to lunch.

'Why not?' she asked, not unreasonably, because this was a weekly highlight for her.

'Because I'm too busy.'

I said the words without thinking.

Those were the words I had promised myself in the Philipinnes I would never say to a child of mine again. I had made this promise to Molly when I got back and could see the words stung her. So I put the books away, took her out to lunch and read the books through the night instead.

Sooner or later though, a straw was going to lightly fall and break the camel's back. Ironically, it was a Celtic fan that did it.

Much of the other highlights for me as a Celtic follower during the reign of Strachan involved the fans rather than the players. The atmosphere at Celtic Park after the departure of St Martin grew increasingly stale, in spite of the success of the team. This was partly because of the ridiculous crackdown on songs you weren't allowed to sing any more, partly because of the poor quality of football on offer and partly because of the hiring policy when it came to stewards. 'Are YOU a fat, ignorant, heavy-handed, power-hungry arsehole with the personality and charm of a raptor? Will YOU get a semi if you throw people out for standing up to sing a song? Why not become a steward at Celtic Park?'

First of those were the Jungle Boys who had got a singing section started and had also instigated some cracking card and banner displays. Some were simple affairs which read *Welcome To Paradise* or *Celtic 67*, another time they had the individual banners of every player in the team at the time, deserving credit for managing to fit Gary Caldwell's humungous head on one. Some of their banners were humorous: one featured a red, white and blue Pinocchio and the words *Murray Must Stay* in reference to the Rangers chairman's assorted promises of rosy financial futures for the Govan team. There was another that aped the numerous pictures of broken Celtic FC crests that seemed to appear on the back pages of Scottish tabloids every time Celtic lost a couple of games. This one had the broken Rangers crest with the grim reaper looking on.

There were some that were a mixture of the two. *Is it cold in this shadow?* asked one above a picture of Jock Stein casting a shadow in the picture of the European Cup. This was a direct response to the chants of 'Big Jock Knew' a charming three line chant sung by animals apparently laughing at child abuse.

The greatest one of theirs was after Artur Boruc was given an official police caution for blessing himself at Ibrox in February 2006. Officially the caution was for breach of the peace. Aye. Right. Shortly afterwards there was a banner which read. *Jungle Bhoys support Artur Boruc. Blessing yourself is not a crime.*

Time after time they organised TIFO displays: cards handed out to fans in the Jock Stein stand which when held up would form the Celtic colours.

Then came the guys modelling themselves on the continental clubs style of Ultras: The Green Brigade who were more aggressively political stating from the off that they were 'a predominantly left-wing, pro-Irish Republican anti-fascist group.' I didn't have a problem with any of that myself, though some sections of the home support did. But when it came to banners and displays everybody was in agreement that the Green Brigade was simply amazing.

They had the most incredibly powerful anti-racism one featuring a green and white fist smashing a black swastika. Smaller versions of this had the anti-fascist slogan *No Passaran* made famous during the Spanish Civil War.

Their second funniest banner came during the Paul le Guen era at Rangers, when the initial talk of *la Revolution* had died down somewhat after they trailed us by more than a double-figure point tally before the winter had even ended. It featured a pastiche of the famous Ascent of Man picture, except this time the monkey became a Rangers fan.

*Revolution? Try Evolution.* It read.

Compared to the rubbish on the pitch by this stage, the Green Brigade and Jungle Bhoys were the best thing about going to Celtic Park. Even the names speak volumes when you compare the Green Brigade to their Rangers 'equivalent' the Blue Order. The Jungle Bhoys sound like a fun bunch of lads, the Green Brigade sounds romantic, libertarian. The Blue Order is a status quo, something rigid and inflexible.

The Celtic banners were always at their funniest when it came to Old Firm games. But nothing prepared me for the banner the Green Brigade would unfurl during the Celtic-Rangers game of 16 April 2008, the greatest banner I ever saw at a football game in my life.

It appeared at half-time. I could see a commotion over on the North side of the Lisbon Lions upper, just to the left of where the Rangers fans were sitting. As the banner dropped you could see it read in big black letters SCOTLAND'S SHAME. With an arrow pointing to the Rangers fans. The humour was unsurpassable, the cleverness unimpeachable and the timing was impeccable, coming as it did when a section of those Rangers fans were once again singing that chant that treats child abuse as a big joke.

You could hear the laughter building as word spread across the ground; Celtic fan nudged Celtic fan and pointed towards the banner. The Rangers fans obviously couldn't see it, which made it all the more hilarious. It was like sticking two fingers up behind the teacher's head in a school photo. Rendered large.

After a while the police stepped in and confiscated the banner, something they hadn't done to the Rangers fans who had displayed one directly behind Artur Boruc at Ibrox that read *Dodgy Keeper - Voodoo No Workie*. Go figure.

The banner wasn't the only significant factor in that game. Recent form including a loss at Ibrox, a nil all draw against Dundee United and a shocking 1-0 loss at home to a ten-man Motherwell team had rendered this and every other game that season 'must wins' for us to have any hope of stopping Rangers winning the SPL.

With Scott Brown turning into £4.4 million of headless chicken, Vennegoor of Hesselink getting slower all year and McManus and Caldwell well into an epic downward spiral, it was up to Boruc, Naka, McGeady and McDonald to keep us in the league up till then.

Scott Brown had been injured which had forced Strachan to go for a midfield pairing of Barry Robson and Paul Hartley. It was this selection that turned things around that season. It was that selection that helped us beat Rangers that day.

Within the first few minutes Robson had sent Christian Dailly flying in a way that made it clear this team was not going to get physically bullied by Rangers in the manner of recent encounters. Hartley did the same to Lee McCulloch. Finally we had a midfield pairing with a bit of dig. Rangers were stunned, Barry Ferguson virtually anonymous as a result. Naka put us ahead with a stunning twenty five-yard strike, then who else but Novo equalised shortly after the half-time banner show. One missed penalty from Skippy, an injury-time winner from his striking partner Jan and a post-whistle scuffle in which Gary Caldwell finally managed to strike something properly, namely David Weir's head, and we had won 2-1. We were still in the hunt for the title!

Now, back to that banner . . . As soon as the match was ended I called Michael Wilson (now the boss of Talk 107 after Mike Graham got punted as another cost-cutting measure) and said that we had to get someone from the Green Brigade on to talk about this on the show. Michael had reservations: he appreciated it was a great story and no other media outlet would even attempt to get the Green Brigade on air, but he made me promise him I wouldn't turn this into a huge Rangers-baiting exercise.

I promised him it wouldn't. After the experiences of the last two years in Glasgow the last thing I wanted to do was stir things up. I got in touch with the Green Brigade and arranged a live interview with a guy called 'Mark'. This was not his real name, and this is crucial to what happened next.

I introduced Mark as a member of the Green Brigade, one of a few groups that had sprung up at Celtic to try and make the act of supporting the club a bit more passionate and exciting. I argued that it was a great example for all supporters to follow in an attempt to put control of the terraces back in the hands of the fans, rather than the corporate monkeys who controlled the game today. I asked Mark to explain why they'd decided to make the banner. And off he went. But not in the measured direction I thought he'd gently meander.

Rangers fans were scum, he effectively said. They were animals who embarrassed Scotland and it needed to be publicly pointed out. He barely drew a breath as he launched attack after attack after attack into them. Michael came into the studio; I faded down my mic so he could speak to me without the audience hearing.

'You've got rein him in here, big fella. This is too one-sided.'

So I cut him off with the line. 'Now listen Mark, you can't say all Rangers fans are animals. That's blatantly not true.' And it isn't. Then I said 'there are good and bad in both sets of supporters, they're as bad as each other at times, surely?'

Did I really think that? Deep down?

If you want to try and set up some form of moral comparison, for me the vileness of Rangers fans who sing 'The Billy Boys' (a song commemorating a violent street gang led by British Fascist Billy Fullerton in 1920s Glasgow talking about being 'up to our knees in Fenian blood') is cancelled out by the equally atrocious Celtic fans who sing about sixty-six people falling down the stairs to their death in the Ibrox disaster of 1971.

It would do extremists from both sides well to remember that Jock Stein helped tend to the wounded and dying Rangers fans that day. The greatest man in Celtic history said that this tragedy must 'help curb the bigotry and bitterness of Old Firm matches.'

*That* is what Big Jock Knew. And Big Jock would be as ashamed at songs mocking the deaths of Rangers fans that day as he would at songs mocking child abuse. But I have never heard songs about the Ibrox disaster sung at any Celtic match I have ever attended, or any Celtic pub I've drunk in. I have heard the odd line shouted by a pissed-up ned on the way into a ground, but he's been told to button it. I have heard 'The Billy Boys' sung every time I've seen Rangers play.

I have seen Nazi salutes at Ibrox and all over the city by guys wearing Rangers tops. A Nazi salute is the vilest of the vile. Some might now say, 'Oh but they sing pro IRA songs at Celtic games and that's just as bad.' No it's not. It's not even true.

And you only ever hear three Irish Republican songs sung at Celtic away games (the only place you hear them, ironically, given that they are banned at Celtic Park . . . ) *Boys of the Old Brigade* is a song about a bunch of poor farmers who were forced to take up arms and defend their country from an invading force in the Irish War of Independence in 1919-1921, no different than rural English workers who were conscripted to help repel the invading force of the Nazis in World War Two, or Scots who joined forces to try and beat the English at Bannockburn.

The IRA mentioned in the song is not even close to being the same IRA that existed in the second half of the twentieth century. Read any history book for more details (I can recommend Tim Pat Coogan's book *The IRA* 'a very sensible and fair-minded assessment of a uniquely controversial organisation' – *The Times*).

'Aiden McAnespie' mourns the death of a twenty-four-year-old Sinn Fein election worker, shot while walking to a Gaelic Football Match on 21 February 1988. He was not a member of any paramilitary group. The British Army claims that it was an accidental discharge from a rifle that just happened to kill him dead from 300 yards. Subsequent testimonies have thrown so much doubt over this claim as to make it laughable if it weren't so sad.

'Go on Home British Soldiers' is a song written in response to the murder of innocent Irish people by British troops on Bloody Sunday 1972 asking that same invading army to go back to their own country and leave them alone or they will be forced to keep fighting for their lives.

None of them glorify death. None of them talk about being up to their knees in British blood. The first two are clearly anti-war songs; the third echoes sentiments expressed by Paul McCartney in his own response to Bloody Sunday 'Give Ireland Back to the Irish', McCartney's song has less swearing; probably because he had less friends and relatives killed that day. The sentiments expressed by the chirpy Beatle in this song did not prevent the British Queen giving him a knighthood in 1996, so why is it so wrong when non-music legend Celtic fans express them? So where are we on the points scale now? Who's got the worst fans? It is for the reader to decide, but at times neither cloaks themselves in glory.

'Mark', however, refused my pleas for moderation. Off he went again: animals this, animals that. Now I was getting worried. It was alright for 'Mark' who could say whatever he wanted. No-one listening knew his name, what he looked like, where he went drinking or where his kids went to school. They knew mine.

Every word that dropped from his lips would be associated with me, because it was my show. In his desire to speak his piece he showed no appreciation that it would be me who would carry the can for his words. I had to cut the interview short in the end. It was too much.

'Mark' was blinkered, he was irresponsible, he was one-sided and he wouldn't listen. He was exactly like I had been in the 90s when I was on Radio 5 live, just another example of the chickens coming home to roost. I don't blame the guy, he was just doing exactly what I would have done if I was him, and exactly the kind of things I did do when I was an indestructible young man in my twenties living in London without a family. Now it was different. Now I knew the net result of these pellets of discord and had had enough of it all. That's why I'd left Glasgow, but it had followed me here to Edinburgh.

I was probably naïve to think I could have discussed the banner and retained some form of perceived journalistic neutrality, but I felt it was an important story to discuss. What really upset me though were comments that evening on The Huddleboard, with people calling me a fanny and a traitor for daring to stick up for Rangers fans. Again, these comments are made by people who have the luxury of being a Celtic fan when and where they want. They put on the scarf and they're a fan, they take it off and they're just a person. I didn't have that luxury, not in Scotland. I was too well-known. I couldn't take off my face, though there were more than a few people who would like to have helped me try.

'Fuck this,' I said to Phoebe that night. 'Fuck all of this. Celtic, Rangers, Catholic, Protestant, Dominik Diamond Fenian Bastard. Fuck all of it. I'm out. Out of the media, out of Scotland. Let's just go.'

'Where?' Phoebe asked.

'Don't know yet. But let's start thinking.'

It's a shame because less than a month afterwards I saw an example of how the best of Rangers fans are every bit as good as the best of Celtic fans. I awoke after a night out with friends in Glasgow and as I was driving away from the hotel I turned on the radio to hear that Tommy Burns had died after his long battle with cancer. I went straight round to Celtic Park.

I'd never been one of those people who go and pay tribute when someone dies. I hate funerals and tend to just blank out death when it happens. I think it goes back to when I was eighteen and I had a really good friend from school, Chris Henderson, and my cousin Alan both die at the same time. The funerals for them really scarred me.

I never met Tommy but for some reason I felt I had to go to Celtic Park that morning. In front of the club entrance there were already hundreds of people and a great sea of green and white scarves and banners tied to railings and lying on the ground among lit candles. But it wasn't the sea of green and white that struck me as much as the splashes of red, white and blue amongst it. There seemed like a hundred Rangers scarves and tops, all with tributes to Tommy Burns on them. It was *that* sight that caused my tears to flow, and does so now even as I write those words. It just showed that people can rise above all that hate sometimes.

Sometimes, but not often enough and I have to admit my own part in stirring this hate up. I have suffered horrible sectarian abuse, but would that have happened if I hadn't been so ferally irresponsible on the radio in my twenties? Did I help turn reasonable people into hateful human beings in response to me throwing the first irresponsible verbal hate stone? It's a question I was asking myself every day.

So now I was getting out, but first I had to get to the end of that season. After beating Rangers in the Scotland Shame game, the Hartley-Robson midfield became a regular occurrence. Every time they played together we won. With the combination of those two, the Holy Goalie, Naka and Aiden it almost didn't matter how much McManus and Caldwell (AKA Hoof and Heid) tried to ruin it in defence, we still won.

While we went on a roll, Rangers floundered. Walter Smith and Ally McCoist had taken a pretty poor Rangers team and made it punch well above its weight through the self-belief they inspired, but once that self-belief had been torpedoed by those

264

two wins at Celtic Park those players returned to being journeymen.

And so it came down to Dundee United away on 22 May – aka Helicopter Thursday. Like the Black Sunday in Motherwell in 2004, the SPL went down to the final game. Once again a helicopter would be hovering with the trophy, ready to deliver it on this occasion to either Tannadice or Pittodrie (where Rangers played Aberdeen) depending on who won. Once again Archie and I were late because once again I was doing a bloody radio show just before the game.

Thankfully we only missed the first few seconds in what was pretty much an incident-free first half, with Aiden McGeady of all people missing a decent chance to score.

At half-time I did a live phone interview with *The Kickabout*, Talk 107's football phone in. I could hardly hear them back in the studio for all the noise, though the interview was marked by the moment a Celtic fan walked past me and shouted into the mouthpiece. 'Haw is that Real Radio? Yer fucking pish!'

Archie and I had started our superstitious blame game we often did at times like this. It went a bit like this.

ARCHIE: We're going to lose because we were late. And we were late at Motherwell on Black Sunday. It's your fault we're late. So you've cost us the league.

ME: We have never seen a 0-0 away game in Dundee. We have never stayed in a hotel in Dundee before. *You* wanted to stay in a hotel. If we don't win it's cos you wanted to stay in a hotel. Therefore *you've* cost us the league.

ARCHIE: You've got that Jock Stein T shirt on. You had that on in Milan each time Celtic got beat.

ME: You HAVEN'T got on your Juninho top. We have *never* been beaten when you'd been to an away game wearing that top.

ARCHIE: I only ever wore it twice!

And so on.

When Naka got booked for a perfectly legitimate tumble in the box the doubts started to creep in. Then the cheer went up around us, the news spreading like a ripple on a pond, slowly turning into a tsunami. Aberdeen had scored! Then to make things even sweeter, Big Jan leapt up to nod home a Paul Hartley corner. Then to make this sweetness a veritable sugar rush, the news came through from Pittodrie that Nacho Novo had been sent off. It got a bigger cheer than anything that night.

Anything apart from the Tommy Burns T shirts. That was the most emotive sight of all: the whole squad parading the SPL trophy, each of them wearing the famous image of Tommy on his knees hands clasped in prayer with the words *You'll Always Be with Us* etched underneath.

I wish I'd lived my life with a fraction of the grace and dignity that man had.

While the football we'd played that year was mince, the tension of the last day and the sadness at the passing, not just of Tommy but of Phil O Donnell that year, gave it an emotional depth and richness.

And then we got hammered. Off on a crawl of friendly Dundee pubs ending up in the musical Mecca that is The Doghouse. I'd played there with the AMs when we supported Little Man Tate and it was responsible for aiding and abetting so many Dundee bands of the time to make it big, best known of which were The View, who used to rehearse in a room upstairs. The Law, another cracking Dundee band, were in there that night, but I couldn't keep the pace. The stress and strain of the last month had built up and I left Archie playing pool with them and wandered back to the hotel.

The next morning Archie claimed he'd got in at 4am to find me sleepwalking around the corridor in nothing but my boxer shorts, apparently looking for a toilet. As if . . .

An addendum to this story, at one point that night I was offered some cocaine. It had been nearly three years since I had touched the stuff. I was in a great mood, it was a party spirit, and it was exactly the kind of occasion when I used to do it. Surely it wouldn't hurt to do a quick line, for old time's sake?

But I didn't. It proved to me that I had completely buried that part of my life. Time now to dig a deep hole and bury the remaining unhealthy parts.

# ONE FINAL TRIP TO CASTLE GRAYSKULL

'How about Nova Scotia? Someone told me that was nice,' said my wife.

And that was it. We were sitting in front of the computer in May 2008 trying to work out where to move to. We'd always spoken about moving abroad when I left Xfm but we felt that as long as I had my *Daily Star* column the money was too good to give up, especially having three kids.

That dilemma was taken out of my hands when the newspaper's owner decided to do away with all of the columnists to save money. I can't complain really. I'd lasted over a decade there and had probably written about everything I could possibly write about at that level. *The Star* has its critics but regardless of the political leanings of the newspaper or its readership, I had total freedom there to write about what I wanted for a decade. That's rare in the tabloids. Admittedly when I did take a liberal or anti-racist stance I clashed with certain sections of the readership (you should have seen the postbag I got when I defended immigration on the basis that my grandfather had been Polish.) But I think it's far more important to be a liberal of sorts on a rightwing newspaper than to be a liberal writing for *The Guardian*.

My column ended in June and I left on good terms, a rarity for me. I did the same at Talk 107. Something had changed. I don't know if it was religion, years of therapy or less drinking but I had a new-found serenity and felt that once again I was being guided by a higher power in another random direction.

It turned out it was towards a totally random part of Canada I previously couldn't have found on a map. I went there with Phoebe and the kids, our brilliant nanny Dida, my mum and her partner Miles. It was my first holiday of longer than a week since I was sixteen and thanks to Zoom airlines going bust we were able to spend a little bit more time there than originally planned.

We fell in love with Nova Scotia immediately, wide open spaces, clean air, cheap housing, friendly people, no crime and a real sense of community. Best of all? Nobody knew who the hell I was. I was simply a dad.

In the space of three weeks we saw twenty houses before buying a nine acre farm on a river. We got back to Scotland at the beginning of September leaving us just four months to get everything packed up, closed down and sold off before we left the UK forever. Time then for one final visit to Ibrox with Archie.

I still had my season tickets for 2008/2009 and still went to every game I could but it was obvious that season was going to be a bad one. We had got away with it at the end of 2008, the SPL won as much by Rangers' own implosion as anything Strachan and the team managed. It wasn't so much that the chickens were coming home to roost for Gordon, his team and the board who had stood there with their head buried in a balance sheet, rather the chickens had laid eggs, hatched them, brought them up and were now looking at schools for them.

I was in Nova Scotia for the first month of the season but had caught the 4-2 loss to Rangers at Parkhead en route to

Boston in a tiny town in Maine on a crackly, buffering computer picture. We were terrible. Scott McDonald looked twice the size he had been the season before and had been dropped, replaced by Samaras, the very model of the inconsistency that haunted Strachan teams. Kenny Miller got two goals, which stung. Not just because he was one of them, then one of us and now one of them again, but because he was still rubbish. Worst of all was the obvious evidence that Artur Boruc was letting the Rangers fans get to him and had entered the error-strewn phase of his Celtic career. I don't have a problem with Celtic players trying to wind up Rangers, but it only works as long as you're harming them on the pitch too. And Artur wasn't. You feel churlish for castigating a legend, but I was at Easter Road a few SPL games later to see him single-handedly lose us the game in a 2-0 defeat. Like Skippy, he was obviously overweight and unfit too. I don't know where they went for their off-season holiday, but it obviously had an all-you-can-eat buffet.

And Gordon himself, the man I had loved interviewing so much years before, had entered the nippy stage of his management, always seeming to be in a huff with someone that season. The press, the fans, people who called up radio shows, Aiden McGeady. It was a shame. But it was obvious that the things he'd said to me he didn't like about management when I interviewed him at Coventry were the things he was facing every week at Celtic Park. It still beggars belief in some ways that a man who achieved so much with Celtic in terms of titles and results left with so little genuine affection or fanfare, but I was there. I watched those games. I understand.

So while I was sad to be leaving, I knew for a fact we would not win the league that season. I said so to Archie every single week, but I still applied for every away game. I still followed the team. But there was one away game I wanted more than any other and I prayed to get that ballot letter. It duly arrived. Rangers v Celtic. December 27 2008. Just over a week before I left Scotland for good. Come on Celtic. One more win at Castle Grayskull.

Old Firm madness is a disease it's nigh on impossible to get rid of. It's thrilling and glorious and malignant and destructive and it is always there. By the time this game arrived I was sick of all the hate, aware of the part I played in creating it and wanted nothing more than a quiet, anonymous life out of it.

But on the day of the game itself? Fuck that. It was back into the madness. And it would be the same if I went to an Old Firm game tomorrow or in ten years time. It's part of me.

I picked up Archie in Pollokshields in my big black Shogun with its tinted windows and headed towards Ibrox, over the bridge and down Nithsdale Road, rebel songs blaring in the car. The further along Nithsdale Road, the more solitary blue shirts appeared, becoming clusters as we hit Dumbreck Road and headed north. The more blue shirts, the more the excitement grew, the more the danger. Crazy thinking, crazy behaviour. Two grown men, eight kids between them, 'Boys of the Old Brigade' on the stereo. Stupid. Stupid. Stupid. The Madness of the Old Firm.

Across the M8 junction now, armies of Rangers fans on each side, The Celtic Song now playing on the CD. Now and again one of them would get close enough to the tinted windows to peer in, now and again one of that subset would clock me. There would be snarl, a 'Fenian bastard' or a gob on the window. More often the police would be waving us through too fast for anything to happen.

Stupid, stupid, stupid, the Madness of the Old Firm. The insanity that takes two guys who know right from wrong, who know that for every action there is an equal and opposite reaction but still go out there and nudge that action along a little bit. Searching in a daft primal male way for what they hope is an acceptable frisson of excitement in a self-contained bubble where it's all a laugh and no-one really gets hurt.

Left down Paisley Road West the blue shirts thin out, then as we turn right down Helen Street the Celtic shirts appear, more still once we pass the Strathclyde Police Station and enter Celtic territory: That little patch of retail park to the North West of Ibrox where supporters buses and cars cram into space then spew their green and white striped denizens out into the cauldron, the smell of early morning beer and fried burger van onions hit the air with every cry of 'For it's a grand old team to play for . . .'

The majority, like us, are responsible adults with proper jobs and kids at home, but their faces too are like ours – a bit redder as they walk down Edmiston Drive. Then you see the Broomloan Stand looming before you, then you get to what I call Madman's Roundabout where the police try in vain to keep you off the road while touts offer ticketless punters their last chance of viewing salvation.

Then there are the police and their wall. Then there's forty feet of no-mans land, then another wall of yellow jacketed constabulary, then there's them. The Rangers fans. The most vocal at the front of the ranks, their own faces twisted and red in a different scarved mirror image of ours.

You cannot help but be caught up in these moments; it's what makes them so exciting. It's what makes them so terrifying. The real world is so dull in comparison. We are so cosseted, so anaesthetised and so protected. We have no idea what it was like for our forefathers to go toe-to-toe with an enemy, human or animal, for the right just to survive. This, in tribal terms, is the closest we get to it.

Then through the turnstiles and into the kiosk, two pies, two chips and two diet cokes just so we don't put on any extra weight. Then up the steps into the arena.

Bang! It hits you. Rangers v Celtic, the noise from that ridiculously large Ibrox PA system. Then the colours. Look towards the North Stand, look towards the Govan Stand. See the lines of demarcation. Were these respective club colours deliberately chosen to be opposite ends of the colour spectrum so they would give each other such visual relief?

Then there's the silliness. The pointing at the armpit and wafting of the nose because Celtic fans don't wash, haven't you heard? Then Andy Cameron runs on with his jaunty trot to announce the teams.

Ours was already depleted thanks to Naka's injury and Gordon Strachan's pathetic spat with Aiden McGeady, but the prospect of Koki Mizuno in midfield to add what we hoped would be a measured dash to the brainless Brown. Yes we had the dimwit duo of Hoof and Heid in defence, along with Lee Naylor at left back whose fall from initial greatness had been as dizzying as any player I'd seen in Celtic colours since I returned to Scotland. But Strachan also deployed that winning combo of Robson and Hartley in midfield which would hopefully give them some protection.

Indeed it did, and we needed it. Rangers were all over us in the first half but we held strong in what was a dire forty-five minutes of football.

In the stands, however, there was only one winner. The Green Brigade scored a double that day, first of all with over 7000 bags of confetti handed out before the game which added a nice bit of colour when the teams trooped out, but they also completely molligated the Blue Order.

For those not familiar with the word 'molligate' it means to humiliate using humour. I first came across it when the legendary Huddleboard member Toi Tim 'molligated' former Rangers striker turned radio pundit Derek Johnstone. Tim and a pal approached DJ at Glasgow Airport and asked if he minded doing a photo. Not at all, replied Derek, bursting with the pride of recognition, only to be met with the classic punch line: 'Thanks Derek. OK, try and make sure you get both of us in the frame' as they handed the camera to Derek and lined up to be snapped by him rather than with him.

Toi Tim was the master of molligation. In another video he got onto the pitch at Parkhead and trained with the squad for a minute before getting rumbled.

The molligation at Ibrox that day concerned a banner that The Blue Order unfurled at half time which showed a hooped figure running onto a bus with the words O'FFENDED on it. Beside it was a sign with an arrow pointing to Stranraer. There had been a lot of recent hoo-ha about the song The Hokey Cokey and its origins as a song mocking the Catholic faith. Rangers fans had gaily seized upon this aspect to use it as a terrace chant leading to it being banned. Now they mocked the Celtic fans for being offended.

But someone in their ranks had tipped off The Green Brigade who, a minute or two after the Blue Order had unveiled their masterpiece, unveiled their own. An identically designed bus, painted in green and white but with the words CHAMPIONS and 4 IN A ROW painted on it, with the figure boarding sporting the skullhead motif of The Green Brigade and a speech bubble coming from his head which read. 'BUS-ted.'

Cue much laughing from the Celtic fans followed by a hurried refurling of the original Blue Order banner.

*That* is a molligation.

Of course the irony is that they had the last laugh that season because we did not win four in a row, but if the team, manager and most importantly the Celtic board had shown a fraction of the dedication, imagination and passion as The Green Brigade we would have.

All I needed to make the day perfect was a goal in the second half. Just one goal. One final goal to see me on my way. It came with the only moment of true footballing brilliance in the whole match. Samaras lobbed a ball over the defence towards Scott McDonald who, right under the noses of Archie and I, took it on his knee, knocking it over the head of Kirk Broadfoot before nipping round the other side of him and volleying it home. It was one of those goals you're lucky as a fan to see close up, almost in slow-motion, indelibly etched on the mind's eye.

We exploded. The sting was taken out of the game by this and it was almost a dull last half hour. But it gave me time and composure to drink it all in, to look around and savour the sights of my fellow fans and those on the other side of the divide and wallow in the terrible beauty of a Celtic-Rangers game.

It was the perfect ending. The one I wanted. After the final whistle Archie and I were strangely quiet as we walked back to the car. I was driving back to Edinburgh so I didn't even go for a pint. The thought that this was the last time we'd do this together weighed heavily on us.

I gave Archie a hug and then I was away. I was away. I was finally away.

Hey baby let the free bird fly!


Hate is a horribly destructive force. I have played my part in that hate and I regret it. I now live in a world without hate. And it's the only way I want to live my life. At some point the hate HAS to stop. It's a cliché but an eye for an eye *will* make the world blind.

Unfortunately you can't really have the game of football without it. It is a tribal event. It's them and us and it is the tribalism that gives it an energy and excitement above and beyond that which the play on the pitch merits.

This is especially true in the SPL. How many Old Firm games of the last ten years have been wonderful displays of football?

A handful. How many have been exciting from beginning to end for a member of the Old Firm? Every single one.

Because the fans hate each other. It's sad, but it's also essential for the game. But it's hate with a small h. It's pantohate. It's a hate that exists for ninety minutes of a match. And this hate is fine when it's translated into roars and cheers and chants and a rage that is contained by four stands. But it's outside of that, when it infects life in Glasgow and beyond, that it's unacceptable.

I took that hate out of the ground and into the media. And it's one thing to run around like a loon when you're single and in your twenties, or in my case, say a lot of daft inflammatory things on the radio. And on the telly. And in newspapers. And in magazines. But that day you have your first child it all changes. You grow up; you get to appreciate that word 'consequences'. The thought of my kids being left without a dad or one of them getting a slap in Glasgow city centre because of something their dad said before they were even born fills me with horror.

But that dangerous side of the Old Firm is still exciting, even when I know it's wrong. It's contradictory I know, but to be a Celtic fan, to be an Old Firm fan, is to walk through contradiction every day as if it's your front garden.

Celtic is a Scottish club AND an Irish club. Rangers is a Scottish club and a Unionist club. There are Celtic fans who run around chanting PIRA and couldn't even find Belfast on a map. There are perfectly decent Rangers fans who sit beside those doing Nazi salutes and do nothing.

Contradiction that marked my own life and media career, which ebbed and flowed as the fortunes of Celtic did at the time: the smart guy who did dumb things; the funny guy who wanted to be taken seriously; the man who acted like a child then demanded to be treated like a grown up; the funny depressive; the exhausted insomniac.

My life as a Celtic supporter and my life in the media was

madness. I loved being part of the madness. I hated being part of the madness. I feared being part of the madness. I accepted being part of the madness. I felt guilty at being part of the madness. And I left the madness.

Nine months after I left Scotland I drove down to Shelburne on the South Shore of Nova Scotia with Phoebe and the kids. It's a fishing town originally settled in 1783 by United Empire Loyalists who were opposed to the revolution and fled America. As a result Union Jacks fly from the houses of their descendants. When I saw those flags I instinctively bristled with fear and apprehension. Then I remembered where I was.

I was in Nova Scotia. New Scotland. A flag is just a flag. And I am just a dad driving a car. Nothing more.

It was the happiest I have ever been.

I turn up the rebel songs and start singing, and catch myself in the mirror, seeing the flash of the Celtic FC crest on the chain around my neck, next to the Crucifix, both of them always close to my heart.

# EPILOGUE

In the eighteen months since I moved to Nova Scotia my life has completely changed, then changed back to what it was like before. With Celtic it's much the same.

I did a bit of writing, a bit of singing and a bit of what Phoebe gets embarrassed at me calling 'farming' because it's half an acre of veg plots and five chickens. But most of all I spent eighteen months with my wife and kids: walking in woods, swimming in rivers, eating together round the table every day and going to Mass every Sunday.

It's been amazing but, like the SPL, there's no money in it.

And just as Celtic had to ring the changes after a year farting around with Mowbray so I've returned to working. In Canadian radio. But I'm loving it.

Nova Scotians are a great bunch. They warmly welcome outsiders and look out for each other. I still get recognised, but here it's as a husband, a dad and a part of this community family here.

No one calls me a Fenian Bastard.

This hasn't made it any easier watching Celtic. The chickens came home to roost as I feared and this looked even worse on a dodgy internet connection. Football is still at the centre of my life. Except I call it soccer now. Sorry.

Molly started playing for our local town Under 12s last summer because it's what her friends did. She'd never kicked a ball before and began as a spirited midfielder who tackled her heart out but couldn't pass longer than five yards. She was Neil Lennon, basically: the man whose name was on my shirt when I first took Molly to Celtic Park, the man who is now the boss.

It's the cheap option for the board. But when Lennon tore into the players after Ross County knocked us out of the Scottish Cup? Twas one of the few moments in 2009/2010 I felt proud. He might become a better coach than the suits deserve.

The coaching setup in Nova Scotia is wonderful. Molly enrolled in the South Shore Regional Training Centre run by John Charman, who worked with Hoddle at Chelsea. He has transformed her into a fast, fearless left wingback about to attend her first Nova Scotia squad trial.

It's fuelled another wave of my passion for the game and I was asked to help coach her team. They're small, but they have skill. We play football on the ground with short passes and wingers who dribble. We play the Glasgow Celtic way.

And the team plays in green and white. Some things are meant to be.